BILL

AND

HILLARY

■

THE MARRIAGE

D0182827

ALSO BY CHRISTOPHER ANDERSEN

The Day Diana Died

Jackie After Jack: Portrait of the Lady

An Affair to Remember: The Remarkable Love Story of Katharine Hepburn and Spencer Tracy

Jack and Jackie: Portrait of an American Marriage

Young Kate: The Remarkable Hepburns and the Shaping of an American Legend

Citizen Jane

The Best of Everything
(with John Marion)

The Serpent's Tooth

The Book of People

Father

Susan Hayward

The Name Game

BILL

AND

HILLARY

THE MARRIAGE

·

Christopher Andersen

WARNER BOOKS

A *Warner* Book

First published in the United States in 1999
by William Morrow and Company, Inc., New York
First published in Great Britain in 2000
by Warner Books

Copyright © 1999 by Christopher Andersen

The moral right of the author has been asserted.

Grateful acknowledgment is made to the following for permission to use
the photographs in this book:
AP/Wide World Photos: 4, 8, 12, 14, 16, 19, 21, 24, 25, 26, 27, 29, 30,
33, 35, 38, 45, 46, 48, 49, 56, 57, 58, 60
Archive Photos/Ernie Sachs: 7
Arkansas Democrat Gazette: 15, 17, 18, 32
Corbis: 9, 51
Corbis/F. Specker; *NY Post*: 34
Corbis/Mitch Gerber: 37
Corbis/Reuters: 31
David Hume Kennerly/Sygma: 59
Gary Speed, *Arkansas Democrat Gazette*: 11
Reuters/Gary Cameron/Archive Photos: 50
Reuters/Gregg Newton/Archive Photos: 44
Reuters/HO/Archive Photos: 40, 52
Reuters/Jeff Mitchell/Archive Photos: 2, 5, 13
Reuters/Mike Theiler/Archive Photos: 41
Reuters/NBC TV/Archive Photos: 53
Reuters/Rick Wilking/Archive Photos: 39
Reuters/Rose Prouser/Archive Photos: 36
Reuters/Win McNamee/Archive Photos: 22, 23, 28, 42, 43, 47, 55
Sygma: 54
UPI/Corbis-Bettmann: 1
Wide World Photos, Inc.: 20

All rights reserved. No part of this publication may be
reproduced, stored in a retrieval system, or transmitted, in any
form or by any means, without the prior permission in writing
of the publisher, nor be otherwise circulated in any form of binding
or cover other than that in which it is published and without
a similar condition including this condition being imposed on
the subsequent purchaser.

A CIP catalogue record for this book
is available from the British Library.

ISBN: 0 7515 3035 2

Printed and bound in Great Britain by
Clays Ltd, St Ives plc

Warner Books
Brettenham House
Lancaster Place
London WC2E 7EN

For my wife, Valerie—still the one

I wonder what history is
going to say about our marriage.

—*Hillary*

Preface

BY ANY DEFINITION, they are one of history's most re-markable couples: he the irrepressible country boy populist oozing ambition and Southern charm, she the brilliant, tough-as-nails Midwesterner with a head for strategy, a taste for power, and, in the end, an unshakable allegiance to the man in her life. To-gether, William Jefferson Clinton and his wife, Hillary Rodham, scaled the heights of power and prestige, only to have his confoundingly reckless behavior bring them to the brink of personal and political ruin.

The first products of the post–World War baby boom to reach the White House, Bill and Hillary carried with them the hopes, dreams, fears, aspirations, doubts, and frustrations—not to mention the emotional baggage—of a generation. They were raised during the Eisenhower fifties, weaned on *The Mickey Mouse Club, Howdy Doody, I Love Lucy,* and *Ed Sullivan.* In high school they danced to the Beatles, the Rolling Stones, and Motown, and sat in stunned silence when they were told of JFK's assassination. Reaching college age in the turbulent 1960s, they picked up placards and marched against U.S. involvement in Vietnam. Their parents had the De-pression and World War II. The Clintons and their contemporaries grew up in an era where widespread divorce, drug abuse, racial conflict, terrorism, and violent crime presented a dark side to the American Dream.

Yet, faced with the disillusionment and growing cynicism of the age, Bill and Hillary shared a profound belief in each other—a conviction that, if they combined their formidable talents, they could make a difference.

They did. In 1993 at age forty-six, Bill Clinton was sworn in as the forty-second President of the United States—the youngest, with the exception of his idol, John F. Kennedy, ever elected. By the time Congress voted to impeach him six years later, the true nature of his tangled relationship with Hillary was more of a mystery than ever.

To be sure, as individuals each was a Gordian knot of contradictions. He could be compassionate yet vindictive, idealistic yet unscrupulous, expansive yet moody, conscientious yet wildly self-destructive. She was the ardent feminist whose power and position were derived from the man she married, the scorekeeper and grudge holder with a seemingly bottomless capacity for forgiveness, the armor-plated politico still capable of being deeply wounded. There could be no greater irony than the fate of this fiercely proud wife, mother, and professional: Destined to be remembered less for her accomplishments than for being the ultimate Wronged Woman, Hillary displayed courage and a quiet dignity in the face of private pain and searing public humiliation.

Like that other great power couple they sought to emulate perhaps too closely—Jack and Jackie Kennedy—the entity known as Bill and Hillary is greater than the sum of its parts. And like their 1960s counterparts, the Clintons are youthful, brilliant, attractive, complicated, sometimes arrogant, often mystifying, always controversial—but never dull.

Sex, money, power, lies, and scandal—each has played a role in the making and unmaking of the Clinton legacy. Yet whatever the judgment of history, the saga of Bill and Hillary is—above all else—a curious, compelling, and uniquely American love story.

BILL

AND

HILLARY

■

THE MARRIAGE

She doesn't know whether to kill him or save him.

—*Mandy Grunwald,*
Clinton advisor

I don't like saying this, but he lied to her. He's a very good liar. And she didn't want to believe the worst about him.

—a close friend
of Hillary

You stupid, stupid, stupid bastard.

—*Hillary,*
to her husband

August 13, 1998
A THURSDAY

CHELSEA BRUSHED HER newly permed hair away from her face, then turned to wave goodbye to her mother before leaving the White House to spend the evening with friends. Hillary Rodham Clinton, looking small and drained and vulnerable at the far end of the cavernous Center Hall in the second-floor family quarters, smiled back bravely. "Have fun," the First Lady said wanly as the Stanford coed, shadowed by her ever-present Secret Service detail, stepped into the elevator that would take her downstairs to a waiting bulletproof sedan.

There was some comfort in having Chelsea home from Stanford University for the summer. Although a continent apart, the two women had nonetheless been riding the same emotional roller coaster for the better part of seven months—seven months during which the most important man in their lives swore to them and to the country that he had never had sexual relations with a twenty-two-year-old White House intern named Monica Lewinsky.

This time Hillary, all too aware of Bill Clinton's past indiscretions as Governor of Arkansas, needed to believe him. During their six years in the White House, Bill and Hillary stood shoulder-to-shoulder in the face of Whitewater and Travelgate and Filegate and

Vincent Foster and Paula Jones—not to mention a dizzying array of lesser scandals and investigations. In each case, in fact, it was Hillary who met with White House lawyers to devise strategies to discredit their accusers and mount counteroffensives.

To be sure, the sexual harassment lawsuit brought by former Arkansas state employee Paula Jones had made Hillary cringe. But the allegations—that he had lured Jones to his hotel room, lowered his pants, and then tried to coerce her into performing oral sex—dealt only with Bill's behavior before he stepped onto the national stage. Besides, while Hillary knew that her husband had been unfaithful in Arkansas with a lounge singer named Gennifer Flowers, when it came to Paula Jones she believed Bill's denials. Paula was merely a pawn of her husband's political enemies, Hillary firmly believed. Over the fervent pleas of the President's advisors, she adamantly opposed any out-of-court settlement in the Jones case—a fatal miscalculation that would ultimately lead to the Lewinsky debacle.

At the time it was inconceivable to Hillary that her husband would have reverted to his old ways—not here under the White House roof they shared, not with the Secret Service lurking in every corner, and certainly not now with the outcome of the Paula Jones lawsuit uncertain and Independent Counsel Kenneth Starr still breathing down their collective necks.

Although Hillary was blissfully unaware of it back then, things had begun to unravel on January 17 when the President gave his deposition in the Jones case. Judge Susan Webber Wright, wearing her best poker face, listened as Bill Clinton denied that he had ever had sexual relations of any sort with Monica Lewinsky. With some coaxing, he did vaguely recall buying one or two small gifts for the intern, but little about what she might have said to him in person or over the phone.

Back in the White House two hours later, President Clinton phoned his secretary, Betty Currie, and told her to come to the Oval Office the next morning. "Betty," he said, "I want to have a little chat with you about Monica's visits to my office." As she hung up the phone, it occurred to Currie that in all the years she had worked for him, Bill Clinton had never prevailed on her to come to the White House on a Sunday—not during any of the budget showdowns, not after the Oklahoma City bombings, not following any natural disaster, not even during the dramatic brink-of-war confrontations with Saddam Hussein.

Hillary, meanwhile, needed to be told *something*. The First Couple canceled their dinner plans with White House Chief of Staff Erskine Bowles, and Bill told Hillary what he hoped she would believe: that he had taken pity on a disturbed young friend of Currie's, that he had tried to help her through some "emotional problems," and in the process the poor deluded girl had convinced herself there was something more between them. As she had in the past, Hillary accepted what she was being told at face value and channeled her anxiety into something constructive: "We spent the weekend," she later said with no hint of sarcasm, "cleaning out closets."

The next day the President, as was his habit, kept Betty waiting for over an hour before emerging alone in shirtsleeves from the Oval Office to speak with her at her desk. She could tell that her boss, who kept his Vesuvian temper hidden from the public, was agitated: A vein in his forehead began to throb, and he drummed his fingers on her desk as he spoke.

"Well, they asked me several questions about Monica during the deposition yesterday," he said, shaking his head. "Now, there are several things you may want to know."

Currie had always willingly covered for her boss. But the little white lies to Hillary about the stream of attractive women in and out of his office was one thing. Lying under oath was quite another.

"You were always right there when she was there, right?" he said.

"Well, Mr. President, I'm not su—"

The President, standing by the desk, leaned toward her. *"Right?"* he demanded again. Currie, intimidated, nodded her head.

"We were never really alone," the President continued. "Monica came on to me, and I never touched her. Right?"

Currie nodded again.

"You can see and hear everything, *right?*" Clinton went on. Currie kept nodding. "You know, Betty, she wanted to have sex with me, but I couldn't do that."

"No, Mr. President," she replied. "No, you couldn't."

"Right. Now, get Monica on the phone," he said, turning back toward the Oval Office. "I want to know what she's up to."

Currie tried four times to page Monica—all without success. The following morning she tried nine more times to locate Lewinsky—to no avail. Shortly before noon she told the President that Monica had returned none of her pages or calls. Clinton merely shook his head and sighed.

On Tuesday evening, January 20, 1998, shaken Press Secretary Mike McCurry called the President. McCurry held in his hand the lead story for the following morning's edition of the *Washington Post*. He hesitated a moment before reading the headline to the President:

CLINTON ACCUSED OF URGING AIDE TO LIE
STARR PROBES WHETHER PRESIDENT TOLD WOMAN TO
DENY ALLEGED AFFAIR TO JONES'S LAWYERS

The President glanced at his watch. It was midnight. At 12:08 he placed a call to his personal lawyer, Robert Bennett. "I'm telling you, Bob," he said, "it's all lies. There was no sex of any kind, period."

No sooner had he hung up the phone than Bill called Deputy White House Counsel Bruce Lindsey. A half hour later, at 1:16 on the morning of January 21, the President woke Betty Currie at home, warned her about the upcoming *Washington Post* article, and went over their story for a second time. Then he called Lindsey again . . .

It was 6 A.M. and still dark in New York City when Vernon Jordan, an influential Washington attorney and longtime presidential confidant, was jolted awake by the sound of his ringing phone. Jordan, who at the President's behest had been trying to find Monica Lewinsky a job out of harm's way in New York, listened as his old friend told him about the story appearing in that day's *Post*—and that it was all "a damned lie." At 7:14, Bill talked to Deputy White House Counsel Lindsey a third time.

Now Bill Clinton faced the most daunting task of all: telling his wife. Hillary had gone to bed shortly before 11 P.M., and had been sound asleep since then—blissfully ignorant of the breaking *Post* story and Bill's frantic efforts to counteract it. It was not unusual for the First Lady to be unaware of her husband's nocturnal activities; like their idols Jack and Jackie Kennedy, Bill and Hillary Clinton slept in separate bedrooms. In fact, the Clintons had not shared the same bedroom—much less the same bed—for at least seven years.

A copy of the newspaper with its damning front-page headline clenched tight in his left fist, the President made his way to "The Residence," the First Family's private quarters on the second floor. Bill walked purposefully past the Center Hall hung with Cassatt, Cézanne, and de Kooning, past the dark Lincoln Bedroom crammed with heavy American Victoriana and the rose-colored Queen's Bedroom before stopping at the First Lady's bedroom at the end of the corridor.

The President raised his hand to eye level and gently knocked on the door, then pushed it open slowly without waiting for an answer. He walked in and sat on the edge of the bed. It was only now that Hillary, like her husband a self-described "dead to the world" sleeper, began to stir.

"What is it?" she asked, propping herself up on one arm.

"Here," Bill said, handing his wife the paper, "you're never going to believe this."

No sooner had she finished reading the article than Hillary flew into a rage. The President loudly proclaimed his innocence, and soon their angry shouts echoed down the corridor—a familiar sound to White House staffers and Secret Service agents assigned to cover the First Couple.

The heated exchange lasted only a few minutes. Hillary had always chosen to believe Bill in the past—now, with the very future of their presidency at stake, she had no choice but to convince herself once again that his denials were genuine. Once the anger had subsided, Bill asked his wife the same question he always asked when they were confronted with a crisis: "So, now what do we do?"

For the next twenty minutes, he quickly briefed her on his discussions that morning with Betty Currie, Vernon Jordan, and Bruce Lindsey. Bill and Hillary agreed that the President would have to go through with the three press interviews already scheduled for that day. But first, he would have to rally support from his inner circle of advisors.

Throughout the day, the presidential refrain to members of the White House staff never varied: "I want you to know that I did not have sexual relations with this woman, Monica Lewinksy" . . . "I haven't done anything wrong" . . . "We never had sex in any way whatsoever—we did not have oral sex."

Bill Clinton told one of his senior advisors, former *New Yorker* writer Sidney Blumenthal, that Monica's friends called her "The Stalker." As for himself, the President told Blumenthal he felt "like a character in a novel—like somebody who is surrounded by an oppressive force that is creating a lie about me and I can't get the truth out." Then, alluding to the hero of Arthur Koestler's dark tale of an individual being relentlessly persecuted by the state, he added, "I feel like the character in the novel *Darkness at Noon*."

Hillary would turn out to be her husband's staunchest ally in what she called their "war" with Kenneth Starr. Believing blindly in Bill, she told a friend in California, "is the only way I can get through this. I *have* to believe what my husband says is true."

Convincing herself of that would be a formidable task; Bill had lied to her so many times before about his extramarital affairs. Less than three hours after Bill woke her up and handed her the *Washington Post* story, Hillary boarded a train for Baltimore, where she was scheduled to give a speech on race relations at Goucher College. "She was upset," said an Education Department official who accompanied the First Lady's party on the trip. "But not visibly so. Just chilly and withdrawn. It was not an enjoyable train ride."

The train had just pulled out of Washington when one of Hillary's assistants received a call on her cell phone. "It's the President," she said warily, handing the phone to Mrs. Clinton. But instead of taking the call, Hillary pulled open a folder and began going over the notes for her speech.

"I . . . I'm afraid she can't come to the phone right now, Mr. President," the startled aide stammered. "May I take a message?"

The President did not leave a message, but he did call Hillary back—twice. "Hillary declined to take them," said the administration official, "even though she was sitting next to the assistant holding the cell phone."

At least one White House staffer would later concede that, at this juncture, "the President was very concerned—frantic would not be too strong a word—that Mrs. Clinton was not returning his calls." If he was worried that his wife might doubt his version of events, the public saw no sign of it. His denials—first on National Public Radio's *All Things Considered*, then in an interview with Jim Lehrer on PBS's *The NewsHour*, as well as in nonstop meetings with aides— were full of righteous indignation.

Yet he did allow the mask to slip when his longtime political advisor Dick Morris called. Credited with being largely responsible for Clinton's election victories, Morris could appreciate his old friend's predicament: He had been summarily dismissed from the 1996 reelection campaign when newspapers carried photographs of him lounging in a Washington hotel suite with a prostitute. Morris blamed the White House "secret police"—his enemies within the administration—for leaking confidential information regarding his sex life to the *National Enquirer*. But Morris did not hold the President responsible, and could be counted on to lend his old friend and benefactor a sympathetic ear.

"You poor son of a bitch," Morris said. "I've just read what's going on."

"Oh, God. This is just awful," the President replied. "I didn't do what they said I did, but I did something. I mean, with this girl, I didn't do what they said . . . but I did do . . . something."

"Bill," Morris said, "what did—"

"And I may have done enough," the President continued, "so that I don't know if I can prove my innocence. There may be gifts—I gave her gifts—and there may be messages on her answering machine."

Morris had never heard the President sound so despondent. Yet he did not see Bill's position as hopeless. In fact Morris was convinced the President could even turn the situation to his political advantage. "There's a great capacity for forgiveness in this country," he said, "and you should consider tapping into it."

"But what about the legal thing?" Bill asked. "You know, the legal thing? You know, Starr and perjury and all . . ."

Morris told the President point-blank that he understood his predicament perhaps better than anyone. "It occurs to me that maybe I'm the only sex addict you know," he said, "and that maybe I can help you."

"You know, ever since the election I've tried to shut myself down," the President went on. "I've tried to shut my body down, sexually, I mean. But sometimes I slipped up and with this girl I just slipped up."

"I know, I know," Morris replied. "Addicts fall off the wagon. This is an addiction just like drugs or alcohol and you just have to recognize it and fight it."

But Bill was also addicted to danger. A consummate risk-taker, he loved the thrill of putting himself in impossible situations and then, Houdini-like, miraculously extricating himself. As Governor of Arkansas, he had been so brazen as to walk up to desk clerks at major hotels around the country and boldly introduce himself.

"I'm Bill Clinton, the Governor of Arkansas," he would say, "and I'm expecting an urgent phone call from the President of the United States. Would you make a suite available to me for a few hours so I can take the call in private?" Then he would have his girlfriend-of-the-moment join him inside the suite for a tryst. "He always got a big laugh out of hiding in plain sight," said one long-time mistress. "It was all so in-your-face, yet nobody suspected a thing. Bill would say, 'Isn't this great? I don't even have to pay for the room!' "

But now, in January 1998, the danger was greater—and the stakes so much higher—than they had ever been. Over the phone, Dick Morris suggested to the President there was a way out of his current dilemma. "Look, Bill, I think the American people will forgive you," Morris said, trying to reassure his old friend. "Why don't you let me take a poll on this? We'll see what the mood is out there."

There was a pause. "Yes," the President said with a sigh. "Yes, go ahead and call me as soon as you get the results."

Morris called up a research firm in Melbourne, Florida, and told them that the identity of the person who commissioned the poll would have to remain confidential. He would pay the $2,000 cost himself, and insisted that nothing be written down—he would take the results over the phone.

Part of the survey would test public reaction to a public apology by the President that Morris penned himself. "For many, many years I have been personally flawed," Morris's speech for the President began, "and have had sexual relations outside my marriage . . ."

That evening, the Clintons hosted more than one hundred guests at a White House Endowment Fund dinner. They emerged from their separate bedrooms and walked in stony silence to the elevator. As soon as the Marine Band struck up "Ruffles and Flourishes," both the President and the First Lady lit up, in the words of one guest that night, "like someone had just plugged them into a wall socket. I watched them all night, and they were totally, I mean totally, charming—just so up and *on* all the time."

They could not entirely ignore the headlines that transfixed the nation for days. "Thank you for coming out," Hillary quipped. "It's been SUCH an eventful week at the White House." According to a journalist at the dinner, the Clintons were "radiant. You would not have had the slightest idea that the man was facing the biggest crisis of his presidency. But if you looked closely something else became obvious. Not once during the entire evening did the President and Mrs. Clinton actually speak to each other. *Not once.*"

That night, as had become their custom, Hillary went to bed around 11 while Bill returned to work in the Oval Office. Not long after, Dick Morris called with the results of his poll.

The results were not encouraging. Reading from his own hastily scrawled notes, Morris told the President that if he gave the speech Morris had written, 47 percent would want him out of office while 43 percent would want him to stay. The remaining 10 percent were undecided. Then Morris read the President the speech he had prepared for his friend.

"For many, many years I have been personally flawed and have had sexual relations outside my marriage. This has caused Hillary great pain and I have tried and tried to curb my behavior as I saw the pain it caused her. After I became President, I was determined to mend my ways. For the most part, I did, but sometimes I fell short and gave in to temptation. I did, in fact, have sexual relations with a twenty-three-year-old woman named Monica Lewinsky while I've been President. I regret my behavior more than I can say. I apologize for it. I take responsibility for it. I wish I were a better man and better able to cope with the pressures of life and work, and I am going to redouble my efforts to walk a straight line.

"When the allegations first surfaced I did, indeed, lie about them and urge Monica to lie."

With this, Morris paused for a split second, anticipating that Bill would interrupt him with a "But that isn't true." But the President said nothing. Morris continued reading the speech.

"I was wrong. I am sorry for it. I am especially sorry for the pain I have caused my wife and daughter. If the American people want me to step down as President, I will do so . . ."

Again, Morris expected an interruption, perhaps a "That goes too far." Still, nothing. Morris continued reading.

"With a heavy heart, but I will do so. If they can forgive me and want me to continue to lead our great nation, I'll do that, too. I've tried to be a good President and I think I've succeeded. I've tried to be a good husband, and I'm afraid I've sometimes failed. As President, as a repentant sinner and as a Christian, I ask your forgiveness, God's forgiveness, and my wife and daughter's forgiveness. My future is in your hands, my fellow Americans."

To Morris's astonishment, the President "was silent throughout the whole thing."

When he broke down the results of the poll further, Morris came to the conclusion that it was not the affair the American people objected to, but the lying and the duplicity. "Well, Bill," he said, "it seems the American people are willing to forgive you for adultery, but not for perjury or obstruction of justice." Going public with a confession or explanation of any kind, Morris went on to explain, could spell disaster.

"Well," Clinton replied, "we just have to win, then."

In this final battle for political survival, as in all the others, Bill would lean heavily on Hillary. Few others in Washington possessed her innate political savvy, or what she herself once called her "take no prisoners" approach to the opposition. She had always been particularly adept at concealing her emotions from the public. Yet when it was reported in the *New York Times* on January 23 that one of the gifts her husband had given Monica Lewinsky was a copy of Walt Whitman's *Leaves of Grass,* Hillary, in the words of an aide, "appeared shaken." In a voice tinged with heartache, Hillary said to no one in particular, "He gave me the same book—after our second date . . ."

Hillary's doubts notwithstanding, there were still those stalwart FOBs (Friends of Bill) who were convinced he could, as Morris put it, "bluff it out." The morning after watching Bill's strained appearance on *The NewsHour,* the Clintons' old Arkansas pal-turned-sitcom-producer Harry Thomason flew out to Washington and met with his old friend. He told the President point-blank that he was being "too wishy-washy . . . You should explain it so there's no doubt in anybody's mind that nothing happened," Thomason insisted.

"You know, you're right," Bill concurred. "I should be more forceful than that."

That Sunday, January 25, the Clintons went ahead with plans to invite a handful of friends to the White House to watch the Super Bowl. Among them was veteran civil rights activist Jesse Jackson, who sat on the couch next to Chelsea and, Hillary would later say, "bonded with her immediately. He made Chelsea laugh for the first time in a long time, and I was grateful for that."

From the vantage point of Reverend Jackson—who quickly recognized the *frisson* between the President and the First Lady—it was apparent that Chelsea needed the extra attention. "She's a very strong young woman," Jackson recalled, "but she was obviously in terrible pain. I did what I could to cheer her up." As for her parents: "The tension," Jackson said, "was palpable."

The American people were unaware that the President and First Lady were no longer speaking to each other when, on January 26, he stood at the presidential podium to deny once again that he had ever had an affair with Monica Lewinsky. This time, he was determined to follow Harry Thomason's advice and be more forceful in his delivery.

"I did not have sexual relations with *that woman*," he swore angrily as he wagged his finger into the camera, "I never told anybody to lie, not a single time, never." Hillary, standing at the President's right with her hands folded demurely in front of her, nodded in agreement.

The next morning Hillary, wearing a brown pantsuit, pearls, an American Eagle brooch, and a newfound air of righteous indignation, went on NBC's *Today Show* to blast her husband's critics. Back at the White House, the President held his right hand to his mouth and watched as his wife told interviewer Matt Lauer the entire affair was part of a "vast right-wing conspiracy" aimed at toppling the Clintons from power.

It was, in fact, a familiar refrain. "Whenever things got really rough," said a former White House staffer, "Hillary always blamed it on dark forces conspiring to get them. It was almost Nixonian at times." Indeed, throughout the Clintons' public life in Arkansas and Washington, Bill and Hillary made repeated reference to the mysterious "them"—unnamed conspirators who would stop at nothing to sabotage Bill's career.

Hillary's conspiracy theory notwithstanding, Lauer persisted. "If an American President had an adulterous affair in the White House," he continued, "and lied to cover it up, should the American people ask for his resignation?"

Hillary, shifting uneasily in her chair, conceded that the public had a right to be concerned, but Lauer pressed her again for an answer. "Should they ask for his resignation?"

"If all that were proven true," Hillary said, "I think that would be a very serious offense. That is not going to be proven true."

It was at that moment, according to Hillary's longtime press secretary Neel Lattimore, that the President must have realized "he had not only betrayed her in their marriage, but also professionally, in a way that he'd never betrayed her before." Unable to face the prospect of telling Hillary the whole horrific truth, he would have to continue the lying—publicly and privately.

His greatest ally in this deception was Hillary herself. To remain steadfast in her conviction that Bill had not repeatedly betrayed her with a White House intern only a few years older than their daughter, Hillary simply stopped reading the newspapers. Even the daily news summaries prepared by her staff were sanitized. Since entering the White House, Hillary had a standing rule about these digests. They were only to include hard news or issue-oriented pieces—no tabloid gossip, and definitely no sex. Now aides were under strict orders from the First Lady not to include anything about the Lewinsky scandal.

Hillary saw no reason why the same hear-no-evil, see-no-evil approach would not work for her daughter. She called Stanford and suggested to Chelsea that, for the time being at least, she should also stop reading the papers.

The next Wednesday, she called Chelsea again—this time to summon her back to Washington for a show of family unity. Sure, Chelsea told her mom. But first she planned to attend the big Thursday night game between the Stanford and University of Arizona basketball teams. She could catch the first flight out to Washington Friday morning and be at the White House in time for dinner.

But the President had other plans for his daughter. At his insistence, Chelsea flew home immediately so she could join her mom and dad at Camp David on Friday—time enough for the wire services to carry photos of the tender family reunion in the large-circulation weekend papers. No sooner had the all-important photos run on front pages across the country than Hillary boarded a plane for Switzerland and Bill headed for the golf course.

Back at Stanford Chelsea heeded the First Lady's advice, turning a blind eye to the blizzard of news reports detailing her father's extramarital activities. Nor did Chelsea have to worry about being hounded by the press or accosted by strangers. During their six years in the White House, the Clintons had simply forbidden the press to interview their daughter. Chelsea was so shielded from the media, in fact, that when she spoke to Tanzanian students on a tour of Africa with her mother, it came as a shock to most Americans. They realized that, after all her years in the White House, they were hearing Chelsea's voice for the very first time.

At Stanford, the curtain around the First Daughter was drawn ever more tightly. No fewer than twenty-three Secret Service agents, most chosen for their youthful appearance so they could blend in with the Stanford student body, zealously guarded Chelsea's privacy. That did not, however, keep Stanford swim team star Matt Pierce from walking up to Chelsea the first day of school and striking up a conversation with her. They began dating, and when the Lewinsky scandal broke Pierce became one of Chelsea's main pillars of support.

But in the end there was no way to shield her from the endless stream of sordid revelations that threatened her father's presidency and, more important for the teenage coed, her parents' marriage. On May 19, she collapsed with severe stomach pains and was rushed to the campus hospital. After a battery of tests ruled out appendicitis, ulcers, or pelvic inflammatory disease, doctors came to the inevitable conclusion that the pains were brought on by stress.

Aware that any sign of doubt or weakness on Chelsea's part might undermine the First Family's business-as-usual profile, the White House issued a press release claiming Chelsea was simply suffering from the flu. In the coming months, as Hillary rightly worried about the impact the scandal was having on her daughter's health, Chelsea would be rushed to the hospital suffering from stress-induced stomach pains at least three more times.

Chelsea's trips to the hospital triggered a flood of painful memories for Hillary. Back in Little Rock, Hillary had looked the other way for years until Bill's womanizing caught up with her one spring day. A few months earlier, a young Governor Clinton had attended an engagement party for the nephew of a wealthy supporter. No sooner had he arrived than Bill took the shocked host aside and pronounced the twentyish bride-to-be "hot." That night, Bill seduced the young woman in front of her fiancé, broke up the engagement, and over the course of several months led her to believe he intended to divorce Hillary and marry her.

When Hillary found out, one of her closest friends said, "something snapped." She began hyperventilating and was rushed to the emergency room. "Hillary had always put up with his cheating," said the friend, "but for some reason that particular affair came as a real slap in the face. It literally took her breath away, and she landed in the hospital with an anxiety attack. She told Bill back then, 'This has to stop!' and he promised he would. She believed him."

Now, decades later, Hillary watched as Bill's infidelity drove their only child to the hospital with bouts of anxiety. That May Hillary flew out to California to spend time with her daughter. The First Lady took Chelsea, her boyfriend Matt, and a few dorm mates to a restaurant for brunch. There her mother's concern was evident in the way she showered affection on the eighteen-year-old. According to one of their waitresses that day, "Hillary kissed and hugged Chelsea openly all the time."

Throughout that spring, Hillary called her daughter every other day to try to boost her spirits and reassure her that none of the stories about her father was true. It was nothing new to Chelsea; for as long as she could remember, she was taught that the world was divided into two camps: those who adored her father and those who wanted to destroy him.

The indoctrination of Chelsea Clinton had begun in earnest when she was only six years old. Before then, safe within the confines of the Governor's Mansion in Little Rock, Hillary could "monitor" whatever the little girl saw or heard about her father. But once she reached school age and learned to read, the Clintons, facing what promised to be a particularly messy 1986 reelection campaign, took steps to prepare Chelsea so, in Hillary's words, she would "not be surprised or overwhelmed if she heard someone say something nasty about her father."

Daddy was going to run for governor again, Hillary announced over dinner. "If he wins," she told a wide-eyed Chelsea, "we could keep living in this house . . ." But first, she went on, there would be a campaign during which Daddy's enemies might say "terrible things" about him. "They might even lie," she went on, "just so people will vote for them instead of Daddy."

Hillary later recalled that Chelsea "struggled" with the idea that a politician might lie. "Why would they do that?" she asked again and again.

"I'll tell you what," Hillary said. "Why don't we play a game. You be Daddy and tell me why we should vote for you for governor."

Chelsea paused for a moment before suddenly turning serious. "I'm Bill Clinton," she said, "I've done a good job and I've helped a lot of people. Please vote for me."

Pleased with herself, Chelsea waited for her parents to shower her with praise. Instead, her father leaned forward, scowled, and wagged a bony finger in her face. "Well, Bill Clinton," he said, "I think you have done a lousy job. You've raised taxes, and you haven't helped people at all. Why, you are a very mean man, and I am NOT voting for the likes of *you*."

With that, Chelsea dissolved in tears. "Why would anybody say things like that?" she wanted to know. Her tears aside, this strange drill continued over the dinner table for weeks. Like two lawyers playing devil's advocate to prepare their star witness for cross-examination, Bill and Hillary peppered Chelsea with questions and insults until she was numb. "Our role-playing," Hillary would later explain, "helped Chelsea to experience, in the privacy of our own home, the feelings of any person who sees someone she loves being personally attacked."

As the exercise progressed over the coming weeks, Hillary watched proudly as Chelsea gradually gained "mastery over her emotions"—a degree of self-control that often seemed to mirror her mother's own.

For the next six years, Chelsea merely shrugged aside whatever negative remarks were made about her parents. But when Bill entered the presidential race in 1992, Hillary took their daughter aside for another heart-to-heart chat. "Before this is over," Hillary warned Chelsea, "they'll attack me, they'll attack you, they'll attack your cat, they'll attack your goldfish."

Outfitted in his-and-hers power suits, their hair meticulously coiffed, Bill and Hillary looked every centimeter the power couple of the nineties when they moved into the White House in January 1993. But since Chelsea had always been shielded from public view, little attention had been paid to her appearance. To the requisite braces and blemishes that are the hallmarks of awkward adolescence, Chelsea added frizzy hair and an unfortunate wardrobe. NBC's *Saturday Night Live* wasted no time taking aim at the First Daughter. Wearing braces, a frizzy wig, and pimples supplied by the makeup department, cast member Julia Sweeney did a devastating send-up of Chelsea. Mike Myers and Dana Carvey, meanwhile, made less-than-flattering comparisons between Chelsea and the beautiful blond daughters of Vice-President Al Gore.

"I'm going to do everything I can to help Chelsea be strong enough so she doesn't let what other people say about her affect her," Hillary told a reporter. "We can't control anybody else."

The cruel jokes soon subsided—in large part because Chelsea was, for all intents and purposes, pulled from public view and enveloped in the protective cloak of the White House. But now, at eighteen, she was no longer living an isolated, insulated existence within the walls of the Executive Mansion. Away from the Clinton Court for the first time in her young life, she was exposed to all the blistering accusations being leveled at her father. As she made one trip after another to the emergency room doubled over with unexplained stomach pains, one thing had become glaringly clear: Chelsea Clinton, despite her parents' best efforts at thickening her skin, was no longer master of her emotions.

That spring of 1998, Hillary was phoning her daughter daily to bolster her spirits. The President also called Chelsea and chatted with her at least once a week. Yet when she returned to the White House in June, Chelsea was stunned to discover that she, too, had been fooled by her parents' public display of unity. Hillary was not only giving her husband the silent treatment, she was refusing to cooperate in shaping his defense. Despite repeated pleas from Bill, the First Lady abruptly stopped meeting with the White House legal team.

Amid press reports of oral sex in the Oval Office and Monica Lewinsky's semen-stained blue Gap dress that surfaced in July, Chelsea sided with her mother. And like the First Lady, Chelsea now refused to speak to her father at all.

Late that month, Chelsea and her mother arrived at a popular Washington restaurant for dinner with friends. As they made their way to their table toward the rear of the restaurant, one patron rose from her table to applaud, then another and another until the entire restaurant was standing on its feet and cheering the two women. Hillary and Chelsea smiled and waved as they sat down, but it was clearly an uncomfortable moment for the First Lady. She knew all too well why she and her daughter were being cheered, and hated the idea that her husband's infidelity had now transformed her into an object of pity.

As Chelsea left on this muggy evening in August for a night out with friends, her mother walked to her bedroom and waited for her husband. For two weeks now, it had been a foregone conclusion that the President would be forced to admit to a sexual relationship with Monica Lewinsky when he testified before Kenneth Starr's grand jury on August 17.

The turning point had actually come exactly two weeks earlier, on August 3, when two of Kenneth Starr's deputies arrived at the White House with a medical technician. With his lawyers looking on, the President rolled up his left sleeve, made a fist, and joked as a needle was inserted and blood drawn from his arm. At that moment, Bill Clinton knew that the DNA sample he was providing would link him inexorably with the semen stain on Lewinksy's blue dress.

On August 12, the President called his old friend and advisor Dick Morris and tried out a confession on him. In a bizarre attempt to shift at least some of the blame to the opposition, he would say he was under such mental strain following the 1995 government shut-down caused by the Republicans that he slipped and had an "improper" relationship with Lewinsky—and that he was profoundly ashamed of his behavior.

Now, on August 13, a Thursday, Bill made the long and lonely journey from the Oval Office to Hillary's bedroom. There was no longer any way he could keep the truth from her. It had all been true. Although he still insisted that he had never actually had sex with Lewinsky—according to Clinton's definition sex meant only intercourse—he had crossed the line. Bill would not go into the details, but he admitted that he had lied all along. As the First Lady sat on the edge of her bed in stunned silence, the President of the United States got down on his knees and, weeping, begged her forgiveness.

Much of what transpired next between Bill and Hillary Clinton was plainly audible to Secret Service agents and household staff members down the hall. In the past, Hillary had thrown books and an ashtray at the President—both hitting their mark. This time, he would later tell one of his oldest political confidants, Hillary rose to her feet and slapped him across the face—hard enough to leave a red mark that would be clearly visible to Secret Service agents when he left the room.

"You stupid, stupid, stupid bastard," Hillary shouted. Her words, delivered at the shrill, ear-splitting level that had become familiar to White House personnel over the years, ricocheted down the corridor. "My God, Bill, how could you risk everything for *that*?"

But it was not in the nature of Bill Clinton to remain silent in the face of his wife's fury. He fought back, loudly arguing, as he would to the grand jury, that he had not slept with Monica Lewinsky and therefore had not committed adultery. What he did with Monica Lewinsky—including fellatio, fondling, and phone sex—was not, by Clinton's narrow definition, sexual activity. "I did not lie to you about that!" he could be heard shouting through the door. "I said I didn't have sex with that woman, and I didn't!"

The screaming continued for a few moments, and then seemed to end as abruptly as it had begun. Spent emotionally and physically, Hillary sank back onto the bed. "How," she asked numbly, "are we going to tell Chelsea?"

Chelsea had taken her cue from her mother and stopped reading the newspapers altogether. But there was no way either woman could avoid feeling the reverberations from the *New York Times* story that ran Friday morning. The front-page article quoted high-ranking White House sources as saying that the President was about to admit to his affair with Lewinksy. Still, Mom and Dad could not bring themselves to sit down with their daughter and tell her the whole truth—not yet.

Hillary would have to summon all her acting skills to get through the next day. "Anyone who thinks Hillary knew what happened before the two of them had their conversation wasn't there that weekend," said an old friend, Harry Thomason's wife and business partner, Linda Bloodworth-Thomason. "The second floor of the White House was a somber place." Although she knew that Bill had no choice but to confess that he had lied about his relationship with Lewinksy, Hillary needed to buy her husband and herself some time to find a way out. She had led him to safety countless times before, and she would do it again. But she needed time . . .

For the moment at least, she would tell friends who called that there was simply no truth to the *Times* report. She instructed her lawyers to tell the press the same thing: Her husband was not about to confess a sexual relationship with Monica Lewinsky.

That Friday afternoon, the First Lady grudgingly went ahead with plans to throw Bill a surprise fifty-second birthday party. She had little choice: The event had been leaked to the press days earlier. Still, since his birthday was not until August 19—still five days away—the President could pretend that he was genuinely surprised when he walked out onto the South Lawn with Hillary at his side and the Marine Band struck up "Happy Birthday."

Those in the crowd who understood Hillary knew at once that something was wrong. Guests whispered among themselves that the First Lady looked exhausted, emotionally spent. Her body language toward the President left little doubt about her feelings toward him. "I thought they'd just had one of their fights in the residence," said one of the birthday guests. "She was so cold that all of us felt frostbitten. I look back on it and I see one very hurt lady. She barely spoke to us."

As Hillary stood by, her face as expressionless as an Inca mask, Bill muttered a few words of thanks to the crowd and then leaned over to blow out the candles on his birthday cake. "I wished," he later said of the moment, "that it would all just go away."

The next day, the President canceled his weekend golf game and holed up in the Oval Office. There, huddled with his lawyers, he got down to the business of crafting his grand jury testimony. Chelsea retreated to her room, where she spent hours on the phone pouring out her heart to boyfriend Matt Pierce. Hillary also locked herself in her room and refused to speak to anyone except her mother, Dorothy Rodham.

As always Mrs. Rodham, who had once dreamed of her daughter becoming the first woman to sit on the United States Supreme Court, urged Hillary to go on the offensive in support of her husband. Given all that was at stake, there was never really any question that she would.

On Sunday morning, the Clintons smiled and waved for photographers as they walked up the stone steps leading into Foundry

United Methodist Church. As they emerged, she made a point of holding his hand. Back in the White House two hours later, she launched into a nonstop series of strategy sessions designed to thwart the special prosecutor and save her husband's presidency. It was, she proclaimed at the first meeting of the day, to be nothing less than "all-out war."

"It was classic Hillary," recalled another Clinton aide. "She was putting all her resources into the political battle and putting everything else aside." According to one of her Arkansas friends, "Hillary didn't want Ken Starr to kill her husband. She wanted him alive so she could do it later."

Bill was too consumed with his own troubles to appreciate how, in the words of one of her Stanford confidants, Chelsea was "destroyed" by her father's stunning admission of infidelity. Contrary to what he would soon tell the American people, the President did not ask his daughter's forgiveness. "President Clinton did *not* apologize to Chelsea. He did not even talk to Chelsea about the Monica Lewinksy thing, and Mrs. Clinton was too angry and humiliated to do it. So Chelsea was more or less left to fend for herself. She wound up getting the news from TV like everyone else."

In meetings with his chief strategists that crucial weekend, it was decided that the only way for the President to contain the scandal was to portray it as strictly a private matter—"not a presidential issue," said one longtime Democratic official, "but a personal one." Even before the President made his public confession, the public would have to be afforded a behind-the-scenes glimpse of a contrite husband and father trying to make things right with his family.

At this propitious moment, Jesse Jackson called Chelsea at the White House and asked if he could be of help. The Reverend had called Chelsea at Stanford several times since the Super Bowl, and the two had prayed over the phone. This time, the voice at the other end of the line trembled with emotion. "Things are really rough for my mom and dad right now," she said, fighting back tears. "Would you be able to come over tonight and pray with us?"

That night Jackson, a stalwart Clinton supporter, continued his spirited defense of the President live on CNN. As soon as he was off the air at 10:30, the Reverend was whisked by government limousine to the White House. A Secret Service agent escorted him directly to the private quarters on the second floor.

Hillary and Chelsea, both wearing sweat clothes—their normal Sunday-evening-at-home attire—met Jackson in the Center Hall. Their faces were drawn, and it was obvious to Jackson that they had both been crying. The three shared a group hug, then walked somberly down the Center Hall to the Yellow Oval Room.

Later describing both women as "devastated," Jackson wasted no time in comforting them. He began by pointing out that even the greatest heroes of the Bible had yielded to temptation. "You ask how can Bill with all his power make this mistake," Reverend Jackson said. "Well, how could King David make it? David was a child prodigy. Slew Goliath. Israel's greatest king. And a talented musician, just as Bill is. And yet he became weak when he saw Bathsheba. Samson, with all of his strength and abilities, in the face of Delilah, he succumbed to the flesh."

Jackson went on to tell Chelsea and her mother that "one's faith is only truly put to the test when you are forced to walk through the storm. And that is what this is all about: faith. Faith and unconditional love."

Shortly before midnight, the President walked in, shook Jackson's hand, and thanked him for coming. "I mean, face it," Jackson said of Clinton, "he is embarrassed by what happened, and Hillary has had to face the humiliation of it all." Once again, Jackson found a biblical parallel. "What's different here is that Ken Starr is able to play God with government funding."

Hillary, taken by surprise, shrieked with laughter. If anything, she hated Starr with a passion unmatched even by her husband. "Where on earth," she asked, "did you get *that* one?"

Bill was not quite so amused. The family needed healing from the Lord, he said gravely. But apparently not the President. He left immediately for a meeting in the third-floor solarium with Harry Thomason, who again took time off from running his television production empire to come to the aid of his embattled friend.

Before excusing himself, Clinton leaned over to Jackson and

asked him to stay and talk one-on-one with Chelsea. "I think she's confused by the whole situation," the President said. "If you could just let her know that these things happen . . ." Hillary then went off to bed, leaving Jackson behind for that quiet chat with Chelsea.

"Of course, at the age of nineteen or twenty, she knows about sex," Jackson said. "She's seen videos, watched television, listened to music. She knows what is expected in marriage, and knows what, in fact, happens."

Jackson started out by comparing Chelsea's parents to Adam and Eve. Their decision to defy God and take that bite of forbidden fruit started the very first cover-up, Jackson explained. "The moral here is," he told Chelsea, " 'You should have stopped talking to the snake in the first place!' "

While Jackson tried to explain to Chelsea that God "is merciful and will forgive your father's sins," the President and Thomason discussed the proper tone for his confession to the American people. In January, before Monica Lewinsky was given immunity to testify against Bill and before the world learned of the existence of physical evidence—a dress stained with his semen—it was Thomason who urged his friend to be more unequivocal in his denials. Now Thomason was urging him not to be too contrite when he gave his televised address, and not to hesitate going after his chief tormentor, Special Prosecutor Kenneth Starr.

Again he heeded Thomason's advice. "You're right," Bill said, his anger building. "That son of a bitch Starr has gone too far. The American people know this has been a goddamn partisan witch-hunt from the very beginning." He slammed his fist on the table, and Thomason, who after all these years still found Bill's rages unnerving, flinched. The White House staff had a name for these frequent tantrums, artfully concealed from the outside world but so familiar to those who worked with Clinton. They called these presidential outbursts "purple fits."

While the President yelled and cursed one floor above, Chelsea and Jackson joined hands, bowed their heads, and prayed. Before he left, the Reverend took Chelsea aside and asked if she'd be all right.

When she nodded, he took her hand. "You have an important responsibility now," he said. "It will be your mission to lift your dad up."

"I love my father," she said, trying to smile. "I'll handle it."

"I know you will," he replied. "I know you will." Jackson left the White House that night no less convinced that the First Lady, though clearly wounded and angry, would survive. "Hillary has been humiliated by all this," he said, "but her strength is just *amazing* . . . I think what's most important is that Chelsea and Hillary are standing with him and I suppose if that strength were not there, he would really be in bigger trouble."

The next day at precisely 12:59 P.M., Bill Clinton walked into the White House Map Room. In her room two floors directly above, Chelsea sobbed over the phone to her Stanford boyfriend Matt Pierce.

The chronically late President, who routinely kept congressional leaders and cabinet members alike waiting an hour or more, had actually arrived one minute before his testimony to the grand jury was scheduled to begin. The jurors themselves were actually across town watching on closed circuit television. But Starr and his staff of six prosecutors had already taken their positions opposite the President and were waiting with their notes spread out before them.

Before they could ask a single question, however, the President read a carefully scripted preemptive statement. In it, he conceded an "inappropriate" relationship with Monica Lewinsky, nothing more. Then the barrage began. A surprisingly testy Clinton spent hours parsing his testimony in the Paula Jones case, insisting he had not committed perjury when he denied having sex with Monica Lewinsky because he did not consider what transpired between them—fellatio, fondling, mutual masturbation, obscene phone calls—to fall under his or the court's definition of sex.

As Starr and his team began to bore in, demanding more specific answers to what the President did or did not do with Lewinksy, he simply invoked his right to privacy and refused to answer. While the President artfully dodged his questioners, a group of his advisors were in the office of White House Counsel Charles Ruff going over the text of Clinton's speech scheduled for broadcast that night.

Political strategist Paul Begala had spent the weekend writing a speech—what aides called the "remorse draft"—that pointedly refrained from making any reference to the special prosecutor. But now Begala, senior advisor Rahm Emanuel, Commerce Secretary Mickey Kantor, and a half-dozen other top aides were handed the draft reworked by the President himself—a carefully couched acknowledgment of wrongdoing followed by a blistering attack on Starr.

About two hours before he was to go in front of television cameras and speak to the nation, Clinton met with his inner circle, again in the solarium. This time Hillary, having a bigger stake in the outcome than anyone with the exception of her husband, sat in. Another of her husband's advisors, administration hard-liner Sidney Blumenthal, took time out from his European vacation to fax the First Lady a series of speeches for her husband to deliver, each more strident than the last.

"Mrs. Clinton was always very outspoken at staff meetings," said one of those present when she walked into the solarium. "She often had more to say than the President—and believe me, she didn't mince words or worry about hurting people's feelings." This strategy session was no exception. As soon as she entered the solarium, Hillary made it clear that she wanted her husband to take on Starr. No matter that the allegations were true—that the President had had an affair with Lewinksy and lied about it—no one would have known had it not been for Starr's relentless pursuit of her husband. "They have persecuted us from the beginning," she said. "The worst thing you can do now is roll over and play dead. Bill, you have got to come out and hammer Ken Starr."

But Begala and the others continued to plead with the President not to attack. He would have none of it. "No other special prosecutor would have dared to pry into the personal life of the President," Clinton said indignantly. "This guy has been out to get me from the beginning, and this is my chance to let the people know it. Besides, there are a lot of people who hate Starr, and I want to talk to them."

His advisors persisted, trying to convince Bill that what the American people wanted to hear now was an apology. Clinton's own lawyers joined in the chorus, urging him to delete the caustic references to Starr. Finally Hillary, who seven months earlier had blamed the whole mess on a "right-wing conspiracy," stood up to leave. "It's your speech," she told her husband bluntly. "You say what you want to say."

That Monday night he said what they *both* wanted to say. After showering and changing from his brown suit into a new blue suit and tie—like his idol John F. Kennedy, Clinton wears as many as three freshly pressed suits per day—the President walked to the dimly lit Map Room at 9:40 P.M. At first he seemed relaxed, and even cracked a few jokes with his aides. But as one aide watched the President rehearse his speech, shoulders slumped as he mouthed the words everyone hoped would stave off impeachment, he noted that Bill Clinton looked "deflated, humbled—like a boy who had just been scolded by his mother."

The President took his seat before the cameras, and Begala affixed the microphone to his boss's tie as the countdown to airtime began. Then Bill Clinton clasped his hands before him and, with all the earnestness of his earlier denials, offered an apology of sorts to the American people.

Upstairs, Chelsea stayed alone in her room while her mother watched the speech with several aides. Hillary's face betrayed not the slightest trace of emotion—not even when he seemed to be apologizing directly to her.

"Good evening," the President began. "This afternoon in this room, from this chair, I testified before the Office of Independent Counsel and the grand jury.

"I answered their questions truthfully, including questions about my private life, questions no American citizen," he added grimly, "would ever want to answer . . . Indeed," he went on to confess, "I did have a relationship with Ms. Lewinsky that was not appropriate. In fact, it was wrong. It constituted a critical lapse in judgment and a personal failure on my part for which I am solely and completely responsible . . . I misled people, including even my wife," he said. "I deeply regret that."

After veering off track to say Starr's investigation had "gone on too long, cost too much, and hurt too many innocent people," he once again invoked Hillary and Chelsea. "Now, this matter is between me, the two people I love most—my wife and our daughter—and our God. I must put it right, and I am prepared to do whatever it takes to do so.

"Nothing is more important to me personally. But it is private, and I intend to reclaim my family life for my family. It's nobody's business but ours. Even Presidents have private lives . . . Our country has been distracted by this matter for too long, and I take my responsibility for my part in all of this. This is all I can do. Now it is time—in fact, it is past time—to move on."

With that, Hillary jumped to her feet and applauded the screen. *"Yes!"* she said. "That'll show them." The President was no less elated. "I think it went well, don't you?" he asked no one in particular. "Yes," Clinton went on, "it's time we put an end to this. The American people are fed up with this shit . . ."

The speech had lasted barely four minutes, but the President's advisors knew instantly that the political damage wrought in those four minutes was incalculable. To complicate matters, in the hours before the speech Hillary had instructed her husband's staff to call Democratic leaders on Capitol Hill and reassure them that Bill's testimony before the grand jury had come off without a hitch. No sooner had Clinton lumbered out of the darkened Map Room than his advisors began talking damage control.

Even they were not prepared, however, for the tsunami-sized backlash. Minutes after the broadcast, members of both parties rushed before the television cameras to voice their disappointment over Clinton's failure to tender what the public wanted—an unequivocal apology to the nation. Veteran Republican Senator Orin Hatch, who had angered members of his own party by suggesting that a simple confession would probably bring an end to talk of impeachment, lashed out at the President. "Wasn't that pathetic," he said of Clinton's attack on Starr. "I tell you, what a jerk." Democratic Senator Dianne Feinstein was no less angry. "My trust in his credibility," she said, "has been badly shattered."

Even old friends like former White House senior advisor George Stephanopoulos and ex–Press Secretary Dee Dee Myers were profoundly disappointed in their old boss. Stephanopoulos said he shared with friends that had remained behind at the White House a sense of "deep disillusionment." Concurred Myers: "He had this one chance to make things right. Now I'm afraid it's too late." Another former advisor, veteran Washington insider David Gergen, blasted Bill for listening to his wife and urged him to "start thinking about the country instead of trying to save his marriage and his own fanny . . . Self-indulgence has been in the saddle too long and is taking him over a cliff."

Nowhere was the feeling of bewilderment and betrayal stronger than among Clinton's political allies—from cabinet members to White House aides—who had put their careers on the line for him. Yet there were no immediate apologies to staff members; these would come only two days later, after Clinton read in the *New York Times* that he had supposedly called in several key staff members and begged their forgiveness. "It was hard to imagine how he could do this to us," White House Press Secretary Mike McCurry admitted, "and how he could be so incredibly reckless . . ."

Not long before, the President had had his frisky Labrador retriever puppy, Buddy, sterilized by the White House vet. "It looks," said one angry staffer, "like they neutered the wrong member of the family."

Incredibly, the First Couple seemed all but oblivious to the hurt feelings of those around them—and to the nearly unanimous negative reviews. "They were as pleased as could be about the speech," said one staff member. "They felt they'd been pulling their punches for months, and now they just came out of their corner swinging. It didn't seem to matter at all that the President of the United States had just confessed adultery with an intern just a few years older than his own daughter, and that he'd been lying about it to us—not to mention the American people—for seven months."

Even odder, said one observer, was the way in which the President and the First Lady were galvanized by their mutual hatred for Ken Starr. "The only thing that seemed to bring Bill and Hillary together at this point," said one staffer, "was sheer rage—their pent-up frustration over Starr and all those right-wingers they kept saying were out to get them."

The euphoria of the moment passed quickly. They had no idea

what to expect from Kenneth Starr's upcoming report to Congress, and Hillary could be certain from past experience that Bill had not told her everything.

The next day, the Clintons were to depart for a long-scheduled stay on Martha's Vineyard, one of their favorite vacation spots. There was concern that the First Lady, having just been humiliated on a scale that could only be described as unprecedented, would now bow out of the trip entirely. When a Clinton aide asked the Hillary camp if the First Lady would at least be willing to issue a statement saying she had forgiven her husband, Mrs. Clinton exploded. "For God's sake, do they have any idea how I feel? Tell them not to pressure me!" she snapped. "I'll do it when *I* decide it's time, not when my husband decides."

Shortly after 11, Hillary went to Chelsea's room, but the door was locked. She then returned to her own room down the hall to sort out her own feelings of anger and self-doubt. "Hillary got mad at Bill, but then she did her own soul-searching," recalled a friend who had known Hillary since they were teenagers. "She asked herself, 'What do I owe him? What couldn't I feel? What couldn't I do? What couldn't I give him?' "

Bill was disdainful of such self-examination. But he wasted no time appointing his personal "accountability group"—a trio of pastors who would visit him once a week in the White House to pray, read Scripture, and basically lead him down the road to moral redemption. One of these, Gordon MacDonald, brought his own expertise to the assignment; a former adulterer, he was forced out of his ministry after it was discovered he had been having an affair with a member of his congregation.

Before they accepted the assignment, the three Protestant clergymen wanted to know if Hillary approved of the plan. "Approve?" one aide later asked incredulously. "Hell, it was Hillary's idea." Indeed, at one of the strategy meetings held over that fateful weekend, it was the First Lady who most strongly advocated depicting the President's transgressions as a purely private matter—a matter for which the family would seek spiritual counseling. Clinton's "God Squad," as the trio of ministers was quickly dubbed by skeptics, was reassured that Hillary approved of them wholeheartedly.

They were also told that they were not to invite the First Lady to participate. "Mrs. Clinton," one of the clergymen said, "did not want to be part of our counseling sessions, period."

During his first weekly session with the God Squad, Bill took out the Bible he always kept on hand and read his favorite passage from Isaiah: "And I shall run and not grow weary . . ." A few weeks later, when it looked as if he would miss Sunday services at the Foundry United Methodist Church, the President phoned Foundry pastor J. Philip Wogamon and asked him to deliver his sermon over the phone. "There's a Sunday morning Bill," Dick Morris had observed, "and a Saturday night Bill."

God's forgiveness was one thing. But Hillary's initial reluctance to back her husband after his confession to the nation had the President's staff worried. They breathed a collective sigh of relief on Tuesday morning when, just before leaving for their family vacation on Martha's Vineyard, Hillary's office issued a statement she herself had agonized over for hours. Her press secretary, Marsha Berry, conceded that "clearly, this is not the best day in Mrs. Clinton's life." But, the statement went on, "this is a time that she relies on her strong religious faith. She's committed to her marriage and loves her husband and daughter very much and believes in the President, and her love for him is compassionate and steadfast. She clearly is uncomfortable with her personal life being made so public but is looking forward to going on vacation with her family and having some family time together."

Indeed, the concept of family—specifically Hillary's desire to hold hers together at all costs—played the largest part in Hillary's decision not to, as one friend advised her, "just pack up and get the hell out of there."

To be sure, she was still devoted to Bill as a public figure, and continued to believe that she, too, would have a role in shaping history. But for Hillary, whose own mother endured what she called a "horrific" childhood after her parents separated, divorce was never an option—not after the birth of Chelsea. "My strong feelings about divorce and its effects on children," she conceded, "have caused me to bite my tongue more than a few times during my own marriage and to think instead about what I could do to be a better wife and partner. My husband has done the same . . . People with children need to ask themselves whether they have given a marriage their best shot and what more they can do to make it work before they call it quits."

Still, as the First Family walked across the South Lawn toward the waiting marine helicopter, it was Chelsea—not her parents—who literally held the family together. As they walked out of the White House, the President extended his hand to the First Lady. Hillary not only refused to take it, she refused even to look at the man who had just confessed to the world that he had been cheating on her. Seizing the moment, Chelsea grabbed her mother's right hand and her father's left hand. Then, holding her head high and flashing a megawatt grin, she literally led her estranged parents toward Marine One. Her father also smiled broadly for photographers, all the while trying to rein in Buddy with his right hand. But Hillary was not smiling for the cameras. She turned her face away from them, her eyes, red and swollen from crying, concealed behind dark glasses.

Later, aboard Air Force One en route to Martha's Vineyard, Hillary stayed locked behind closed doors with Chelsea while her husband worked on the *New York Times* crossword puzzle. When he reached 46 Down—a four-letter word meaning "meal for the humble"—he leaned back and shook his head. "Well, here's one," he said ruefully, "that's appropriate for today." Then he penciled in the answer: CROW.

When they arrived at Martha's Vineyard, Vernon Jordan, the man who had helped Monica Lewinsky find a job allegedly in exchange for her silence, was waiting on the tarmac. Jordan greeted all three Clintons with smiles and bone-crunching hugs, then led them to the crowd of well-wishers waving placards that read MV LOVES BILL and WELCOME BACK. The President and his wife kept their distance from each other, and seemed to be going through the motions as they worked the line.

Chelsea, on the other hand, waded into the crowd like a seasoned pro, stopping to thank well-wishers for their support and even kneeling down to chat with their children at eye level. "Chelsea took it upon herself to be the emissary," said family friend Rose Styron, "and she was terrific. She made everyone feel great."

"It was pretty obvious that Chelsea was trying to take up the slack," agreed one of the local officials who had turned out to greet the President. "She had assumed the role of family cheerleader, and in the process managed to get the focus off her parents, who were definitely not even *looking* at each other, much less talking to each other."

The mood was no different once they reached their vacation "cottage"—a nineteenth-century shingled mansion on twenty waterside acres belonging to wealthy developer Richard Friedman. When he checked in to see how his guests were doing, Friedman was surprised to find the President alone in the backyard, playing fetch with Buddy. "Hillary and Chelsea were inside," observed a local reporter who had staked out the house. "It was as if he was afraid to go inside and face the music."

Less than a full day later, the White House announced U.S. missile attacks on terrorist bases in Sudan and Afghanistan, and Bill seized the opportunity to return to Washington. Before he rejoined his family, Clinton told his staff to make sure that either Hillary or Chelsea—preferably both—would be on hand to greet him when his plane landed. When he emerged from Air Force One, neither his wife nor his daughter was there to meet him. "The President was livid," said a staffer. "It didn't look good, and he knew it."

For the next several days, Bill and Hillary spoke barely a syllable to each other. While the President took long walks on the beach with Buddy and his ever-present Secret Service detail in tow, his wife made telephone calls to friends, read, and tried to bolster Chelsea's spirits.

Hillary was not the only one concerned that, for all her irrepressible public cheerfulness, Chelsea might suffer another anxiety-provoked attack of stomach pains and wind up in the emergency room yet again. One day a member of her father's staff passed Chelsea a note: A few of her Stanford classmates also happened to be spending the summer at the Vineyard, and they wanted to "rescue" her from her predicament—at least for a few hours—by spiriting her away for some sun and fun at the beach. She promptly took them up on their offer.

Hillary was happy to see that Chelsea did not appear to have been emotionally annihilated by the spectacle of her father's confession. It was more than the First Lady could say for herself, though she could still manage to rise to the occasion in public.

At one of several small get-togethers thrown for the Clintons, veteran CBS correspondent Mike Wallace, a longtime Vineyard resident, was making idle conversation when he casually asked Hillary if she had ever had a stress test.

She looked up at Wallace and deadpanned, "I'm having one now."

For his part, Clinton, the man who knew how to work a room better than anybody, suddenly seemed lost and deflated. At a dinner party thrown in their honor at the palatial Martha's Vineyard home of investment banker Steven Rattner, the Clintons kept their distance—arriving separately, leaving separately, and virtually oblivious to each other in the interim.

From the moment he walked through the Rattners' front door without his wife, Clinton had what one guest described as "the hangdog look of a little boy who has just returned from the woodshed." Another guest felt pity for the President: "How lonely and forlorn he looked—so unsure, as if he didn't know if anybody was going to speak to him or not."

He was right. In those first days after the President's admission to the nation, even his staunchest supporters had been scarcely able to contain their rage. "I wish," one guest whispered to writer Gail Sheehy, "I had the guts to tell him what I really think."

To bolster Clinton's sagging spirits, his hosts went in search of someone—anyone—to have his picture taken with the President. Instead of a stampede toward Clinton, there was only embarrassed silence. Not even the teenaged children who were skulking about the house could be persuaded to pose with the disgraced leader. "They were furious with him, outraged, male and female alike," recalled a mother of one of those who refused.

The President was going through one of those rare periods characterized by, as Dick Morris put it, "lassitude, lethargy, and recriminations"—recriminations not over what he might have done differently at the outset, but what actions he might have taken to avoid getting *caught*. It did not help matters when, over dinner, Clinton launched into a full-scale attack on the special prosecutor. "He just didn't get it," one of Clinton's dinner companions said. "None of us were particularly fond of Ken Starr, but this was one time the President really should have just let it alone." When he wasn't talking about Starr, Clinton debated biblical interpretations of adultery with another guest at the table, famed Harvard legal scholar Alan Dershowitz.

The mood was very different at Hillary's table, where the First Lady charmed her dinner companions as she alternately told funny stories and held forth on a wide variety of topics. "When she wants to," Dick Morris once allowed, "Hillary can be the warmest, most charming person you ever met. But she often uses that to conceal what's going on beneath the surface."

What no one saw—indeed, what the proud and private Hillary would not let them see—was what one friend described as the "deep hurt and pain" she was experiencing. "It's like you go through a death and you can't live for weeks and weeks and weeks. And then the healing process begins."

In the past, Hillary always relied on the power of prayer to get her through the rough patches—and there were many—in both her public and her private life. Over the course of the Lewinsky scandal, she phoned her childhood pastor from Chicago, Don Jones, and her old Little Rock pastor Ed Matthew as well as the Reverend Wogamon of Foundry United Methodist for advice.

Hillary Clinton had also sought spiritual guidance from decidedly less traditional sources. In the spring of 1996, she turned to "reflective meditation" sessions with New Age psychic philosopher Jean Houston. Hillary confided in Houston that she had always felt the presence of Eleanor Roosevelt in the White House. At Houston's urging, Hillary actually sat in her room and "talked" to Eleanor Roosevelt. "I was a huge admirer of Eleanor Roosevelt—I wanted so much to be like her, to make a real contribution as First Lady," Hillary said. "But after three years in the White House I felt stymied. I wanted to know what this brilliant woman would have done if she were alive today." At this time it was not unusual for White House staff members to hear Hillary, behind closed doors, having animated—if one-sided—conversations with Eleanor's ghost. "I try to figure out what she would do in my shoes," Hillary recalled. "She usually responds by telling me to buck up or at least to grow skin as thick as a rhinoceros."

Hillary was not the only First Lady to make a psychic connection with long-departed White House occupants. Jackie Kennedy Onassis recalled that when she felt overwhelmed as First Lady, which was often, she would "go and sit in the Lincoln Room. It was the one room in the White House with a link to the past. It gave me great comfort . . . When you see that great bed, it's like a cathedral. To touch something I knew he had touched was a real link with him. I used to sit in the Lincoln Room and I could really feel his strength. I'd sort of be talking with him. Jefferson is the president with whom I have the most affinity. But Lincoln is the one I love."

In much the same way, Hillary loved Eleanor Roosevelt, but she identified most with Jackie Kennedy. It was here on Martha's Vineyard that Hillary had the opportunity to get to know Jackie—and vice versa. Before the Clintons, every president from Lyndon Johnson to George Bush had tried and failed to establish some sort of social rapport with Jackie. Bill Clinton was different—not only the first baby boomer elected President, but the first inspired by JFK's example to enter politics. Moreover, Bill's youth and easy charm evoked memories of Camelot. "You know," Jackie had told her former brother-in-law Senator Edward Kennedy, "in some ways he reminds me of Jack."

So much so that Jackie and her son, John Kennedy Jr., supported Clinton in the primaries over Massachusetts favorite son Paul Tsongas. A month before the 1992 Democratic National Convention, Jackie invited Hillary to lunch at her New York apartment at 1040 Fifth Avenue. Topic A: how best to protect Chelsea from the voracious Washington press corps.

At the convention itself, Jackie was moved by the famous film clip of a starry-eyed, sixteen-year-old Bill Clinton shaking hands with John F. Kennedy in the Rose Garden Jackie had created. "I think," Ted Kennedy said, "that established an emotional link for her."

Both Bill and Hillary made no secret of the fact that they idolized Jack and Jackie Kennedy—"they worshipped at the Kennedy altar," as one Clinton staffer put it—to the point where Bill became obsessed with mimicking JFK's private as well as his public behavior. "He was always saying 'That's what Jack Kennedy would have done' to justify his actions," said an aide. "Hillary knew her husband saw himself as another JFK, and I think sometimes the implications of that—just how far he was willing to go to be like his hero— worried her."

Now, as she walked along the beach at Martha's Vineyard, Hillary's thoughts went back to that August five years earlier when Jackie had first invited the Clintons to the Vineyard. No sooner had they boarded the *Relemar,* the seventy-foot yacht belonging to Jackie's longtime love Maurice Templesman, than the First Family was whisked off for some Kennedy-style daredevil fun.

The *Relemar* dropped anchor off a tiny deserted island, and everyone went for a swim. Jackie's daughter, Caroline, and Chelsea jumped thirty feet off the *Relemar*'s highest diving platform. Goaded by her husband into following them, Hillary was terrified when she climbed to the top and looked down.

"Jump!" the President shouted at his wife as she trembled at the top of the platform. "Don't be a chicken, Hillary. Go ahead and jump! Jump! JUMP!"

With her husband and now several Kennedy men yelling at her to jump, Hillary was about to take the plunge when suddenly she heard Jackie's voice above the others. From down in the water, Jackie yelled, "Don't do it, Hillary! Don't do it! Just because they're daring you, you don't have to!" Heeding Jackie's advice, Hillary slowly descended the ladder to a less harrowing height before making the leap into icy water.

The details of that day would remain etched in Hillary's mind forever—the cool breeze and brilliant sunshine, lunch on the deck of the *Relemar*, the visit to Jackie's seaside compound, and the long walk along her pristine private beach. Throughout it all, the two

First Ladies spent hours sharing their thoughts and dreams and fears. Hillary later used just one word to describe the visit: "magical."

Just nine months later, in May 1994, Jackie died of non-Hodgkin's lymphoma at the age of sixty-four. But in the months before Jackie died the two women spoke on the phone often. "You've got to do things that are right for you," she told Hillary. "Don't model yourself on anybody else. You have to be yourself."

Yet who but Jackie could come close to understanding what it was like to be Hillary Rodham Clinton? The American public had remained blissfully unaware of President Kennedy's rampant womanizing until the mid-1970s—more than a decade after JFK's assassination—and though she had been spared the sort of humiliation on a global scale that Hillary was now forced to endure, Jackie had felt the pain of betrayal.

So, on the island where the two First Ladies had forged a special friendship, Hillary turned to her New Age guru and used the same New Age reflective meditation techniques she had used to conjure up the ghost of Eleanor Roosevelt—this time to "talk" with Jackie. As she walked on the beach, or alone in her rooms at the First Family's borrowed estate, Hillary's thoughts went back to that sunny, breezy, cool day aboard the *Relemar*—and the moment she stood on the narrow diving platform, staring down in abject terror at the glistening surface of the water below. She could hear Bill laughing as he dared her to step off into the abyss.

That moment at the top of the diving platform was a metaphor for the choice she now faced. She could retreat into the shadows, salvaging what remained of her own pride and leaving Bill to fend for himself. Or she could, as Bill was praying she would do, jump into the icy waters and rescue him from himself as she had countless times in the past.

"So should I, Jackie?" she asked the only woman who might have an inkling of what it felt like to be Hillary Rodham Clinton at the crossroads in 1998. "Should I do it? Should I do what Bill says and . . . jump?"

Politics gives guys so much power and such big egos they tend to behave badly toward women. I hope I never get into that.

> —*Bill,*
> in 1969

You know why people go into politics, don't you? Because of their unsatisfied sexual desire.

> —*Bill,*
> in 1984

Bill always had this sense about him that he collected girls.

> —*Carolyn Yeldell Staley,*
> longtime friend

I think we're all addicted to something. Some people are addicted to drugs. Some to power. Some to food. Some to sex. We're all addicted to something.

—*Bill*

It was never in the game plan to grow up and fall in love with someone from Arkansas. I had never *known* anyone from Arkansas.

—*Hillary*

2

FROM THE VERY beginning, said Hillary's friend and fellow lawyer Terry Kirkpatrick, "she was absolutely, totally crazy about Bill Clinton. 'Besotted' is not a word I would normally apply to Hillary, but I think she was besotted." For his part, young Bill Clinton saw in Hillary a combination of intellect and raw ambition that made her the perfect life partner for someone with his sights set on the White House. But there was never any question that Bill would love Hillary—or any one woman, for that matter—to the exclusion of all others.

"Bill loves Hillary as much as he could love any one woman," his friend and onetime business partner James McDougal observed. "But to say Bill Clinton is not designed for monogamy is putting it mildly." Agreed one of Bill's Arkansas neighbors: "Of course he's promiscuous. Can you blame him? Look at the environment he grew up in. And that family! Oh, my."

It has become cliché in recent years, but the term "dysfunctional" seems a woefully inadequate way of describing Bill Clinton's twisted family history of violence, promiscuity, adultery, divorce, bigamy, poverty, illegitimacy, and addiction. All of which, according to psychiatrist Jerome Levin, left Bill Clinton predisposed "both biologically and socially to an addiction of his own—an addiction to sex."

Bill Clinton never knew the man who was listed on his birth certificate as his natural father; W. J. Blythe II was killed three months before his son William Jefferson Blythe III arrived via cesarean section in the middle of a raging summer thunderstorm on August 19, 1946. Yet Blythe Sr.'s reputation as a charming if sexually indiscriminate rogue presaged that of the son he would never live to see.

Born the sixth of nine children, W. J. Blythe grew up dirt-poor in rural Sherman, Texas. When the banks foreclosed on the Blythe family farm during the Depression, W.J. hit the road selling everything from auto parts to tractors. Inexhaustible—he got by on five hours of sleep a night—handsome, charismatic, and irresistible to women, he traveled throughout the South collecting wives and lovers along the way.

In 1935, W.J. married Adele Gash, divorced her the following year but nevertheless fathered her son Henry Leon—Bill Clinton's half brother—in 1938. He then impregnated another woman, but to avoid marrying her entered into a sham marriage with his first wife's sister Faye. That marriage ended in 1941, and in May 1941 Blythe married Wannetta Alexander in Kansas City, Missouri, eight days before the birth of their daughter Sharon (Bill Clinton's half sister).

Virginia Cassidy was a student nurse working the late shift at Tri-State Hospital in Shreveport, Louisiana, in the summer of 1943 when Blythe rushed into the emergency room with a lady friend. From the moment she laid eyes on him, Virginia later said, she was overwhelmed by a "fireball of feeling." The young woman he brought into the ER was doubled over in pain and would soon have an emergency appendectomy, but the twenty-year-old Virginia scarcely noticed; she was more concerned with whether the handsome young stranger and the patient were married.

"I was weak-kneed," she later recalled. "All I could think of was, I've got to know if they're married or not." She tried calling him by the last name of the woman he brought in.

"I beg your pardon," he replied. "We're not married. We're friends."

With her garish makeup ("When it comes to lipstick, I say the brighter the better"), painted-on eyebrows, tight sweaters, and stiletto heels, Virginia already had a reputation as an unabashed tease. It did not seem to matter that Virginia was engaged to her high school sweetheart, Richard Fenwich. Before leaving the hospital, Blythe stopped by the nurses' station, walked up to Virginia, and touched the ring that was on the fourth finger of her left hand. "What does that mean?" he asked.

"Nothing," she said without skipping a beat, and promptly slipped it off.

"I was shameless," Virginia later recalled. "In those days we talked fast, played fast, fell in love fast." Two months later, on September 3, 1943, Virginia Cassidy and Bill Blythe were wed in a civil ceremony presided over by a justice of the peace in Texarkana, Arkansas.

Only trouble was, Blythe was a bigamist. He had not bothered to divorce his third wife, Wannetta. It would be another seven months before that marriage would legally end on April 13, 1944. Unbeknownst to Virginia, who claimed she never even bothered to ask if Blythe had been married before, their marriage—the union that presumably produced a future president—was invalid.

Nor did he bother to share another important detail with his new bride. The previous April, Blythe had received his draft notice and was now ordered to report for duty. Just five weeks after he married Virginia, Blythe boarded a troopship bound for Europe.

Virginia already knew something about conflict—particularly the domestic variety. Her mother, Edith, despite a fondness for applying layer upon layer of cosmetics and a tendency to flirt with doctors, was for the most part a respected private nurse in the tiny town of Hope, Arkansas. There and throughout Garland County, she was known for tending to her many patients with humor, patience, and kindness.

At home, however, Edith was a tireless taskmaster and consummate control freak who demanded nothing less than blind obedience from the rest of the family. She could be moody and violent, and routinely exploded at Virginia's mild-mannered father, Eldridge, sending him scurrying for cover as she hurled dishes, glassware—basically anything she could get her hands on—in his direction. Edith also aimed her wrath at their hapless only child, shrieking at little Virginia and whipping her with a strap, switch, or coat hanger over even the tiniest infraction.

James Eldridge Cassidy was as gregarious, generous, and dependably even-tempered as his wife was volatile. And, like Virginia's mother, Eldridge Cassidy was also something of a fixture in Hope—a town best known for the size of its watermelons. While Edith cut quite the flamboyant figure making her rounds in full registered nurse regalia—crisp white uniform, nurse's cap, billowing blue cape, and all—he delivered ice to Hope's homes and businesses from the back of a refrigerated truck.

Later, when respiratory problems forced him to quit the ice business, Eldridge borrowed the money to open a grocery store. The small establishment catered to both whites and blacks, who came in through the same door, pulled items from the same shelves, and paid at the same cash register—far from the norm in still strictly segregated rural Arkansas. As a storekeeper, Cassidy soon became one of the most popular men in town—and with good reason. He sold moonshine under the counter after Hempstead County elected to go dry, and extended credit to anyone who asked—a practice that, sadly, would ultimately cost him his business.

Eldridge adored his "Ginger," and father and daughter were bound by a shared fear of the mean-spirited Edith. Although he did not stand up to his wife and prevent her from physically and emotionally brutalizing Virginia, Eldridge did try to make up not only for his wife's cruelty but for the Cassidys' meager financial circumstances. So that she would not be mocked by the daughters of the town's more affluent families, Eldridge had made sure that, even in the depths of the Depression, his daughter had new school supplies and never had to resort to wearing secondhand clothes.

Virginia inherited her father's outgoing nature, but—from their shared fondness for rouge and eyeliner to their hair-trigger tempers—it was the ambitious, willful Edith whom she would grow up to most closely resemble. At Hope High School Virginia excelled academically, consistently making the honor roll while throwing herself into a wide range of extracurricular activities, from the science and press clubs to student council. As popular and fun-loving as she was studious, Virginia wrote under her photograph in the 1941 senior class yearbook, "I'd like to be serious but everything is so funny."

Virginia was not about to let her new husband's departure for Europe in the autumn of 1943 spoil her fun. Even before Bill Blythe and the rest of the 125th Battalion reached Italy, his bride had earned her nursing credentials and moved back in with her parents. There she resumed the carefree existence she had led before she left Hope, dating old boyfriends and dancing until dawn.

It was not until December 10, 1945, that Blythe and the wife he barely knew reunited in Hope. Soon she was expecting, and the couple moved to Chicago, where Blythe had gone back to work for his old company selling heavy equipment. After several months living in a run-down hotel while they searched in vain for affordable housing, Virginia returned to Hope to live with her parents during the final months of her pregnancy.

That spring of 1946, Bill Blythe finally found their dream house in suburban Forest Park, Illinois. On May 17, a Friday, he jumped into his midnight-blue Buick and headed south to pick up his wife and bring her back to their new home.

He never made it. Blythe was halfway to Hope, passing other motorists as he barreled down Route 61 at breakneck speed, when his left front tire blew out three miles southwest of Sikeston, Missouri, shortly after 10:40 P.M. The car careened across the highway and into an open field before flipping twice and coming to rest upside down.

Blythe somehow managed to pull himself through the driver's side window and stagger toward the highway, his only injury a bruise on his forehead. He was only several yards from the road when he stumbled and fell face first into a drainage ditch. Within minutes, William Jefferson Blythe had drowned in less than six inches of water.

Virginia's husband, the reputed father of a future president, was probably still alive when several drivers he had passed only moments earlier pulled to the side of the road and ran toward the overturned Buick. When they reached the car and peered inside, the radio was still on but no one was inside. Warily, they put their shoulders to turning the car right side up, fully expecting to find the driver's crushed body beneath the wreckage. Again, they found nothing. It would be more than two hours before someone spotted Blythe's hand sticking up from the muck of the drainage ditch. (Virginia would not find out about Blythe's earlier marriages until reporters uncovered the information in 1993, leaving her "hurt and confused." Still, she insisted, "I'll go to my grave knowing *I* was the love of his life.")

Twelve weeks after Virginia buried her husband, William Jefferson Blythe III was born—an event that, given the fact that Virginia's husband had returned from Europe just eight months before and the boy was born full-term, started local tongues to wagging. It did not help that, over the course of the nearly three years her husband was overseas, she was a fixture on Hope's dance hall and party scene.

Over the years Virginia would try to explain away the gossip by claiming that Blythe had actually returned from the war in November, and that the delivery was induced at her doctor's insistence after she took a nasty spill. But the doctors and nurses who were present at Billy's birth insisted the baby was born full-term, and pointed to his eight-pound, six-ounce birthweight to prove it. Doubts concerning Bill Clinton's paternity persisted, even in the mind of Bill Clinton. To one of his closest confidants in Arkansas he confessed that he had grown up "wondering who my father really was."

The newly widowed Virginia brought little Billy home to the Cassidys' white clapboard house at 117 South Hervey Street. "You know, you never think you're going to get married again," she would recall years later. "Never, never. It never crosses your mind. All I was looking at was this baby who was going to be left up to me to support."

He may have been fatherless, but inside the house on Hervey Street little Billy Blythe was the center of his own universe—doted on not only by his mother but also by his "Mammaw" Edith and his "Pappaw" Eldridge. The competition between the two women for the little boy's attention and affection was nothing short of fierce. Mammaw, only forty-five when her grandson was born, felt every bit up to the task of raising him. Although Virginia tried to exert her authority as Billy's mother, it was the iron-fisted Mammaw who determined when Billy would get up and when he would nap, what he would eat and how much, when he would be toilet trained and how. The boy, Virginia later said of the "unrelenting" routine imposed by Edith, "napped, played, ate, burped, slept in an unwavering cycle."

Billy had not yet celebrated his first birthday when Virginia, resigned to the fact that her mother was actually raising the child, left him behind to train as a nurse anesthetist at Charity Hospital in New Orleans. By specializing in anesthesiology, Virginia could command higher pay—enough, she devoutly prayed, to break away from the controlling Edith. Still, it was heartbreaking for Virginia to leave her infant son behind—"the hardest thing," she later said, "I would ever have to do."

Billy understood just how great the sacrifice had been. His earliest memory, he later said, was of being taken by Mammaw to visit his mother in New Orleans. When the trip was over, Virginia sank to her knees on the platform and wept as their train pulled out of the station.

Still, for all practical purposes it was Edith who mothered Billy in those early, formative years. Using a system of homemade flashcards, Mammaw began teaching him to read when he was two. The following year she began taking him to Sunday school at Hope's First Baptist Church.

Virginia, meantime, had a new man in her life—a fast-talking, likable, big-spending Buick dealer from neighboring Hot Springs who, like Billy's widowed mom, loved to stay out partying until sunup. His name was Roger Clinton, but to his drinking and gambling buddies he was known simply as "Dude."

Clinton, thirteen years her senior, was the very much married father of two when he began seeing Virginia in early 1948. He was also an unrepentant batterer; when she filed for divorce in August 1948, Ina Mae Clinton described several harrowing incidents that left her bruised and bloodied.

Virginia may or may not have been aware of his penchant for violence, but she knew full well that he was carrying on with other women even as he professed his undying love for her. None of it seemed to matter; Roger Clinton was an irrepressible carouser and, Virginia said at the time, "right about now I need a little fun in my life."

Virginia proved to be more than a match for Roger. When they visited friends, she would "climb up on the counter, obviously under the influence of something like Roger's moonshine, and sing this absurd song I had made up—'I'm the Hempstead County Idiot.' Which I obviously was." Before long, she announced her intention to marry Clinton—in part, she later confessed to a friend, because as the wife of the local Buick dealer she could have her pick of new cars off Roger's lot.

Mammaw and Pappaw were outraged. Edith warned her daughter that if she went ahead with her marriage plans, they would fight her in court for custody of three-year-old Billy. But Virginia was determined, and married Roger on June 19, 1950, just a few blocks from the Hot Springs racetrack, Oaklawn Park, in a small white house that served as the parsonage for a church. Rather than risk provoking her mercurial mother, Virginia did not object when Edith kept her son from attending the ceremony.

Billy's grandparents backed down on their threat to seek custody, and the little boy moved with his mother and her new husband into a one-story, three-bedroom white wood frame house at 321 Thirteenth Street. He was the chubbiest child in the neighborhood, but other than that there was little to distinguish Billy from the rest of the kids in Hope—or America, for that matter. Caught up in the Hopalong Cassidy mania of the early 1950s, he wore Hoppy's trademark all-black cowboy outfit with silver buttons, toted a toy version of the cowboy's trusty silver-barreled revolver, and even carried an official Hopalong Cassidy lunchbox to school. At Miss Marie's School for Little Folk ("Miss Mary's kindergarten" to local folk), his favorite playmate was Mack McLarty, who was also the son of an auto dealer—albeit a markedly more successful one.

Accustomed to being the center of attention at home, Billy was determined even at age five to gain the affection of those around him. "It was kind of sad, really," said a childhood friend. "He was always kind of jumping up and down, pushing himself to the front. There was never any reticence or shyness like there is with other kids. It was always 'love me, love me.' "

One day during recess, the other children poked fun at their pudgy, clumsy classmate, daring him to jump rope in his cowboy boots. When he did, they yanked the rope up to trip him. He came crashing to the pavement, shattering his leg in three places. As Billy lay on the ground, screaming in pain, the other children stood in a circle and teased him. "Billy's a sissy! Billy's a sissy!" they taunted. From the boy's standpoint, it was not a complete disaster. For five weeks he lay in bed with his leg suspended vertically, his every whim catered to by his mother and Mammaw. The boy snacked, read comic books, and held court as the same children who had cruelly taunted now came to gaze in wonder at his ankle-to-thigh cast.

Meanwhile, Roger and Virginia, now employed as a nurse in nearby Hot Springs, kept up the frantic pace of their social life. They drank, smoked, gambled, and went club-hopping until dawn while Billy was left in the care of his grandparents. At local night-spots that offered live entertainment, Virginia became known for jumping onstage, uninvited, seizing the microphone, and belting out her favorite country songs.

Despite her nightlife shenanigans, Virginia was not an alcoholic. Nor did she allow her vices to interfere with her work or her role as a wife and mother. The same could not be said for Roger, who grew increasingly belligerent as he drank himself into a stupor vir-tually every night.

Before long, Virginia's world had spiraled out of control. "Our house was just bedlam, from the time we got home until dawn's early light, by which time Roger would usually have yelled himself to sleep." Often Virginia's little boy cowered in his room, staring at the photo of Bill Blythe he kept by his bed and flinching every time he heard the sound of Roger striking his mother.

When things became even more chaotic than usual, she would sneak her son out of the house and they would spend the night at a motel. One evening Virginia decided to take Billy to visit his great-grandmother—Edith's mother—at the Hope hospital where she lay dying. Roger told them not to go, and when she said she was leaving anyway he pulled out a pistol and fired.

"Before I knew it," she recalled, "I heard a gunshot and a bullet smacked into the wall next to me . . . I was stunned." She "grabbed Billy by the hand and we were out of there. We went across the street to the neighbors' house, and they called the police." Within minutes a squad car pulled up to the Clintons' front door and "Daddy," as Billy now called his stepfather, wound up spending the night in jail.

Billy was enrolled in Brookwood Elementary School in September 1952. But by Christmas, Roger Clinton sold his Buick agency and moved the family to Hot Springs, where they eventually settled into a two-story house at 1011 Park Avenue. Although he would later capitalize on being the candidate from "a town called Hope," Billy Clinton, as he was now called, was a product of the wide-open resort and gambling mecca that blended white-steepled Baptist churches with strip clubs, cheap motels, bars, betting parlors, and houses of ill repute.

Hot Springs owed its initial fame to the therapeutic powers of the local water; people came from all over the country to visit the spas and bathhouses that lined Central Avenue. But by the 1920s it was a center of gambling and prostitution, a result of the cozy relationship between Arkansas politicians and organized crime. So profitable were the town's various illegal operations that top mobsters from New York and Chicago—Al Capone, Lucky Luciano, and Bugsy Siegel among them—flocked to Hot Springs each year for a piece of the action.

In the town where he really grew up, hypocrisy was a way of life. "Growing up there," said Hot Springs prosecutor Paul Bosson, "you were living a lie." Virginia fondly remembered that "you could carry your drink around with you downtown, even on Sundays." She insisted she never gave a thought to the fact that many of Hot Springs's most high-profile businesses were patently illegal. "When it came to a vote on legalization of gambling in Arkansas," she later wrote, "I never was so shocked."

Even in this gaudy, neon-lit realm of the senses, Virginia stood out. "I'd never met anyone like Virginia before," said her longtime friend and next-door neighbor Carolyn Yeldell Staley. "She seemed so . . . exotic." Mrs. Clinton was painting her eyebrows even higher ("I've lost twenty-five years of sleep drawing on my face every morning. No telling what I could have accomplished if I had been born with eyebrows") and was now gluing on false eyelashes. "Some people say they make me look like a spider," she said, "but I like 'em."

During the day she battled furiously with Hot Springs doctors who preferred male anesthesiologists to female nurse anesthetists. Afternoons she would come home and complain to her son about the office politics that raged at the hospital. "They are all plotting against me," she told him, "trying to destroy my career." Whether real or imagined, the notion that his mother was the victim of a dark conspiracy had a profound impact on the way Clinton viewed the world and his place in it.

Virginia was not one to let office politics stand in the way of her having fun. After nightfall, she put down the top of her convertible and sped from nightclub to racetrack to sporting club to dance hall—usually with her husband, but sometimes with other men she picked up along the way. The Vapors, where Liberace sometimes performed, was one of Virginia's favorite haunts, along with the Southern Club, the Pines, and the Oaklawn racetrack.

Billy, left as many as four and five nights a week in the care of a churchgoing nanny named Mrs. Walters, still lay awake listening to his parents' battle when they returned home. Fueled by jealousy as well as whiskey, Daddy raged more ferociously than ever.

Adding to the chaos, Edith suffered a cerebral hemorrhage not long after her daughter and her adored only grandchild left Hope for Hot Springs. Mammaw recovered from the stroke, but by the time she was discharged from the hospital she was dependent on morphine.

Again, Billy was witness to countless family scenes, this time as his mother confronted his grandmother over her drug addiction. In desperation, Virginia was forced to commit Mammaw to the Arkansas state asylum at Benton, a Dickensian snake pit that would later be described by federal officials as one of the worst institutions of its kind in the country.

For the next three months, Billy went along with his mother on her Sunday visits to the asylum, watching helplessly as each reunion dissolved into a bitter shouting match. When Virginia, satisfied that her mother had overcome her addiction, finally agreed to let her out of Benton, Mammaw returned home determined to play an even larger role in her grandson's life.

Billy was now more determined than ever to make his own world separate and apart from this chaotic family environment. "The violence and dysfunction in our home made me a loner, which is contrary to the way people view me because I'm gregarious, happy, all of that," President Bill Clinton would eventually admit. "But I had to construct a whole life inside my own mind."

Virginia enrolled her Protestant son in St. John's Catholic School "for the order and the discipline." He excelled at everything, and was so eager to please that the nuns found him more than a little obnoxious." To satisfy his desperate need to be liked by all who came in contact with him, Billy talked in class constantly. When a question was asked, his hand was always the first to go up. If another student was chosen, he blurted out the answer anyway. A straight A student otherwise, Billy Clinton was crestfallen when his teachers gave him a C for deportment.

His second-grade teacher more than made up for Billy's only C when she took Virginia aside and told her how impressed the entire faculty was with her son. "Someday," she told Billy's mother, "he is going to be president."

"Oh, yes," she replied almost matter-of-factly. "That's what I tell him every day."

At age eight, Billy put on his Sunday best, tucked his Bible under his arm, and marched solemnly—and alone—to Park Place Baptist Church. While Virginia and Roger were sleeping off their hangovers, Billy even had himself baptized.

For the fourth grade, Virginia's boy made the switch to public school. He enrolled in Ramble Elementary School and within a few days, said his classmate David Leopoulos, "most kids knew who he was and wanted to be around him." Despite the fact that his stepfather refused to adopt him and his legal surname continued to be Blythe, the popular newcomer referred to himself only as Billy Clinton.

At about the same time, Virginia learned that she was pregnant. "Isn't that just the way we women do things?" she marveled. "Here

I was, married to an alcoholic who was abusing me and my son, and I go and let the man make me pregnant."

Roger Cassidy Clinton arrived about a month before Billy's tenth birthday, on July 25, 1956. Still, he would never be able to compete with the primacy of his older brother within the Clinton family. Virginia was an affectionate mother to Roger, but she was besotted with Billy, who for all intents and purposes was the man of the house by the time he entered junior high school.

Unabashedly proud of her firstborn son, Virginia transformed the house on Park Avenue into a veritable shrine in his honor. The walls were lined with photos of Billy, along with framed awards, certificates, and letters of commendation he had earned. "We used to joke," a neighbor quipped, "that all Virginia needed were candles."

From the outset, Billy was a nurturing and protective older sibling. The mere fact that little Roger was Daddy's natural son did not shield him from the emotional trauma that Billy had endured his entire life. Now the two boys huddled together in the upstairs room they shared, clasping their hands to their ears as they tried to shut out the yelling and the all-too-familiar sound of Daddy pummeling their mother. From the beginning, little Roger idolized the big brother he called "Bubba." (From this point on, Virginia was "Dado.")

By 1959 the violence had escalated drastically. In March of that year Roger became wildly jealous of his wife's flirting with other men at a dance early that year. In full view of dozens of other couples, he threw her to the floor, kicking her and punching her until she bled. In Hot Springs, where spousal abuse was tolerated, no one intervened.

At home a few weeks later, he attacked her again, this time taking off her high-heeled shoe and beating her over the head with it as he had done with his previous wife. Billy called Virginia's lawyer, Bill Mitchell, who then summoned police. Virginia promptly filed for divorce, but within a matter of weeks the couple had reconciled amid his promises to halt the abuse and to quit drinking.

Instead, the drinking and the abuse would continue for another two years. Then, one night in 1961, Roger Clinton arrived home roaring drunk and, in Virginia's words, "spitting fire." He pursued her into the bedroom. "I was really afraid this time," she remembered, "and I kept moving, kept dodging him, kept pushing chairs in his way."

His little brother's hysterical crying—at one point four-year-old Roger ran outside and grabbed a stick with which to defend his mother—and the mounting ongoing mayhem finally proved too much for Billy, whose room was directly across the hall. Exhausted from screaming and very drunk, Roger Sr., wearing only a pair of boxer shorts, sat slumped at the foot of the bed when Billy burst through the door. At fourteen, he was already an inch taller than his stepfather.

"Daddy, stand up," Billy said. Roger, as drunk as Virginia had ever seen, tried to get up but couldn't.

"You must stand up to hear what I have to say to you," the boy said. "Daddy, I want you on your feet." Finally, he pulled Roger up by the arms and looked him straight in the eye. "Hear me," he said, "never . . . ever . . . touch my mother again."

That night, Virginia called the police one more time. Roger, refusing to put his clothes on, was hauled off to jail in his underwear. Before he left, Roger turned to Billy and snarled, "Next time, I'll mash your face in."

Over the next two years, Virginia secretly saved up enough money to finance a life for herself and the children without Roger. Then, in April 1962, she filed for divorce on grounds of abuse and mental cruelty, and moved with her sons into a modest ranch-style house she purchased on Scully Street. The house was half the size of the one they had been living in, and was in a far less desirable part of town. But to Virginia and Billy it represented nothing less than freedom.

In her depositions, Virginia recounted humiliation after humiliation, beating after beating. "I am afraid of him when he is drinking," she told the court. "He has continually tried to do bodily harm to myself and my son, Billy, whenever he attempts to attack me when he has been drinking."

Billy also provided testimony. In his written affidavit, he told of "breaking down the door" to confront this stepfather. "He has threatened my mother on a number of occasions," Bill stated, "and because of his nagging, arguing with my mother I can tell that she is very unhappy and it is impossible in my opinion for them to continue to live together as husband and wife."

Ironically, three weeks later Virginia petitioned the same court to legally change Billy's name to William Jefferson Clinton from William Jefferson Blythe III. (Oddly, even as an adult Clinton was so uncertain as to the details of his paternity that he incorrectly referred to himself as "William Jefferson Clinton IV.")

The fact that the senior Clinton declined to legally adopt the boy apparently was of little consequence to Virginia. In her deposition, she argued that "there are no pleasant associations with the name of Blythe, as Billy never knew his father, and has always been known by his friends and in various organizations and school records as William Jefferson Clinton."

Billy did not have to be persuaded. "The name doesn't matter," he later said, "it's the man." But at the time, he felt that the name mattered very much as a symbol of his bond to his vulnerable younger brother. "I thought it would be a gesture," Billy later explained, "of family solidarity."

There was another reason Bubba, as he was now known to the rest of the family, wanted to be legally anointed a Clinton. His uncle Raymond Clinton, Roger's wealthy and influential older brother, was one of Garland County's more respected—and politically influential—figures. Over the years, Billy would increasingly come to regard Uncle Raymond as both surrogate father and something of a political mentor.

The divorce of Virginia and Roger Clinton was finalized on May 15, 1962, giving Mrs. Clinton custody of her two sons, half the proceeds from the sale of the house at 1011 Park Avenue, the family's 1960 Buick LeSabre, and a chandelier. Clinton was ordered to pay a minimum of $50 a month child support for little Roger, but not a penny for Billy.

Within a matter of days, Virginia began to doubt her decision. Roger had repeatedly begged her to drop her divorce action, and even after the final decree he persisted in his efforts to win her back. Clinton would show up on her doorstep unannounced, tearfully promising to change his ways and pleading with her to reconsider. At times, he would park his car across the street and just sit for hours watching the family that had once been his. On other occasions he would "weep and carry on for hours," Virginia recalled, before collapsing in an exhausted heap on her front porch.

"It was so sad," said Virginia, "I couldn't stand it." She was convinced that, without her, the man she once loved would simply self-destruct. That August, less than three months after their divorce was granted, the couple remarried.

"Mother," a wary Billy warned her, "you're making a mistake."

To be sure, within months of their remarriage, little Roger came upon his father in the laundry room holding a pair of scissors to his mother's throat. The boy ran to his older brother screaming, "Bubba! Bubba! Daddy's killing Dado!" Again, Bill stood up to his drunken stepfather, literally shoving him onto the front porch and locking the door behind him.

Long the center of his mother's world, Billy now totally eclipsed her husband. Virginia's son had become the man of the house at fifteen. "Dado" insisted Billy move into the master bedroom, while she and Roger shared smaller quarters down the hall. Gradually Roger, his body ravaged by decades of smoking, drinking, and carousing, now simply faded into the woodwork. He still drank, but now alone and only at home. When Virginia returned home after working late at the hospital, she would poke her head into the family room and see the man she once feared slumped in his chair, staring vacantly at the black and white images flickering across the TV screen.

Even though Billy was convinced that it was only a matter of time before the mayhem resumed, he did not share his concerns with anyone outside the immediate family. In fact, none of Billy's friends, classmates, or teachers were aware of the turmoil that had raged behind closed doors inside the Clinton household.

"Billy never said a single thing to any of us about his father's drinking or the violence that he witnessed. Nothing," Carolyn Yeldell Staley said. On the contrary, added another high school classmate, "Billy went out of his way to lead us to believe that his life was pretty much picture-perfect. That was his reputation in the community, after all. He did everything humanly possible to promote his image as the all-American boy. The thing is, it wasn't a question of his hiding his private pain. I don't think he was feeling pain. He was so good at the deception that he tricked himself into believing everything was just fine at home."

Still, Billy's classmates would have been shocked to learn that, in Roger's absence, Virginia now occasionally took her underage son to nightclubs as her "date." Although he never drank—seeing what liquor had done to his stepfather had made the boy deathly afraid of becoming an alcoholic—Billy did dance with his mother and made sure she got home safely.

If Billy had a talent for self-deception, he had his mother to thank for it. Virginia realized when Billy was still in primary school that the nightly mayhem he witnessed could do irreparable damage to the boy's psyche. By the time he reached high school, the situation had gotten so bad that famously stoic Billy finally complained to his mother that he was finding it difficult to think of anything else.

So, she told him, "brainwash yourself. Put the bad things out of your mind—just push them aside so they don't interfere with the important things in your life." But for Billy, the word "brainwash" conjured up horror-movie images of vacant-eyed zombis. So Virginia tried something else: "Construct an airtight box in your mind," she said. "Keep inside it what you want to think about. The inside is white, the outside is black . . . This box is strong as steel."

Virginia's concept of "boxing things off" would become Billy's salvation, enabling him not only to focus on those things he cared to think about with laserlike intensity, but to neatly package and dispose of all unpleasant thoughts.

Yet there were some unpleasant things he seemed only too eager to confront, and from an early age. While he was still in elementary school, Billy, who often played with the black children who came into his grandfather's store, questioned the right of people to discriminate on the basis of color. He told his mother it did not seem fair to him that black children should go to separate schools, eat in separate restaurants, sit in the balcony at movie theaters, and ride in the back of the bus. But Virginia, who like most Southerners of her generation never questioned segregation, staunchly defended her racist views.

At whites-only Hot Springs High, widely regarded as one of the state's top secondary schools, Billy breezed through his studies effortlessly, leaving plenty of time for Key Club, Beta Club, student council, and volunteer work at his mother's hospital. "When I was a kid," Bill Clinton later recalled, "I thought I was busier than anybody else I knew."

This frenzy of activity masked a fear that would plague Billy his entire life. "He just hated more than anything else," his mother said, "being alone."

In the ninth grade, a civics teacher named Mary Marty "quickened" Clinton's interest in politics, he later recalled. Billy was the only student in Marty's class who supported Jack Kennedy; the rest, mimicking their parents' political views, were die-hard Nixon supporters. So when the class restaged the landmark televised 1960 Kennedy-Nixon debates, there was no doubt who would play the part of JFK. At fourteen, Bill Clinton was already imitating the man on whom he would pattern his entire life—both political and personal.

Music also played a large role in his life during this period. Billy sang in the choir at Park Place Baptist Church, and to please his mother, an ardent Elvis fan, gamely crooned "Love Me Tender" at family gatherings. He also shared Elvis's fondness for peanut butter and banana sandwiches, which he whipped up in the kitchen and consumed with gusto every afternoon after school. (Virginia later placed a bust of Elvis in a corner of her dining room, and purchased a puka-shell necklace that once belonged to the King. "Sometimes," the mother of the future president rhapsodized, "I can still smell Elvis's Brut cologne coming from the porous shells . . . But I ask you: Does that make me an Elvis nut?")

It was as a tenor saxophonist that Billy excelled. He originally took up the instrument to drown out the sound of his parents' quarreling and "to create something that was beautiful, something I could channel my sensitivity into."

He joined the Hot Springs High marching band (the school's fight song was "Dixie"), went to band camp in Fayetteville every summer, and was eventually named the best high school saxophone player in the state. Billy also played sax for The Stardusters, Hot

Springs High's dance band, and formed his own three-man jazz combo, The Kingsmen.

Equally popular with boys and girls, Billy was no less a faculty favorite. His crew-cut looks, outgoing personality, insatiable curiosity, and drive to succeed made him a favorite youth speaker on the Rotary and Lions Club luncheon circuits. "He was," allowed Billy's bandleader and mentor Virgil Spurlin, "simply outstanding at everything he set his mind to—a leader in every sense of the word."

Billy had entertained vague notions of becoming a foreign diplomat until he stumbled on his true calling in the summer of 1963. That June, he attended the American Legion's Boys State summer camp and, while the other young leaders campaigned for the vaunted title of governor, mapped out his strategy to get elected to the less-desirable post of senator. Bill's friend since kindergarten days, local football hero Mack McLarty, handily beat out the competition in the governor's race. But it was Bill who, as one of two newly elected senators, would be going to Washington to represent Arkansas at Boys Nation. "He'd had his eye on the national stage all along," McLarty said.

At Boys Nation, Clinton—one of the few Kennedy Democrats in a sea of Barry Goldwater Republicans—and his fellow fledgling politicos drafted party platforms, engaged in spirited mock debates, and passed resolutions. They also got an up-close look at the real players in Washington. Bill visited all the monuments, visited Congress and the Supreme Court, and lunched with Arkansas's two senators, J. William Fulbright and John McClellan.

A product of Arkansas's notoriously corrupt Democratic political machine, Fulbright had nevertheless risen to national prominence as a liberal during his eighteen years in the Senate. From 1959 until 1975 the former Rhodes Scholar would serve as chairman of the powerful Senate Foreign Relations Committee, clashing often and openly with President Lyndon Johnson over the war in Vietnam.

At their lunch that day, Clinton and Fulbright hit it off instantly. The cherub-cheeked sixteen-year-old from Hot Springs impressed the veteran senator with both his confident manner and his grasp of issues foreign and domestic. It helped that Clinton had stayed up the night before memorizing every detail he could about Fulbright's long and illustrious career. Fulbright, Clinton said later, "had a real impact on my wanting to be a citizen of the world."

Yet what may have been the defining moment of his young life was yet to come. On July 24, a brilliantly sunny Wednesday, two buses pulled up to the White House and disgorged the one hundred teenage senators from Boys Nation. There, in the Rose Garden that would eventually be named for the widow of the assassinated president, they were to be addressed by John F. Kennedy.

During the bus ride from their spartan quarters on the University of Maryland campus, Billy Clinton—already savvy in the ways of political self-promotion—repeatedly asked his American Legion advisor if he could get his picture taken with the President. Not willing to leave anything so important to chance, Billy rushed ahead of his fellow student leaders and positioned himself scarcely a dozen feet from the presidential podium.

After President Kennedy concluded his remarks, he waded into the sea of fresh-scrubbed, white-shirted teenagers. Billy was the first to thrust his hand forward. At six-foot-two and over 180 pounds, he was impossible for the President to miss. JFK seized the boy's outstretched hand and, for one historic moment, their eyes locked as a Reuters photographer clicked away. Billy had his picture with the President, but it was far more than just a treasured memento. The image would not only serve to remind him he was destined for greatness, it would help him convince others of the same thing. "He whipped out that picture at the drop of a hat," said a classmate. "When he didn't, his mother did."

Like millions of high school and college students who grew up during the Eisenhower fifties, Billy idolized Ike's handsome, youthful, and dynamic successor. But to actually shake hands with the larger-than-life JFK and have that instant preserved for posterity signified something greater to Billy. For the first time he had seen the world outside the narrow confines of Arkansas, and he had walked the corridors of power. He knew that someday, and in very different circumstances, he would return there.

"He was just aglow," Virginia said when her boy returned home from Boys Nation. "I'd never seen him so excited about something. When he came back from Washington, holding this picture of himself with Jack Kennedy, and the expression on his face—I just knew that politics was the answer for him."

He may not have been a quarterback like his boyhood chum Mack McLarty, but Billy Clinton possessed a sex appeal all his own. Now that he was gaining fame as the local boy who shook JFK's hand ("Shake the hand that shook the hand of John F. Kennedy" was his new opening line), girls were hanging around the band room and even lingering outside the house on Scully Street in hopes of getting noticed.

Notice them Billy did. Whether he was playing the saxophone in a state band competition, tooling around town in his black Buick sedan, or holding forth with his friends over double-thick chocolate shakes at the local A&W drive-in, the golden boy of Hot Springs High School always seemed, as one of his classmates put it, "on the hunt."

He had known his first "real girlfriend," a pert blonde named Dolly Kyle, since junior high school. When they met, she was eleven years old and he not quite thirteen. Stolen kisses behind the high school gym led to adolescent fumblings in the backseat of Bill's Buick. Off and on, the affair would continue—despite the fact that both Billy and Dolly eventually married other people—for another thirty years. She called him Billy. He called her "Pretty Girl."

"It started out a very simple, very sweet love story," Kyle said. "We had grown up together and shared so much—we were the classic childhood sweethearts. Even at the beginning he was a very thoughtful, very considerate lover. And exciting, yes. Billy was very passionate."

No less so about his standing in the community. If he was a draw on the local service club circuit before having his picture taken with President Kennedy, Billy was now in more demand to speak than the mayor. The Heart Association, the Elks, the Veterans of Foreign Wars, the Soroptimists, the Boys Clubs, and various garden clubs all invited him to bring along the picture that had run in the *Hot Springs Sentinel Record* and describe the moment in the Rose Garden. Young Mr. Clinton was all too happy to oblige.

Billy was sitting with the seven other students taking advanced calculus on November 22, 1963, when the teacher got up to answer the telephone. He listened for a moment, then hung up without saying a word. "He was totally ashen-faced," Bill later said of that moment. "I have never seen such a desolate look on a man's face."

"The President," Bill's calculus teacher said, "has been shot in Dallas." Within two minutes, the phone rang again. John F. Kennedy was dead.

A gasp of horror went up from the other students, several of whom turned toward Bill to see his reaction. There was none. He simply froze, expressionless. Shock quickly gave way to rage. "You could feel the anger," Bill's classmate Jet Jamieson told writer David Maraniss, "building up inside him."

By the time he graduated six months later, Billy was a bona fide local legend—the native son who shook the hand of Jack Kennedy only months before he was gunned down. He was also probably the most popular boy at Hot Springs High. Most seniors would have been fortunate to find their photograph or name listed in the high school yearbook five or six times at most; Billy Clinton appeared no fewer than twenty-eight times.

If possible, the faculty held him in even higher esteem than his peers did. "God has richly blessed you," Edith Irons, his guidance counselor, wrote in his yearbook. "I know in a few years I shall 'read' about you . . ."

For all his charisma, Billy Clinton was not first in his class (he ranked fourth), nor was he the valedictorian. But after all 363 members of the Hot Springs High School class of 1964 were given their diplomas, it was Billy who brought a close to the ceremonies with a stirring benediction—in essence, his first political speech to a voting age audience. "Now we must prepare to live only by the guide of our own faith and character," he said. "We pray to keep a high sense of values while wandering through the complex moral haze which is our society. Direct us to know and care what is right and wrong . . ."

When he was finished, Virginia ran up and embraced him. "Bubba," she said, standing on tiptoe to kiss the son she seldom called by his given name, "you were magnificent. You have made me so proud."

Ever since he shook hands with JFK, Bubba knew that he wanted to return to the capital and attend Georgetown University's prestigious School of Foreign Service. But as much as she admired Hot Springs High's star pupil, Edith Irons cautioned him to apply to several colleges "just in case." The supremely confident Billy, however, applied to only one school, and his gamble paid off.

In May he took Dolly Kyle out to a drive-in, then parked at a favorite necking spot. He told "Pretty Girl" that he had just been accepted at Georgetown. He was excited, he told her, because it was a "foundation for anything I might want to do."

Such as? she asked.

"I want to be President," he replied unselfconsciously. "Of the United States."

"Oh," she said, realizing for the first time how closely he resembled JFK. Kyle would later say she spent the rest of the evening fantasizing about what it would be like to be the wife of President Billy Clinton. She would, she mused, play Jackie to his Jack. "I knew how closely he identified with Kennedy," she said, "and I imagined we would create another Camelot." Even then, when he was a high school senior, Clinton's presidential aspirations were "no laughing matter. Anybody who knew Billy knew he could do anything he set his mind to. Anything."

That September 1964, Virginia made the journey to Washington with Bubba and helped him move into Room 225 at Loyola Hall, a redbrick dormitory in the center of Georgetown's East Campus. When mother and son stepped inside and introduced themselves, Bill's roommate Tom Campbell later recalled, their personalities "filled the room."

Even before he left Hot Springs, Bill, as he now called himself, mapped out a strategy that would, he told his mother, ultimately lead to the White House. The first step was to get elected freshman class president.

Toward that end he enlisted the help of two well-connected classmates: Tom Campbell and Tommy Caplan, who boasted his own, more impressive connection to the late president. Caplan, the well-to-do son of a Baltimore jeweler, had organized teenagers in support of JFK during the 1960 campaign, and had even persuaded the administration to adopt his proposal for a "Youth-to-Youth" junior peace corps.

Initially, Caplan, like several other Clinton classmates, was wary of the affable Arkansan—particularly after Clinton went out of his way to tell Caplan's roommate that he wasn't interested in Caplan's wealth or his social connections. But he soon came to the conclusion that Clinton's gregariousness was natural, that it masked no hidden agenda. Another Georgetown friend, Dallas native Kit Ashby, was similarly impressed. "From the very beginning, his most memorable and attractive characteristic was his friendliness," Ashby said. "He had an inner quality which I simply enjoyed being around."

That autumn Caplan took his new friend and fellow Kennedy aficionado to meet the President's longtime secretary, Evelyn Lincoln, who was at the National Archives organizing her late boss's effects—a process that would wind up taking Lincoln years. An openmouthed Clinton, for once speechless, walked among the icons of the Kennedy era—his rocker, the humidors, the framed family photographs, the carved scrimshaw. "People were always in awe just being around the President's things—particularly so soon after the assassination," she said. "Bill Clinton was even more awestruck than most. Lots of people told me President Kennedy was their idol, that they wanted to be just like him. But he said it with such . . . conviction."

As a student, Clinton made a point of carefully studying his teachers and then telling them what they wanted to hear. "He was so blatant about it," said one of the few Georgetown students who did not warm to Bill. "He would suck up to the point where it was just nauseating. His friends would kid him about it, but he gave them this wide-eyed 'Who me?' look. The only person he was fooling was himself. And the teachers."

Bill's political approach was equally premeditated. At eighteen, he already knew the value of voter research. Georgetown University politics had long been dominated by New Yorkers—specifically students from the more affluent Long Island suburbs. And while the

School of Foreign Service boasted a significant number of Protestant and Jewish students, the vast majority of freshmen at the Jesuit-run institution were Roman Catholic.

Campbell, a Long Island native and a Catholic, helped drum up support from that all-important group and handed out flyers while Caplan helped him formulate a platform. But it was Bill's determination to shake hands with every single freshman on campus ("Hi, I'm Bill Clinton and I need your vote") that resulted in a landslide victory.

Over the next four years, he would employ his tried-and-true aw-shucks brand of down-home Southern charm and self-deprecating Gomer Pyle good humor to win converts. Among students who were doing everything they could to distance themselves from their hometowns and their families, Clinton was an unabashed booster of his native state. Even then, he saw the romance in coming from a place called Hope ("Where the watermelons are as big as Volkswagen Beetles") as opposed to the less savory connotations inherent in the name of the place where he really grew up, Hot Springs.

By way of ingratiating himself to a whole new constituency, Clinton later ran for sophomore class president promising to form a welcoming committee for incoming freshmen. Once he was elected, it was Bill who stood at the main gate with a band of fellow sophomores, greeting the new arrivals and their families, helping them locate their rooms, and broadening his own political base in the process.

That included the women on campus, most of whom were enrolled in the school's language institute. Bill appealed to them directly, then singled out several influential coeds to work on his behalf mimeographing position papers and distributing leaflets. He so impressed one, another candidate for class president named Helen Henry, that she dropped out of the race and went to work campaigning for him. "I simply had to admit," she said, "that he was perfect for the job."

One of his most ardent supporters was Denise Hyland, the tall, blond, poised-beyond-her-years daughter of a New Jersey surgeon who was studying French at the language institute. They had met in February 1965 when he came up and asked her out to dinner. By spring they were seriously involved.

Bill shared his political dreams and desires with Hyland. "That," she allowed, "was a major part of his appeal." They often spent evenings strolling hand in hand along the Mall, discussing civil rights, the Cold War, and the worsening situation in Vietnam against the backdrop of the Capitol, the Washington Monument—and the White House.

Not unexpectedly, Bill plunged headlong into the college experience, enlisting in as many campus organizations as time would allow. He joined the Air Force ROTC, then dropped out after a single semester. He pledged with a service fraternity, Alpha Phi Omega, which, not coincidentally, ran the elections on campus. And he continued going to church—a nearby Presbyterian one, since his friend Kit Ashby informed him there were no "good" Baptist churches in the neighborhood.

Unlike most college students capable of sleeping ten or more hours at a stretch, Bill Clinton thrived on the absence of sleep. It was a trick learned from his Western civilization professor, Carroll Quigly, who pointed out that most great men required no more than five hours' sleep a day. By taking a series of five- or ten-minute naps scattered throughout the day, Clinton discovered he could cram that much more into his already frenetic schedule. With a nod to his father's early death, he confided that he often felt that he was in "a race against time. None of us know how long we've really got, do we?"

Clinton visited home as often as he could, and usually brought one of his Georgetown friends with him to sample the simple joys of rural America. They were not disappointed. Campbell, the first to make the journey to Hot Springs, was impressed by the "exotic" atmosphere—"the heavy Southern air, the warmth, the darkness."

Before he brought Tom Caplan home for Easter, Bill marveled to his mother over the phone, "He's been to Europe, but he's never been to Arkansas." By the time she was finished with the rich Yankee college boy, Virginia boasted, "I had him reaching for the butter in the center of the table like everybody else." One evening, Virginia recalled, Caplan took her aside. "He told me, 'I'll just put it to you as plain as I know how: There ain't nobody anywhere in this world this good—nobody. Until I saw how genuine he is, I could not trust him.' "

That summer of 1966, Denise Hyland left to study in France and Bill went home to Arkansas to get his first real taste of grassroots politics. Billy, as he was still known on his home turf, wanted to go to work on Judge Frank Holt's campaign for the Democratic nomination for governor. Holt was handpicked by the Democratic Party machine, and favored to win. Having an inside track with the future governor couldn't hurt, Bill reasoned, but first he had to approach his influential uncle Raymond Clinton to pull some strings. "Ray Clinton's boy" got the job.

As the most junior member of the campaign staff, Billy floundered until he was assigned the job of driving Judge Holt's wife, Mary, and their two daughters around the state. Over the next several weeks they crisscrossed Arkansas, stopping at towns with names like Altheimer, Fifty-Six, Arkadelphia, and Evening Shade.

Having been raised by his mother and Mammaw, Billy was in his element. The Holt women, in turn, were "utterly charmed" by their good-looking, energetic young chauffeur-companion. He even made Judge Holt's loss at the polls more bearable, reassuring them that their father was a great man and that the outcome of a single election would not change that.

It was then that Bill got his first lesson on snatching victory from the jaws of political defeat. The day Judge Holt lost the election, young Clinton asked the candidate's nephew if he could help Clinton land a job in Senator Fulbright's office. Jack Holt picked up the phone and called Fulbright's administrative assistant, Lee Williams.

The next Friday, Williams phoned Clinton in Hot Springs and offered him a choice—either a part-time job paying $3,500 or a full-time job with a $5,000 salary.

"How about two part-time jobs?" Clinton asked.

"You're just the guy I'm looking for," Williams answered.

That day Bill packed up and drove to Washington. First thing Monday morning, he reported for work as one of the Senate Foreign Relations Committee's "back room boys"—ambitious college students who sorted mail, ran errands, and generally did the bidding of Senator Fulbright and his senior staff.

By the time Clinton joined Fulbright's office, the senator, who had helped shepherd through the Tonkin Gulf Resolution expanding presidential warmaking powers, was now the administration's harshest critic on the issue of Vietnam. Bill, his student draft deferment firmly in place, did not share Fulbright's antipathy toward the man who succeeded his idol as President—at least not at first. Bill was a firm believer in Johnson's Great Society, and took some measure of pride in the fact that a fellow Southerner was responsible for sweeping civil rights legislation.

From Berkeley to Columbia, campuses across the nation had become hotbeds of protest by early 1967. Everywhere students were marching against the war in Vietnam—everywhere except at Georgetown, where frat parties and beer busts remained the order of the day. Caught in this time warp with the rest of the student body, Clinton was "for the war"—not for any ideological reason, but because he "just wasn't against it."

Bill's schedule included grueling eight-hour workdays at the Foreign Relations Committee and a full class load. But since he was still managing to squeak by on five hours' sleep a night, he saw no reason to curtail his political career on campus. Now arguably the university's best-known underclassman, he never doubted for a minute that he would be swept into office as junior class president.

He was wrong. Many of his previous supporters felt that Bill, now seen as a symbol of the student body establishment, was taking them for granted. His opponent, Terry Modglin, a self-styled campus renegade who promised to confront the school's administration with a series of demands, won in a landslide—but only after Bill's campaign manager was caught ripping all of Modglin's posters off the walls, stuffing them into Clinton's car, and dumping them in a vacant lot.

This dirty trick, which Bill denied knowing anything about, sealed Modglin's landslide victory. Although he made a gracious concession speech, Clinton took the defeat hard. Over the last two years he had made a point of meeting nearly all the two thousand-plus undergraduates. They knew him, and that made the rejection personal.

Bill quickly turned his attention to his studies, and to his work on Capitol Hill. The year 1967 would be remembered by many baby boomers for San Francisco's psychedelic "Summer of Love" and the antiwar counterculture it inspired. But for Bill Clinton, it was the summer to get in shape for his next great challenge.

At Fulbright's urging, Bill had decided to apply for a coveted Rhodes Scholarship. Rhodes Scholars (Fulbright had been one in the 1920s) were a handpicked few chosen to pursue all or part of their postgraduate education at Oxford University. But the full scholarship was generally awarded to scholar-athletes, and Bill, despite his size, had never excelled at any sport. He was so notoriously clumsy at sports, in fact, that his fraternity brothers teased him mercilessly about his prospects for ever becoming a Rhodes Scholar.

Determined to at least look the part, Bill began running a half hour every morning in hopes of losing weight. Unfortunately, after his morning jog he usually rewarded himself with a hamburger and french fries—a routine that one friend called "completely self-defeating." He would nonetheless continue this practice well into middle age.

Only thirty-two Americans would be selected from thousands of candidates for a Rhodes placement. But, despite his decided lack of athleticism, Bill did have certain advantages: His academic credentials were impeccable, his record as a student leader was outstanding, and he boasted a recommendation from Senator Fulbright, a Rhodes alumnus who was so inspired by his Oxford experience that he established a scholarship of near-equal prestige in his own name. To further improve his chances, Bill offset his lack of athleticism by getting himself appointed chairman of the Student Athletic Commission. Since Rhodes Scholars were selected by region, Bill was also careful not to apply as a resident of Washington, where he would have faced stiff competition from scores of qualified candidates. Instead, he dramatically improved his odds by filing as one of only a half-dozen applicants from Arkansas.

That summer at home, Bill helped his mother face another crisis.

Two years earlier, Roger had been diagnosed with a particularly virulent form of oral cancer. Refusing to undergo surgery that might leave him disfigured, the once-handsome "Dude" opted instead for radiation treatment.

Bill had written to his stepfather from Georgetown, where he now shared a house on Potomac Avenue with four friends. He tried to offer words of comfort and encouragement, but they could not mask smoldering feelings of anger, confusion, and regret. "I believe, Daddy, none of us can find any peace unless they face life with God," he wrote, "knowing that good always outweighs bad and even death doesn't end life. You ought to look everywhere for help, Daddy. You ought to write me more. People—even some of my political enemies—confide in me . . .

"Of course I know I have never been much help to you—never had the courage to come and talk about it," Bill went on. "The reason I am writing now is because I couldn't stand it if you and Mother were to break up after all these years. I just want to help you help yourself if you can.

"I think I ought to close this letter now and wait for your answer but there are a couple of things I ought to say first—(1)I don't think you have ever realized how much we all love and needed you. (2) I don't think you have ever realized either how we have all been hurt . . . but still really have not turned against you.

"Please write me soon Daddy—I want to hear from you . . . Don't be ashamed to admit your problem . . . We all have so much to live for; let's start doing it—together."

The letter, signed "Your son, Bill," reduced Roger Clinton to tears.

When Roger traveled to Duke University in Durham, North Carolina, for treatments, Bill drove the 265 miles from Georgetown to visit him. "There was nothing else to fight over, nothing left to run from," Bill recalled of those visits. "It was a wonderful time in my life, and I think in his."

A few days before Thanksgiving break, Virginia picked up the phone and summoned Bill home to Hot Springs. The only father he had known was dying. When he arrived, Bill encountered a small army of nurses—all coworkers of his mother—hovering over

Roger's bed, checking his pulse, consulting his chart, and then murmuring to one another in the hallway.

Trying to preserve what little remained of his fifty-seven-year-old stepfather's dignity, Bill picked Roger up—by now he weighed scarcely one hundred pounds—and gently carried him to the bathroom when he could no longer summon the strength to walk. Virginia was less charitable. For years, she later revealed, little Roger had prayed that his father would die so that the family could "move on." Now Virginia joined the boy in praying for Daddy's demise.

In his final days, Virginia refused even to see her husband ("It was not a pretty sight to see"). When he managed to hang on three weeks longer than expected, she bitterly characterized his lingering death as "one last act of terrorism" leveled against the family.

Bill stayed with his stepfather during those last few nights, and when it was over watched as the ambulance attendants lifted Roger's body onto a stretcher and rolled it out of the house. He was fatherless again—if Roger had ever really been a father to him—but, Virginia mused, "at least they made their peace."

Two months later, Virginia called her son with the news that the vexatious Edith had died of a stroke at the age of sixty-six. Now that they were in heaven, she said with chilling candor, Roger and Mammaw would never "feel the need to shriek through the night again."

Bill shared his mother's sense of sadness mingled with relief. "Never have I been so sorry to be away from you as I was when Mammaw died," Bill wrote to his mother from Georgetown, adding slyly, "surely you will get some years of peace now."

For his part, Bill was consumed with the task of becoming a Rhodes Scholar. "He is so competitive," Virginia observed, "and he doesn't want anything given to him. A lot of that comes from me, it sure does. I don't give up easily. Like never."

En route to his final qualifying interview in New Orleans, Bill picked up a copy of *Time* magazine that contained a particularly interesting article about heart transplants, an area of medicine he knew virtually nothing about. The next day, the selection committee included in its interrogation a surprise question concerning . . . heart transplants. "I couldn't," Bill later marveled, "believe my luck." After being told he was one of only four students chosen from the South, Clinton broke down.

Back in Hot Springs, Virginia waited by the phone for word from Bill, refusing to report to the hospital even when she was summoned for an emergency. She had given her son a London Fog raincoat for luck, and when the phone rang at five in the afternoon she nearly "passed out from all the excitement."

"Well, Mother," her son asked, "how do you think I'll look in English tweeds?"

Meantime, Bill's final few months at Georgetown would prove to be among the most tumultuous in modern American history. As American casualties mounted in the wake of February's bloody Tet Offensive, Senator Eugene McCarthy assumed the mantle of the antiwar movement and nearly defeated incumbent Lyndon Johnson in the New Hampshire presidential primary. Emboldened by McCarthy's upset victory, New York Senator Robert Kennedy promptly declared that he, too, would seek the Democratic nomination, running on an antiwar platform. Bill, ever in the thrall of the Kennedys, unhesitatingly switched his allegiance from McCarthy to RFK. When Lyndon Johnson made the stunning announcement that March that he would not seek reelection, Bill predicted to his friends that Kennedy would wrest the nomination from LBJ's anointed successor, Vice-President Hubert Humphrey.

But race—not Vietnam—would continue to be young Clinton's primary political obsession. As enamored of Martin Luther King as he was of Camelot, Bill memorized King's stirring "I Have a Dream" speech and launched into it at the slightest provocation.

King's assassination on April 4 triggered rioting in black neighborhoods across the country, and while much of inner-city Washington went up in flames, the Georgetown campus remained safely out of harm's way. Bill, who like other GU students had been insulated from the unrest that had engulfed much of the rest of the nation, would eventually make the decision to get involved. But first he had to drive to the airport to pick up an old high school sweetheart who was arriving in Washington for a national Catholic women's conference and escort her to her hotel.

Dolly Kyle, the woman he liked to call "Pretty Girl," was now married and eight months pregnant with her second child. "Billy," as she would always refer to him, drove her at breakneck speed through Washington, past barricaded storefronts and burning tenements toward the Mayflower Hotel. According to Kyle, they spent the night together, consummating their relationship although she was due to give birth in a matter of weeks.

The next day, Bill volunteered to deliver food and medical supplies to the inner city for the Red Cross. He slapped a Red Cross decal on the side of his white Buick convertible, then sped past scores of gutted buildings to a church that was serving as a shelter for families made homeless by the fires. Along for the ride was Bill's Hot Springs neighbor, Carolyn Yeldell Staley. For Staley, who had been exchanging love letters with Bill for months, the trip to Washington was "a revelation"—and not just because it afforded her an up-close-and-personal look at the riots. She realized for the first time that Bill was cheating on her, juggling at least two other girlfriends while he tried to play the gracious host. "He would actually talk to this one girlfriend of his, Ann Markesun, while Carolyn was standing in the same room just a few feet away," said a fellow student. "We couldn't figure out what the hell he thought he was doing—it was totally dishonest of him to string these girls along—but Bill seemed to thrive on that sort of risk."

In fact, during his senior year Bill Clinton cut a wide swath through the women of Capitol Hill. According to one of his roommates, when he and Denise Hyland decided to end their romance "it was as if a bell had gone off and suddenly he was dating a new woman practically every night." In each case, as several lovers would attest, Clinton adamantly refused to wear a condom ("I hate them")—a preference he made so widely known it became a running joke among his friends. "He also," said one longtime girlfriend, "insisted on leaving the lights on."

Grim reality intruded again on the morning of June 6, 1968, when Tommy Caplan shook his roommate awake. "Bill, Bill!" he said. "Bobby Kennedy's been shot! He's dead." The night before, they had watched on television as RFK was declared the winner of the California primary, then went to bed moments before Sirhan Sirhan pumped bullets into Bobby's head, neck, and right side. Now Bill, disbelieving, sat in stunned silence on the edge of his bed.

The evidence that life is fragile at best was all around him: his father and stepfather dead, his three idols—Jack Kennedy, Martin Luther King, Bobby Kennedy—all cut down in their prime. Bill returned to Arkansas that last summer before Oxford determined to make a difference—and hell-bent on having fun.

He had figured out one way of accomplishing both. First, he worked feverishly on behalf of Senator Fulbright's reelection campaign, driving to virtually every courthouse in Arkansas to persuade the state's judges to stick with the incumbent—and, not so incidentally, introducing them to a rising young star named Bill Clinton.

The second part of his plan—the fun part—involved dating the daughters of the judges and other local officials he managed to win over. Bill needn't have worried. Even as he kept in touch with Ann Markesun and old flame Denise Hyland back home, he rekindled his relationship with Carolyn Staley while simultaneously pursuing a serious romance with the newly crowned Miss Arkansas, Sharon Ann Evans. That last summer in Arkansas before he left for England, Bill was, in the words of one close friend, "a very, very, very busy boy."

In October 1968, Bill and the thirty-one American Rhodes Scholars set sail from New York bound for Southampton aboard the luxury liner S.S. *United States*. Seas turned rough the second day out, and one of Clinton's fellow scholars, Robert Reich, spent the rest of the trip throwing up in his cabin. One afternoon, Bill showed up offering some sympathy, a plate of crackers, and some ginger ale before returning to the ship's bar and his never-ending pursuit of women. "I thought you might be needing these," he said as he placed the tray on a table. "Heard you weren't doing so well."

Over the decades this otherwise forgettable expression of concern for a fellow passenger in distress would take on a life of its own. In later versions, Bill would essentially be credited with nursing Reich back to health. But it did mark the beginning of a friendship between the future president and the brilliant, diminutive (four feet ten inches compared to Clinton's six-foot-two) student activist who would become his Labor Secretary.

As for the rest of the Rhodes Scholars aboard the *United States*, most were disarmed by Clinton's easygoing manner. Others instantly recognized the ambition that smoldered beneath the surface. Daniel Singer remembered him being "very politically ambitious . . . nobody was ever in any doubt that he would do anything other than run for president." Stanford's Rick Stearns remembered Bill telling him "that he planned to go back to Arkansas to be governor or senator and would like to be a national leader someday"—all within forty-five minutes.

As thrilled as they were to be embarking on their Oxford adventure, another issue weighed heavily on the minds of all the American men aboard ship: the draft. Graduate deferments had been abolished back in February 1968, and a month later the Garland County draft board had reclassified Bill 1-A. But his well-connected Uncle Raymond, the local wheeler-dealer whose influence helped Bill land a job in Fulbright's office, had already swung into action.

Pressuring friends with draft board contacts, even cornering Senator Fulbright at the dedication of a dam, Uncle Raymond would work tirelessly to keep his gifted nephew from being drafted—and, contrary to presidential candidate Clinton's later denials, informing Bill of his actions every step of the way. "We kind of leaned over backwards," admitted draft board executive secretary Opal Ellis, "to let him go to Oxford. As old as he was, he would have been at the top of the list to be drafted, but we were proud to have a Hot Springs boy with a Rhodes Scholarship . . . The board was very lenient with him. We gave him more than he was entitled to."

Freed, at least temporarily, of the anxiety of worrying about his draft status, Bill plunged into the Oxford experience with characteristic gusto. Founded in the early twelfth century, Oxford, located fifty miles northwest of London, was originally made up of three colleges—University, Balliol, and Merton—but eventually expanded to include thirty-one separate colleges. Its reputation as a center of learning was without parallel.

Bill was enrolled in University College—"Univ" to the student body—ostensibly taking a popular interdisciplinary grab bag of courses called "PPE": politics, philosophy, and economics. But contrary to its vaunted public image, the Oxford experience proved to be anything but grueling academically. The regimen consisted of a one-hour tutorial twice a week, an infrequent essay assignment, and no exams.

At Oxford, recalled Rhodes Scholar David Segal, "Hard work is not only unnecessary, it's essentially frowned upon." Agreed another Clinton contemporary: "You could just sit back and coast. It was all fish and chips, Guinness stout, parties, cards, women. We spent a hell of a lot more time in the pubs than we did in any classroom."

Bill wasted little time figuring this out. He routinely skipped lectures, made no particular effort to distinguish himself, and like many other Rhodes Scholars would depart Oxford after two years without ever earning a degree. He did, however, write one eighteen-page essay on "Political Pluralism in the USSR" that so impressed his instructor it was later used as a model.

"He was a very good student, receptive and intelligent," said Bill's tutor, Zbigniew Pelczynski. "But he was generally better at arguing verbally than on paper." As for Clinton's approach to his studies: "He had the mind of a politician . . . laying out all the different lines of thought and then synthesizing them, rather than independently developing his own line of thought."

Bill did devour books while he was at Oxford—more than three hundred, he claimed, during his first year alone. His taste was eclectic: Jean-Jacques Rousseau, Dylan Thomas, Thomas Hobbes, John Locke, biographies of Gladstone and Disraeli, as well as books that hinted not too subtly at his ultimate goal. Among these: *Presidential Leadership* and Carl Sandburg's six-volume biography of Abraham Lincoln.

For the most part, Bill focused on the one thing that mattered most to him regardless of what continent he was on: making personal contacts that might serve his political future.

When he was told that he was not the only Arkansas boy on campus, Bill sought out Cliff Jackson, who was attending nearby St. John's College on a Fulbright Scholarship. The two dated American girls who happened to be roommates, and played on the same Oxford basketball team—something neither would have had the courage to try back home.

To fully immerse himself in the English experience, the famously clumsy and out-of-shape Bill even joined the rugby team. "He had an appetite for the game and he was an excellent member of the team," said Chris McCooey, secretary-captain of the University College rugby team during the two years Bill played as a second-row forward. "He was always good fun, so it didn't matter about his skills." McCooey also remembered that Bill was "fairly unfit and not at all athletic—too lumpy for that."

No matter. Team sports merely enabled Bill to expand his circle of friends—a circle that seemed to be growing exponentially. Whenever he met someone new, Bill pulled a three-by-five index card from his pocket and scribbled down the person's name, number, and whatever salient information he might be able to glean from him in the course of a normal conversation. Each afternoon he got together with his new friends for a pint, but only after making certain he had recorded the names of all the people he had encountered that day.

Bill's favorite haunts were the Turf Tavern and The Bear, where as the guileless country boy abroad, he managed to charm his hosts with tall tales of the South—all delivered in what Robert Reich described as his "syrupy" Arkansas accent over his favorite drink, a mixture of beer and lemonade called shandy.

He was animated, engaging, and—despite a tendency to dominate a conversation to the exclusion of everyone else—supremely courteous. There were those, however, who viewed Bill as a transparent opportunist. "It was the eyes that gave it away," Philip Hodson later said. "They moved on before he had finished talking to you." Yale's Douglas Eakeley was more blunt. Even then, Eakeley said, Bill Clinton was the "classic Southern glad-handing politician."

At his small flat in Helen's Court behind University College, Bill held forth over sips of sherry on the pressing topics of the day: the Cold War, race relations, and—above all else—Vietnam.

In fact, to know Bill Clinton then was to know a man obsessed with the war in Southeast Asia, and determined to find historical parallels that would bolster his growing feeling that America's involvement was indefensible. Along with his newfound moderately left-of-center stance came a change in appearance, from the fashionably shaggy prep look that had served him so well at Georgetown to the studied scruffiness of the European neopacifist.

Clinton was not alone among young intellectuals of his generation. In liberal salons everywhere, the only guests more sought after than Maoists were scowling, gun-toting members of the Black Panther Party. It was the year of Radical Chic.

His growing outrage over Vietnam aside, Bill resisted attempts by pro-Hanoi factions such as the Oxford Revolutionary Socialist Students to recruit him. The more radical Americans on campus, including a handful who had belonged to the Students for a Democratic Society (SDS), berated him for not joining in anti-American demonstrations. For all his pontificating on the subject of Vietnam and Washington's misguided policies in the region, Bill was careful not to appear too radical "lest," as one of his British classmates observed, "it cost him future votes back home." Added Cliff Jackson: "They called him a hypocrite, a fake, and a phony because he wouldn't stand up for his convictions."

When antiwar protesters stormed the U.S. Embassy on Grosvenor Square that year, the Rolling Stones' Mick Jagger pulled up in his Bentley, jumped out, and began mingling with demonstrators. Between signing autographs and allowing himself to be shot by press photographers, Jagger linked arms with marchers and for a time actually led the protest before climbing back into his limousine. When he got back to his town house on Cheyne Walk, Jagger scribbled the incendiary lyrics to "Street Fighting Man," which promptly became the movement's anthem.

Unlike their British counterparts for whom such protests were pleasantly diverting, Bill and the other Americans at Oxford actually had something to lose. Lieutenant General Lewis B. Hershey, the crusty Selective Service director, wanted to strike a blow against the antiwar movement by drafting its student leaders immediately. The Federal Bureau of Investigation, the CIA, and several other U.S. intelligence-gathering organizations were also keeping close tabs on American activists abroad. Aware that his position vis-à-vis the draft was tenuous at best, Bill nevertheless did attend meetings of Group 68, a loose-knit band of Americans that was financed by the openly pro-Moscow British Peace Council.

Vietnam and the draft were not Bill Clinton's only preoccupation during this period. While still writing to several women back in Washington and in Arkansas, he pursued new conquests with a zeal that wowed both his countrymen and their British hosts. "There were big noisy parties, with wine, marijuana, and casual sex," recalled Alessandra Stanley. "It was a time of revolving-door relationships, and Clinton pursued a lot of women—including the girlfriends of his friends."

While he would never tire of seducing big-haired, blond beauty pageant contestants, Bill now broadened his tastes. He wrote Virginia, who now dyed the sides of her hair jet-black but left what she called a "skunk stripe" of white down the middle, saying he was involved with a woman he found attractive "but not in the traditional sense of the word." Then, he added, "You wouldn't understand, Mother."

It was an uncharacteristically sarcastic remark for Clinton to make to his mother, who never wavered in her fanatical devotion to him. When she decided to get married a third time—to Hot Springs beauty parlor operator George Jefferson Dwire—the groom flew Bill in from London to surprise her. When her son walked through the front door, Virginia broke down sobbing.

Bearded and unkempt, Bill was scarcely recognizable to the people who had known him as Hot Springs's saxophone-playing over-achiever. But his new stepfather warmed to him instantly. Even before the wedding, Jeff Dwire confessed to Bill that he had been married three times before—and that he had done jailtime. Seven years earlier, Dwire had conned a number of people into investing in a film about the notorious gangster Pretty Boy Floyd. The movie project was a scam, and in 1962, Dwire was charged with forty-two counts of embezzlement. After a plea bargain, he went to federal prison in Texarkana, Texas.

"Virginia knew he'd been in prison and Bill knew too," said Bill's cousin Ann Blythe Grigsby. "But they are both very compassionate people. Dwire had paid his debt to society and that was good enough for them." Not long after the wedding, Bill began circulating a petition in an unsuccessful attempt to secure a pardon for his new stepfather.

Never one to waste an opportunity, Bill managed to expand his network of contacts. Before leaving to enroll in Oxford, he had asked Sharon Ann Evans if, in her capacity as Miss Arkansas, she could get him introduced to Arkansas's Republican Governor Winthrop Rockefeller. She did. Now he somehow wangled an invitation to the Rockefeller estate, Winrock. There he charmed the governor and his First Lady, Jeanette. "I have a feeling," the governor said after reading Clinton's florid thank-you note, "that we haven't heard the last of him."

Before returning to England, Bill spent time with Carolyn Yeldell Staley—who had been holding out hope that they might still have a future—and the lushly beautiful Evans. But once he was back at Oxford, Bill resumed his romance with one of the new breed of unconventionally attractive women he had been referring to in his letter to Virginia—one of those women whose appeal she "wouldn't understand."

Foremost among these was Tamara Eccles-Williams. He called her, simply, "Mara." Clinton, Eccles-Williams later said, "never had much money, but he was a very easygoing and a very caring person. Bill was very . . . cuddly."

Ann Markesun apparently thought so. In March 1969 she and Bill rendezvoused in Munich and toured the Bavarian Alps with another couple. But as soon as he returned to London, he met the stunning Sharon Evans at Heathrow. For the next ten days, Bill showed Evans the sights and introduced her to his friends. They had heard quite a lot about the homegrown beauty and were eager to meet her.

"I am in love with Sharon," he had told Frank Aller, the Rhodes Scholar from Spokane. "She's the woman I am going to marry— the future mother of my children." One Sunday afternoon the couple was at Trafalgar Square, transfixed as some twelve thousand antiwar protesters streamed toward the American Embassy.

"Y'all, I want to go," Evans said. "I've never been to a demonstration."

"Gosh," Bill replied with a nod, "I'll go too." As it had earlier that year, violence erupted, and the couple from Arkansas beat a hasty retreat. Afterward Bill put her back on a tour bus. Once the purported future mother of his children was out of sight, he returned to Mara Eccles-Williams.

According to one friend, Clinton had sexual relations with "a minimum of thirty women—and I stress the word 'minimum.'" When Stearns asked him to share the secret of his success with women, Bill did not hesitate to tell him. "I listen," he replied. "There is nothing in the world more flattering to a woman or man than to have someone really *listen* to what you're saying."

Katherine Gieve, another girlfriend from the period, agreed. She felt the garrulous American with the megawatt smile was "always thinking about people. He made a relationship between abstract ideas and the meaning of people's experiences. My abiding impression of Bill is that he was a softie. He wasn't afraid of expressing his feelings."

Or of heeding other people's. Mandy Merck, a leading British feminist of the 1970s, also felt Bill was "an incredibly empathetic soul." So much so that, after they had gone out together a couple of times, she got up the nerve to tell him she was a lesbian. Bill was the first man she had ever told.

Katherine Vereker, the comely daughter of a philosophy professor, was another of Bill's conquests. Along with Sara Maitland, who later carved out a career for herself as a novelist, Vereker routinely invited Rhodes Scholars for tea in their attic flat.

"Lady Sara," as the Americans called Maitland, was in the process of distancing herself from her wealthy background. Surrounded by thin-lipped pseudointellectuals, she reveled in the company of the terminally affable Southern giant. She also took pride in the fact that her teas offered Clinton and his friends the opportunity to meet women.

"A lot of Rhodes Scholars had a hard time at Oxford because of the shortage of females," she explained. "Bill liked female company and found the boys' world that was Oxford more difficult than men who had come from private schools. We became such good friends. It wasn't just S-E-X."

It was, to an extent, drugs—primarily hashish and marijuana, which were invariably served up with the tea and sherry. But, as he would later attest, Bill was not particularly adept at ingesting controlled substances. Not for lack of trying, apparently. "We spent enormous amounts of time trying to teach him to inhale," Maitland said, conceding that Clinton had on several occasions lit up joints in an effort to get high with his friends. He had never smoked cigarettes, and as a result he began hacking whenever he began to take smoke of any kind into his lungs. "God knows," Maitland said, "it wasn't for lack of trying."

For Bill and the other Americans at Oxford, the cozy evenings spent socializing over tea, sherry, and hashish in Lady Sara's pillow-strewn parlor provided a momentary distraction from the looming specter of Vietnam. One of his friends, the China scholar Frank Aller, had summoned the courage to defy his draft board and refuse induction.

While Clinton and the others admired Aller, none followed his lead. A number went to considerable lengths to be classified 4-F. One played rock music at ear-splittingly high levels in hopes of destroying his hearing. Several sought psychiatric deferments, hoping that sympathetic British physicians would diagnose them as just mentally disturbed enough not to serve.

Bill could not disguise the fact that he was, in his own words, "disgustingly healthy." After staving off the draft for a full year following his 1-A reclassification, Bill received his induction notice on May 3, 1969. That he ever received a draft notice at all was something he would later dismiss as something so inconsequential he scarcely remembered it.

He felt differently that day, however. After receiving his notice, Bill phoned his mother in Arkansas and pleaded with her and his new stepfather to see what other strings could be pulled to secure another postponement. Frantically he ran to the flat of a friend to tell him the news, but no one was home. Under the best of circumstances, Bill had a visceral fear of being alone. Now, in what he had come to regard as a dark night of the soul, Bill Clinton had no one to turn to. A wave of panic came over him, and he began pounding furiously—until the knuckles of his hand were bruised. Then he sank to the floor—and wept.

I'm going for brains and ability—not glamour.

—*Bill*

I know he's ready to go after anything that
walks by.

—*Hillary*

Hillary hated to lose.

> —*Don Jones,*
> Hillary's youth pastor

She loves talking about ideas. But ask her about herself, and she shuts down emotionally.

> —*Jan Piercy,*
> Wellesley classmate

I tried to run her off, but she just won't go.

> —*Bill*

I have to kick his ass every morning.

> —*Hillary*

3

TALL, DIGNIFIED, AND famous for his soft-spoken elo-
quence, Massachusetts Senator Edward Brooke strode to the
podium and looked out at the Wellesley College graduating class of
1969. A liberal Republican and an African American, Brooke had
been chosen to deliver the college's commencement address because, as one professor put it, he was "comparatively safe—neither
hawk nor dove, but a bridge between left-leaning students and their
more conservative parents. No one was going to boo Edward
Brooke, and you couldn't say that about very many politicians back
in the sixties."

A young woman wearing granny glasses and no makeup sat a few
feet away on the stage, listening patiently to the senator as she waited
her turn. Brooke began with a nod to student activists. "The protest
movement reflects and stimulates the healthy criticism taking place
throughout the nation," he conceded. "It is a very significant fact
that America has identified more precisely than ever before the nature and magnitude of its social problems." But he went on to
specifically attack the hard-line Students for a Democratic Society
for advocating violent protest. "Whatever the romantics may say
about violence in our national life, the use of force is repugnant to
the spirit of American politics," Brooke said. "So long as society
retains a capacity for nonviolent political change, resort to violent
political action is anathema."

After Brooke finished speaking, graduates responded with polite applause. At a time when the fabric of American society seemed to be coming apart at the seams, his remarks had seemed tepid at best.

Now the plain-looking girl in the granny glasses stood and walked confidently to the podium. Student body president Hillary Rodham had spent days carefully crafting her remarks, but a sense of outrage was slowly welling inside her. It seemed impossible that just two years earlier Hillary, as president of the school's Young Republicans, had campaigned on Brooke's behalf.

"It was a defense of Richard Nixon," she later recalled of Brooke's address, "a pro forma commencement speech—you know, 'The world awaits you, we've got great leadership, America is strong abroad.' " That was not how Hillary or her classmates saw things. "We'd had assassinations. We were in the midst of a war everybody was confused about and most people didn't like. Civil rights, you know, all the great issues of the day were just kind of subsumed in Brooke's onward and upward speech."

For the next ten minutes, Brooke sat a few feet away in polite but stunned silence as the upstart girl chosen to speak for her Wellesley sisters lashed out. "Senator Brooke," she said, "part of the problem with empathy for professed goals is that empathy doesn't do anything. We've had lots of empathy. We've had lots of sympathy. But we feel that for too long our leaders have used politics as the art of the possible. And the challenge now is to practice politics as the art of making what appears to be impossible, possible."

If Brooke's address seemed cliché, Rodham's remarks—an incoherent grab bag of peace-and-love rhetoric—was at times painfully self-indulgent. "We are, all of us, exploring a world that none of us understands and attempting to create within that uncertainty. But there are some things we feel, feelings that our prevailing, acquisitive, and competitive corporate life . . . is not the way of life for us."

She ended by reciting a poem written by a classmate, Nancy Scheibner:

> The Hollow Men of anger and bitterness
> The bountiful ladies of righteous degradation
> All must be left to a bygone age.

When Hillary was finished speaking, her classmates sprang to their feet and gave her a standing ovation that lasted seven minutes. "It was brash, it was brilliant," her classmate Jan Dustman Mercer said, "and I can remember squirming in my seat. At the same time, you know the inner me was saying, 'All right!' "

But there were many in the audience who were seething over what they perceived as the young woman's impertinence. One of those who for a moment contemplated going up and yanking her off the platform was Marge Wanderer, who was there to see her daughter Nancy graduate.

But Nancy, like the rest of the Wellesley student body, was in awe of Hillary Rodham. "Take a good look at her," Nancy Wanderer told her mother. "She'll probably be the president of the United States someday."

Or, as Dorothy Rodham kept telling her daughter from the time Hillary was in second grade, at least Chief Justice of the United States Supreme Court. Although Hillary would claim she inherited her driving ambition from her up-by-the-bootstraps father, Hugh Rodham, she was influenced as much if not more by her mother.

Indeed, Hillary's parents and Bill's parents had much in common: All four endured hardscrabble childhoods, came of age during the Great Depression, and started their families in the wake of World War II. Dorothy Howell may have had the heaviest cross to bear. Her French-Scottish mother was only fifteen and illiterate when Dorothy was born in the slums of South Chicago in 1919. Dorothy's father, a descendant of Welsh-English immigrants, was a seventeen-year-old fireman-in-training.

Following their divorce eight years later, the Howells sent Dorothy and her three-year-old sister to California to live with her grandparents. Hillary would later say she was "incredulous" and "furious" that two small children would be put on a train and allowed to make the three-day journey alone.

Things did not improve once Dorothy and her sister arrived in Pasadena. Her grandparents, both British immigrants, were openly hostile to the children. Dorothy's grandfather scarcely acknowledged her existence, and her grandmother was—not unlike Virginia's mother, Edith—a strict and capricious taskmaster who routinely abused her both physically and emotionally. Dorothy's father seldom visited; her mother vanished completely.

At fourteen, Dorothy escaped to a job as live-in baby-sitter for a local family. Freed from the oppressive influence of her grandparents, she blossomed at Alhambra High School, where she joined the Scholarship Society, the Spanish club, and the Girls Athletic Association. After graduating in 1937, she moved back to Chicago and applied for a job as a secretary at the Columbia Lace Company, where in 1939 she met and started dating Hugh Rodham, a short, dour, dark-haired salesman seven years her senior.

Hugh Rodham's Welsh immigrant parents had both gone to work in Scranton, Pennsylvania, when they were young children. The second in a family of three boys, he went to work in the coal mines during the Depression but still managed to attend Pennsylvania State College on a football scholarship. After graduating with a bachelor's degree in physical education, he decided he could earn more as a salesman and went to work for the same company that employed his father, Scranton Lace Works.

After a five-year courtship, Hugh and Dorothy were finally married in 1942. After Pearl Harbor, Hugh put his college degree to use instructing navy recruits in the Gene Tunney program, a physical conditioning technique named after the former world heavyweight boxing champion.

After his discharge from the navy at war's end, Hugh started his own custom drapery business in Chicago. They were living in a one-bedroom apartment in Chicago when, on October 26, 1947, Dorothy was rushed to Edgewater Hospital on the city's North Side. There she gave birth to eight-and-a-half-pound Hillary Diane Rodham—a docile, even-tempered child who impressed her mother as "very mature even then."

When Hillary was three, the Rodhams moved to Park Ridge, a leafy, prosperous, Republican-to-the-core suburb situated just northwest of Chicago. There were no minorities to speak of—no Asians, Hispanics, or Jews owned homes in Park Ridge, and the only African American among the town's thirty thousand–plus residents at the time was a foster child.

It was here, in a brick Georgian house at 236 Wisner Street with arching windows and tall shade trees, that a frustrated Dorothy put her own dreams of earning a college degree on hold and settled into the *Ozzie and Harriet* role of stay-at-home housewife. Hugh, too, lived out his life according to the classic 1950s scenario. A brusque, tobacco-chewing workaholic, he prided himself on the condition of his lawn—he paid Hillary and her younger brothers, Hughie and Tony, one shiny copper penny for every weed they pulled in the hot summer sun—and the gleaming new Cadillac he bought for himself every year.

Despite her decision not to pursue a career of her own outside the home, Dorothy was "determined that no daughter of mine was going to have to go through the agony of being afraid to say what she had on her mind. Just because she was a girl didn't mean she should be limited." When Hillary rushed home one afternoon to say that she was afraid of a bigger girl, the local bully, Dorothy told her, "There's no room in this house for cowards. The next time she hits you," Hillary's mother continued, "I want you to hit her back."

Hillary did just that, and in front of a group of admiring boys. A delighted Hillary ran back to her mother with the good news: "I can play with the boys now!"

From that point on, Dorothy later recalled, "boys responded well to Hillary. She just took charge, and they let her."

Hugh was even more demanding when it came to his children. All three were taught to master the stock tables in the *Chicago Tribune* almost as soon as they learned to read. When it came to sports, Hillary, no less than her more athletically inclined brothers, was expected to live up to her full potential. Once it was determined that she could not hit a curveball, Hugh took her to the local playground every Sunday after church for two months. For hours, Hugh and his sons took turns pitching to Hillary until she was better at slamming a curveball than any of the Rodham men.

Hugh Rodham also took a firm hand in their political indoctrination. An old-school Republican, Rodham supported Ohio Senator Robert Taft in his 1952 bid against Dwight Eisenhower for the GOP presidential nomination because he felt Ike was too liberal. It was a sentiment shared by Rodham's neighbors; at the time Park

Ridge was a stronghold of the right-wing John Birch Society. Accordingly, Hillary and her brothers were required to watch gavel-to-gavel television coverage of the Republican National Convention, but forbidden even to turn the set on while the Democratic Convention was under way.

Dorothy rebelled in her own quiet way. Unbeknownst to Hugh, his wife was a closet Democrat. In 1960, while her husband sang the praises of Vice-President Richard Nixon ad nauseam, Dorothy quietly cast her vote for John F. Kennedy. "How on earth," Dorothy Rodham later quipped, "do you think Hillary ever became a Democrat?"

Just as Virginia Clinton had provided her son with the airtight mental "box" as a tool for coping with adversity, Dorothy pulled out a carpenter's level to teach her daughter how to maintain her emotional equilibrium. She held the level in front of Hillary, pointed to the bubble in the center, and then tilted the level so that the bubble slid to one end and then to the other. "Imagine having this carpenter's level inside you," she said. The trick, Dorothy told her daughter, was to remain calm, determined, focused, always in control—whatever it took "to keep the bubble in the center."

Outwardly, Hillary's childhood seemed nothing short of idyllic. The streets were so safe that, from the age of five, she was allowed to walk alone the several blocks to Eugene Field Elementary School. During the winter months, the Rodham children built snowmen and went ice-skating on one of the local ponds. Most of the year, they got where they wanted to go—school, friends' houses, the baseball field, the local movie theater—on their bikes. "We didn't even know what bike locks were back then," she later said. "Nobody needed them." As a student at Ralph Waldo Emerson Junior High School, Hillary rode her bike to her favorite destination—the local library—"unaccompanied and unafraid."

Yet she was fearful of one thing—disappointing her formidable dad. Hugh Rodham had a reputation around Park Ridge for being something of an oddball—moody, antisocial, and, when he did deign to speak to his neighbors, blunt-spoken to the point of rudeness. If he went to watch his sons play baseball, Rodham would plop a lawn chair down in left field—as far away from the other spectators as possible. Whenever anyone called on the Rodham household, Hugh did not budge from his chair or acknowledge the visitor's presence in any way. "Her dad was very strange," neighbor Rawls Williams said. "A sort of recluse, really."

Hillary's unrelentingly authoritarian father was, in the words of neighbor Carolyn Susman, "a looming presence in all their lives." Indeed, when his daughter proudly handed him her report card, Rodham would look at her straight A's and hand the card back to her. "It must," he invariably replied, "be a very easy school you go to."

His fondness for Cadillacs aside, Rodham was also a notorious pennypincher. Even in the dead of winter, he turned off the heat at night so that Hillary and her brothers woke up shivering. "I used to go to my father and say: 'Dad, I *really* need a new pair of shoes,' " Hillary recalled. " 'My shoes have holes in them,' and he'd say, 'Have you done your chores? Have you done this? Have you done that?' "

There was plenty to do. Hillary and her brothers mowed, weeded, raked leaves, took out the garbage, shoveled snow, washed the dishes—all without receiving an allowance or, worse yet, hearing any words of praise from Hugh Sr. When she was finished with her chores and seated at the dinner table, Hillary would ask her father for a dollar to go to the movies.

"Here," he replied, unceremoniously plopping another potato on her plate. "That's your reward."

Years later, when she asked her father for a dress to wear to the junior prom, he grudgingly agreed to buy her one—but only so long as it was "plain and cheap." Hillary told a friend she was "surprised" he bought her a dress at all. "It's probably," she surmised, "because my parents are going to be chaperones . . ."

Hugh's drill sergeant mentality extended to corporal punishment, which he administered with some frequency. When the otherwise perfect Hillary got in trouble for talking in class, she could expect a spanking from her dad when he got home from work. Of his many warnings to the children, perhaps his favorite was, "You get in trouble at school, you get in trouble at home."

Unlike Roger Clinton, Hugh was a model of probity. There

were no drunken scenes, no screams in the night, no calls to the police in the middle of the night. But in a deliberate, measured way, Hillary's father conducted his own unremitting psychological reign of terror on the family that only craved his approval. "Hillary adored her father," a neighbor said, "the way a kidnapping victim eventually comes to love her captor. Hillary gives him credit for giving her backbone, but Hugh had such a mean streak you had to feel sorry for her and her brothers. Hillary might have been crushed if it weren't for her mother."

But Dorothy did not want to deny Hillary's father his share of the credit. "Maybe that's why she's such an accepting person," Mrs. Rodham mused. "She had to put up with him."

Nevertheless, Hillary would later claim that, "as a girl growing up, I never felt anything but support" from both her parents. "Whatever I thought I could do and be, they supported. There was no distinction between me and my brothers or any barriers thrown up to me because I was a girl." To be sure, Dorothy Rodham would later concede that she refrained from giving her daughter "advice on clothes and makeup and how to attract boys." But there were times when even Dorothy was "annoyed. I used to think, 'Why can't she put on a little makeup?' " Still, what Dorothy wanted most was to see her daughter become the first woman on the United States Supreme Court. "But," Dorothy said, "Sandra Day O'Connor beat her to it."

While Bill Clinton piled up honors and awards seven hundred miles to the south, his future wife was building an impressive résumé of her own. At Maine Township High School, Hillary was at various times a member of the student council, the Cultural Values Committee, the pep club, the debating team, the Girls Athletic Association, the National Honor Society, the brotherhood society, the Organizations Committee, and the school's *It's Academic* quiz show team. She was on the staff of the school newspaper, served as junior class vice-president, performed in both the spring musical and the school variety show, and was one of eleven National Merit Scholars chosen from her class of fourteen hundred at Maine Township High School.

Still, classmates questioned her motives. "She was very ambitious," fellow student Arthur Curtis said. "I was an overachiever, and it was impossible to upstage her." Another classmate, Penny Pullen, remembered the day it was announced that the Daughters of the American Revolution were going to bestow a "Good Citizens Award" on the one Maine Township High student who best personified the qualities of "dependability, service, leadership and patriotism."

"I'm going after the DAR award," Hillary told Pullen matter-of-factly. "It'll look good on my résumé."

Pullen was taken aback by Hillary's candor. "Nobody 'went after' it. I mean, it was not appropriate to go after it . . . you got the award because of your concern for your country, not so you could get the award." Perhaps, but Hillary got the award.

Such calculated ambition, coupled with Hillary's drab appearance and apparent lack of interest in the opposite sex, resulted in her being cast as something of a social wallflower. At one point, the campus newspaper cruelly joked that the piously aloof Miss Rodham would become a nun—"Sister Frigidaire."

Notwithstanding such gibes, Hillary was, unlike her father, open to new influences. Her social conscience received a jump start one summer when, at the age of thirteen, she joined a group of baby-sitters organized by the First United Methodist Church to care for the children of migrant workers—the hundreds of Mexicans and African Americans who were trucked in from the South to harvest crops just a few miles outside Park Ridge.

The following year, she signed on with the Reverend Don Jones's "University of Life" youth group at First United Methodist. Jones was a self-described existentialist who sought to expose Hillary and the other members of his youth group "to the experience of social service and life outside Park Ridge."

Toward that end, Jones introduced his charges to the ideas of theologians Reinhold Niebuhr, Dietrich Bonhoeffer, and Paul Tillich; the writings of e.e. cummings, Wallace Stevens, Stephen Crane, and J. D. Salinger; the films of François Truffaut, the music of Bob Dylan, and the paintings of Pablo Picasso.

On one of several field trips to a recreation center on Chicago's gritty South Side, Jones took a print of Picasso's *Guernica* and propped it up against a chair. The painting, which graphically depicts a bombing raid by pro-Franco forces on a village during the Spanish Civil War, was seen very differently by the ghetto kids and their well-heeled counterparts from Park Ridge.

While Hillary and friends spoke of the horrors of war in the abstract, the inner-city kids related the mayhem to their everyday lives. One girl looked at the painting and told Hillary, "Just last week, my uncle drove up and parked on the street and some guy came up to him and said you can't park there, that's my parking place, and my uncle resisted him and the guy pulled out a gun and shot him . . ."

On another occasion, the Reverend Jones took Hillary and the others to meet Saul Alinsky, the left-wing firebrand whose 1937 book *Reveille for Radicals* became the bible of the protest movement. The quintessential outside agitator, Alinsky organized rent strikes, sit-ins, and picket lines, vowing all the while to "do whatever it takes to bring power to the people." Matters of taste did not concern him; Alinsky once proudly led a "fart-in" in the Chicago headquarters of a major corporation. Hillary would later describe Alinsky as a "great seducer" of young minds.

On April 15, 1962, Jones brought Hillary's group to Orchestra Hall to hear Dr. Martin Luther King deliver a lecture called "Sleeping Through the Revolution." Then he brought his young charges backstage to meet Dr. King personally. In what would be a parallel to Bill's meeting with JFK, an awestruck Hillary shook the civil rights leader's hand. There was a difference, however. Unlike Bill, the decidedly less emotional and sentimental Hillary would never see this or any such single symbolic event as a turning point in her life. "She was," a friend said, "far too level-headed and practical for that."

No matter how blasé, no American who was old enough to comprehend what had happened that day in Dallas would be left unaffected by the cataclysmic events of November 22, 1963. No sooner had word raced through the hallways of Hillary's high school than the entire student body was hastily summoned to an assembly. When the principal confirmed that John F. Kennedy had been assassinated, a collective gasp went up from the crowd. Several teachers broke down and wept openly, triggering the same reaction in scores of students.

Although she later described this moment as "the absolute turning point in my life," Hillary was still very much under her father's political spell, and her views mirrored those of her conservative Republican father. In high school, she quoted constantly from Barry's Goldwater's *The Conscience of a Conservative*, and in her senior year campaigned for the 1964 Republican nominee as a "Goldwater Girl." That year she also ran for senior class president but lost. She wrote a letter to the Reverend Jones pouring out her heart about how difficult it was to reconcile herself to defeat. What emerged from the letter more than anything else, said Jones, was just how much "Hillary hated to lose."

In 1965, Hillary graduated in the top 5 percent of her class and was voted Most Likely to Succeed. That September, her parents drove her in the Rodhams' Cadillac to Wellesley, the exclusive women's college situated beside Lake Waban some fifteen miles southwest of Boston. "Aside from a few trips away with girlfriends, Hillary hadn't really been away from home," Dorothy recalled of that emotional moment when they said goodbye. "After we dropped her off, I just crawled into the backseat and cried for eight hundred miles." Dad, on the other hand, was unimpressed by the fact that his daughter had been accepted at such a prestigious school, and later said he viewed the trip as "an inconvenience."

With its five hundred wooded acres and neo–Gothic architecture, Wellesley was generally regarded as one of the nation's most beautiful campuses. Despite boasting one of the largest endowments of any private learning institution in the country, Wellesley also charged more tuition than any of the other elite women's colleges known as the Seven Sisters (Barnard, Vassar, Radcliffe, Mount Holyoke, Bryn Mawr, and Smith).

Best known in academic circles for its library and art collections, Wellesley had in fact broken considerable ground since it opened its doors in 1875. It was, among other things, the first women's college to have its own science laboratories. Yet when Hillary arrived in the autumn of 1965, Wellesley was still rightly known as part college and part finishing school—a bastion of tradition and political conservatism catering to the daughters of power and privilege.

Hillary certainly fit the stereotype when she arrived. A prim, demure presence at the afternoon teas held for incoming freshmen, Hillary threw herself into campus activities and was immediately elected president of the campus Young Republicans. She immersed herself in schoolwork, but soon grew restless. "After six weeks of little communication or companionship," she wrote the Reverend Jones back home, "my diet of studying gave me indigestion. The last two weeks of February were an orgy of decadent indulgence—as decadent as any upright Methodist can become." Whether she wrote of holing up in the library, entering "party mode," or "playing hippie"—which consisted of painting a flower on her arm and wearing tie-dyed clothes for a month—Hillary carefully planned every move, every phase. "She was totally, utterly self-conscious in everything she did," said a Wellesley classmate. "Spontaneity was anathema to Hillary."

On weekends, she began tagging along with the other Wellesley girls and took the train to Cambridge. She was soon dating Geoffrey Shields, a law school–bound Harvard junior who came from Lake Forest, another affluent Chicago suburb. Shields had been both a star football player in high school and, like Hillary, an inexhaustible overachiever. Yet even he was intimidated by Hillary's steely sense of self.

"The time when she seemed to lighten up the most was when there was a good, interesting, heated debate about issues," Shields said, "particularly issues that had a practical impact on the world—racial issues, the Vietnam war, civil rights, civil liberties." That first year, however, Hillary argued on behalf of the Johnson Administration and U.S. involvement in Vietnam. Meantime, the relationship with Shields, which he later described as "romantic but platonic," lasted three years.

Both Hillary and Shields underwent an ideological metamorphosis in 1966. When she returned to Wellesley as a sophomore that fall, Hillary not only resigned as president of the Young Republicans but declared she no longer was one.

At the time, protests over civil rights and Vietnam were already erupting on campuses across the country. But at staid, antediluvian Wellesley, student activism was muted in both content and form. As a member of the student senate, Hillary argued on behalf of greater minority enrollment (there were only ten African Americans at Wellesley at the time), and an end to curfews as well as school prohibitions against males setting foot in the dormitories. Still, Shields conceded, "she was hardly a bomb-throwing radical. She liked to get things accomplished in a calm, rational, methodical way."

By her junior year, the transformation was complete. In Boston Hillary took part in antiwar protests, and in March 1968 ventured north to New Hampshire to campaign for peace candidate Eugene McCarthy in the Democratic primary there.

Three weeks later, Hillary was strolling across the campus when someone raced up to her with the news that Martin Luther King had been shot. Hillary ran back to her dormitory, threw open the door, and hurled her book bag against the wall. "She was distraught," recalled her roommate, Johanna Branson. "She was yelling. She kept asking questions."

"I can't stand it anymore!" Hillary screamed. "I can't take it." Then she and several other students put on black armbands and went to Boston to join thousands of protesters "marching in anger and pain."

In her senior year, Hillary took a few more tentative steps to the left. She invited hell-raiser emeritus Saul Alinsky to Wellesley to speak, and interviewed him for her thesis on LBJ's Community Action Program, a cornerstone of the Great Society. She was also profoundly influenced by the writings of Marxist theoretician Carl Oglesby, who condoned violence as a legitimate tool for social change and advocated pitting elements of America's "ruling class" against each other.

Ultimately, she drew the line at extremism, but only on the grounds that it would alienate the majority that was needed to accomplish real social change. So, while she continued to support civil rights leaders who followed the example set by Martin Luther King, Hillary rejected the Black Power call-to-arms of SNCC, Stokely Carmichael's Student Non-Violent Coordinating Committee.

As her senior year drew to a close, Hillary pondered what to do after graduation. Even though she adhered generally to his anti-establishment philosophy ("You know, I've been on this kick for twenty-five years," she would say after becoming First Lady), Hillary turned down an offer to work with Alinsky as a paid community organizer in Chicago. "She just didn't think she could bring about real social change that way," said her political science professor, Alan Schechter. According to Schechter, who gave Hillary's senior thesis an A, she wrote that "organizing the poor for community actions to improve their own lives may have short-term benefits for the poor but would never solve their major problems. You need much more than that. You need leadership programs, constitutional doctrines."

"The only way to make a real difference," Hillary told one friend, "is to acquire power." According to Schechter, his prize pupil decided the best way to accomplish this was by finding a way to "use the legal system" as an agent of change.

If she was going to law school, then Hillary decided she had one of two choices: Harvard or Yale. She was leaning toward Yale, which at the time put less emphasis on corporate law than the marginally more prestigious Harvard. But to be certain she was making the right choice, Hillary visited Harvard Law School, where a friend introduced her to "a tall, rather imposing professor, sort of like a character from *The Paper Chase*."

"I'm just trying to decide," she told the professor, "whether I should go to Harvard Law or to your closest competitor."

The professor stared down at her and replied disdainfully, "Well, first of all we don't *have* any close competitors. Secondly, we don't need any more women." Then he turned and walked away.

"That's what made my decision," Hillary later said. "That fellow's comments iced the cake."

Meantime, Hillary's defiant speech at Wellesley's graduation ceremonies made media waves, landing her in *Life* magazine as one of the eloquent new voices of her generation. Wearing oversized glasses and tight striped pants, her straight auburn hair cascading over her shoulders, Hillary perched on the edge of a chair and gesticulated with her hands while the photographer clicked away. The less-than-flattering shots nevertheless made her an instant campus celebrity, although she was beginning to have her doubts. The day the magazine hit the stands, Hillary called Geof Shields and asked, "Did I go too far?"

She certainly had no regrets the day of the speech itself. What no one knew was that, beneath her graduation gown that day, Hillary had worn a bathing suit. Immediately after the ceremony, Hillary had gone to Lake Waban, stripped off the gown, and dived in—all in direct violation of college rules that strictly prohibited swimming in the lake. It was to be her final, solitary act of rebellion—at least as far as Wellesley was concerned.

One evening in November 1970, Hillary was hunched over her books at the long table that ran down the center of the Yale Law Library's third-floor reading room. Surrounded by legal pads, notebooks, and phone book–sized legal texts, she occasionally stole a glance at the tall, shaggy-maned man with the scraggly beard pretending to be engrossed in a conversation at the far end of the room.

Bill Clinton was listening politely as Jeffrey Gleckel, an editor of the *Yale Law Journal*, tried to convince him to sign on with the journal. At first Clinton seemed to be listening intently as Gleckel pointed out that students chosen to write for the *Journal* had their pick of judicial clerkships and teaching positions, not to mention entrée into the country's top law firms.

"He was telling me I could clerk for the U.S. Supreme Court if I was a member of the *Yale Law Journal*, which is probably true," Bill later remembered. "And then I could go on to New York and make a ton of money. And I kept telling him I didn't want to do all of that. I wanted to go home to Arkansas. It didn't matter to anybody in Arkansas if I was on the *Yale Law Journal* or not. I just didn't want to do it. And all this time I was talking to this guy about the *Law Journal*, I was looking at Hillary at the other end of the library."

Soon Gleckel realized he was losing his audience—if he ever really had it. "Little by little, it seemed to me his concentration was disappearing," Gleckel recalled. "He listened but was saying much less. His glance began to wander and he seemed to be looking over my shoulder. I was trying to find a way to look in an inconspicuous manner and so I sort of turned around halfway as an excuse to scratch my leg or something and there I saw, seated at a desk with a stack of books and notepads, Hillary Rodham."

She was wearing Levi's bell-bottoms (which she occasionally alternated with baggy black silk pajama bottoms), a long-sleeved peasant blouse, sandals, and thick owlish glasses. Eyewear was her one fashion indulgence; at one point, she owned over a dozen pair, each with a different distinctive frame, from round wire-rimmed granny glasses to Gloria Steinem aviators to huge plastic rims in a variety of colors. She still shied away from makeup, and in those rare instances when her legs were visible, even her classmates were taken aback by the unmistakable fact that she did not bother to shave them.

Despite his fondness for blondes in the Arkansas beauty pageant mold, none of this seemed to deter Bill. He kept up the charade of listening to Gleckel until Hillary got out of her chair and walked across the room. "Look," she said, "if you're going to keep staring at me and I'm going to keep staring back, we should at least introduce ourselves. I'm Hillary Rodham."

Taken aback by her boldness, Bill drew a blank. "I was dumbstruck," he claimed. "I couldn't think of my name."

Gleckel confirmed Clinton's account of that meeting. "I could see something was about to happen," he said, "so I just politely excused myself."

Hillary and Bill had, in fact, met earlier—when, during the first week of school, their mutual friend Robert Reich made a pro forma introduction over trays in the cafeteria. There was no chemistry then, but over the next few weeks both Hillary and Bill had eyed each other, waiting for the right moment to make a move. She watched from the sidelines as he stood in the middle of a small crowd passionately extolling the virtues of his homegrown watermelons. "That's Bill Clinton from Arkansas," her friend informed her. "And that's all he ever talks about."

He, meanwhile, trailed her after a class they shared but failed to find the right opening. It was a problem the terminally flirtatious Bill had never faced before. But Hillary was different. "I could just look at her and tell she was interesting and deep," he said. Besides, she was also "frightening, intimidating—a challenge," he conceded. "She was a star. I was genuinely afraid of her."

He was not alone. Hillary complained to one of her other twenty-nine female classmates that men seemed put off by her directness. If Bill felt intimidated, he did an expert job of concealing this fact from her. That, in turn, was part of his appeal. "I've actually found a guy," she proclaimed, "who is not afraid of me. Not one bit."

Hillary, although a year younger than Bill, had already been at Yale Law School a year when they finally did connect in the fall of 1970—a year during which she had firmly established herself as one of the campus's most visible activists.

As soon as she arrived, Hillary sought out the leaders of the antiwar movement on campus. Ironically, one of these newfound friends—future movie critic and author Michael Medved—would eventually call for her husband's removal from the White House. Another, Greg Craig, would become a powerful Washington lawyer and wind up defending President Clinton against perjury and obstruction of justice charges in the well of the U.S. Senate.

"There was nothing radical about her as far as we were concerned," Craig later recalled. "She was against the war, and so was practically everyone else in her age group." More the pragmatist than the firebrand, Hillary joined the Youth Advisory Board of the League of Women Voters and pressed for the mainstream organization to support lowering the voting age to eighteen.

When she was asked to address the league on its fiftieth anniversary, Hillary showed up wearing a black armband in honor of the four students shot and killed by National Guardsmen at Ohio's Kent State University. Her speech was a scathing indictment of the establishment, particularly corporate America. "How much longer can we let corporations run us?" she railed. "Isn't it about time that they, as all the rest of our institutions, are held accountable to the people?"

Through her involvement with the league, she had met two people who would play key roles in her life: noted civil rights lawyer and children's rights pioneer Marian Wright Edelman, and influential Washington lawyer Vernon Jordan.

The spring of 1970 was a time of turmoil. The trial of Black Panther founder Bobby Seale was about to begin in New Haven, and Huey Newton, newly sprung from San Quentin on $50,000 bail, flew in to whip up support. He was met at the airport by Donald Sutherland and Jane Fonda, who raised her fist in a Black Power salute as Newton got off the plane. Seale and seven other Panthers had been indicted for the torture-murder of a fellow Panther, who had presumably informed police of a New York bombing conspiracy.

In anticipation of rioting as thousands of Panther supporters poured into New Haven, local merchants boarded up storefronts to stave off looters. Yale students, meanwhile, called for a strike in sympathy with the Panthers, listening as Newton denounced fascist "Amerika" and called for full-scale revolution.

To make sure there were no violations of the Panthers' civil rights, Hillary organized a group of students to monitor the proceedings for the American Civil Liberties Union. Students protesting in support of the Panthers had been teargassed on the campus green. But when someone set fire to Yale's International Law Library, she presided over a hastily called meeting of the law school student body to decide what should be done.

Sitting cross-legged on the edge of the stage, Hillary cut through all the posturing and the grandstanding of opposing factions and hammered out a middle-of-the-road approach. "It was pure Hillary," her classmate Kris Rogers said. "She was focused, and she would not put up with any fuzzy thinking." Another friend, Carolyn Ellis, remembered that when everyone walked out of the room, no one "could remember what the meeting was about— only that we were awed by her."

Spurred on by stories of her own mother's horrendous childhood, Hillary began doing research into the plight of disadvantaged children as a summer intern in Marian Wright Edelman's office. Edelman assigned the eager young law student to work with Senator Walter Mondale's subcommittee studying migrant labor. Hillary interviewed dozens of laborers about the grim conditions in migrant labor camps, and by the time hearings began she was fuming.

Minute Maid, a newly acquired subsidiary of The Coca-Cola

Company, was one of the companies being investigated. When Coke president J. Paul Austin arrived to testify at the hearings, Hillary walked up to him and waved her finger in his face. "We're going to nail your ass," she said to the startled executive. "Nail your ass!"

By her second year at Yale Law School, Hillary was a bona fide campus star. But she could not help but be intrigued by the man she later described as "a sunny Southerner with Elvis sideburns."

"Hillary was a straight shooter—there was absolutely no b.s. about her," said another classmate, Harlon Dalton. "In Bill Clinton's case, she saw right past the charm and saw the complex person underneath. I think he found that irresistible."

The "complex person underneath" was all the more complex for having come through a tumultuous year of his own. While Hillary Rodham forged a name for herself at Yale, Bill was trying to figure a way out of being drafted into the armed forces and shipped to Vietnam.

Bill's options were few. He had no intention of entering the service as a buck private. Neither was he going to join his friend Frank Aller in resisting the draft—an action that could doom his chances of ever holding national office.

Before he left Oxford for home that June, a somber Bill told anyone who would listen that he would probably be fighting in Vietnam by late summer. "Everyone was terribly upset," Sara Maitland recalled. "Bill was going off to war. It was traumatic for all of us." His friends threw a going-away bash for him that lasted three full days, ending only when partygoers drove Bill to Heathrow and put him on a plane bound for the United States.

None of his Oxford companions—particularly the women who agreed to go to bed with him because he might not come out of Vietnam alive—were aware that he had already started the wheels in motion to stave off service. In the weeks before his departure from London, Bill made several calls to his stepfather, Jeff Dwire, instructing him to contact a number of officials in Hot Springs who might be able to get him into a National Guard unit or a Reserve Officer Training Corps program.

Bill did not stop there. In a frantic flurry of phone calls from

England—all, amazingly, collect—he approached a dozen friends in the United States asking them either to intercede on his behalf with draft officials or to find him a spot in the ROTC.

Bill stopped off in Washington on the way back to Hot Springs. On Capitol Hill, he approached his old boss, the powerful Senate Foreign Relations Committee chairman J. William Fulbright, and asked the senator to use his influence to find him a National Guard or ROTC appointment.

Bill's search for a way around the draft continued in Arkansas, only now with a new sense of urgency as the number of American dead was fast approaching forty thousand. Cliff Jackson, the young Fulbright Scholar he got to know in England, had returned to Arkansas that summer to work for the executive director of the state's Republican Party, Van Rush. Bill asked Jackson to use his influence with Rush to "quash" the draft notice.

Jackson would eventually become Clinton's nemesis. But for now, he shared Bill's ambivalence about the war, and decided to comply with his request. Rush went to Willard "Lefty" Hawkins, director of Arkansas's Selective Service office, who in turn approached the head of the ROTC program at the University of Arkansas, Colonel Eugene Holmes.

Gene Holmes, a thirty-two-year veteran, had survived the Bataan Death March and three years in a Japanese POW camp. His brother had been killed in the war, and now two of his own sons were serving in Vietnam. With his induction date fast approaching, Bill, his beard now gone and his hair neatly trimmed, drove to Colonel Holmes's residence in Fayetteville on July 17. Sitting in the decorated war hero's living room, Bill made the case over the course of a two-hour interview that he could better serve his country as an officer than as a draftee.

The next day, Holmes was deluged with calls from state and local officials who urged him to bend the rules and admit Bill into the ROTC program. Even the draft board weighed in on Clinton's behalf. "The general message conveyed to me," Holmes recalled, "was that Senator Fulbright was putting pressure on them and that they needed my help." Holmes, who later said he was eager "to help a Rhodes Scholar serve in the military as an officer," made the necessary arrangements to enroll him in the University of Arkansas ROTC program. Not only would Bill not be required to report for duty as a draftee on July 28, but he would be allowed to complete law school in Arkansas before serving as an officer. "He knew," said Jackson, "that by the time he got out of law school three years later the war would be over."

Still, Bill agonized over whether he was doing the right thing. A month after formally signing up with the ROTC program, Clinton poured out his feelings in a letter to his friend Rick Stearns. "Nothing could be worse than this torment," he wrote. "You see, I haven't explained it very well—the anguish is not that apparent . . . it's ravaged my whole image of myself . . . I honestly feel so screwed up tight that I am incapable, I think, of really giving myself, of really loving. I told you I was losing my mind . . ."

A few days later, on September 12, he stayed up all night at his mother's house on Scully Street writing a letter to the chairman of the draft board in which he said he had "no interest in the ROTC itself. I was only trying to protect myself from physical harm," he continued. "Please draft me as soon as possible." He carried the letter with him for months, even showed the letter to several friends, but never mailed it.

Instead, Holmes allowed Bill to return to Oxford with the understanding that he would be back "in a month or so" and begin classes at the University of Arkansas Law School. Bill, who swore to Holmes that he did not oppose American involvement in Vietnam, joined some forty like-minded student organizers at the Martha's Vineyard estate of wealthy antiwar activist John Sullivan. The ostensible purpose of this student activist summit was to find ways they could continue the work they had begun a year earlier while working in the presidential campaigns of Eugene McCarthy and Robert F. Kennedy.

One of those Bill befriended at the Martha's Vineyard gathering was David Mixner, a twenty-three-year-old zealot who nearly died after being tossed by police through a plate-glass window at the 1968 Democratic National Convention in Chicago. Mixner, who later become one of President Clinton's chief advisors on gay rights, was also one of the founders of the militant Vietnam Moratorium Committee.

On the way back to England, Bill stopped off at the Moratorium Committee's Washington headquarters and volunteered to help organize their antiwar efforts abroad. With Colonel Holmes and the folks back in Arkansas firmly convinced he would be coming home in October to begin his ROTC training at the University of Arkansas, Bill now threw himself into the antiwar movement.

In the fall of 1969, American students wishing to participate in demonstrations against the U.S. government in London were put in contact with Bill Clinton. At more than a dozen antiwar meetings at Oxford, he emerged as the leader. And on October 15—Moratorium Day—Clinton was front-and-center among several hundred Americans who participated in a teach-in at the London School of Economics and then marched on the U.S. Embassy in Grosvenor Square.

A month later there was an even larger protest at the American Embassy. This time, Bill and nearly five hundred other protesters wore armbands and carried cards, each scrawled with the name of an American soldier killed in Vietnam. The following day, he led a prayer service at a nearby church and, with other protesters, again marched on the embassy carrying foot-high wooden crosses. When they arrived at Grosvenor Square, Clinton and the others piled the crosses at the embassy gates while stern-faced marine guards looked on.

Two weeks later, the first draft lottery since the Second World War was broadcast live on national television. Young men would be drafted according to the order in which their date of birth was drawn from a large glass bowl. That year, Bill's birth date of August 19 was the 311th date picked, virtually ensuring that he would not be drafted. (The highest number taken, it turned out, was 195.)

Three days later Bill, now confident that he was no longer within the grasp of his draft board, mailed a letter to Colonel Holmes in which he told the career military man what he really thought of the military. Decades later, as he pursued the presidency, the letter would come back to haunt him.

"First, I want to thank you, not just for saving me from the draft," Clinton wrote, "but for being so kind and decent to me last summer, when I was as low as I have ever been. One thing which made the bond we struck in good faith somewhat palatable to me was my high regard for you personally. In retrospect, it seems that the admiration might not have been mutual had you known a little more about me, about my political beliefs and activities . . ."

Bill went on to explain that he worked for the Senate Foreign Relations Committee "for the experience and for the salary but also for the opportunity, however small, of working every day against a war opposed and despised with a depth of feeling I had reserved solely for racism in America before Vietnam . . . I have written and spoken and marched against the war . . . After I left Arkansas last summer, I went to Washington to work in the national headquarters of the Moratorium, then to England to organize the Americans for the demonstrations planned for Oct. 15 and Nov. 16.

"From my work," he continued, "I came to believe that the draft system itself is illegitimate . . . Because of my opposition to the draft and the war, I am in great sympathy with those who are not willing to fight, kill, and maybe die for their country, right or wrong . . . One of my roommates is a draft resistor who is possibly under indictment and may never be able to go home again. He is one of the bravest, best men I know. That he is considered a criminal is an obscenity."

He went on to say the decision not to resist the draft and enter the ROTC instead was "the most difficult in my life. *I decided to accept the draft in spite of my beliefs for one reason: to maintain my political viability within the system. For years I have worked to prepare myself for a political life characterized by both practical and political ability and concern for rapid social progress. It is a life I still feel compelled to try to lead.*"

Once he received his draft notice, Bill continued to explain, "despite political convictions, I was having a hard time facing the prospect of fighting a war I was fighting against, and that is why I contacted you. ROTC was the one way left in which I could possibly . . . avoid both Vietnam and resistance."

The letter rambled on until Bill admitted that he "had no interest in the ROTC program in itself and all I seemed to have done was to protect myself from physical harm. Also, I began to think I had deceived you, not by lies because there were none, but by failing to tell you all the things I am telling you now."

Once he had actually committed himself to ROTC and his 1-A draft status was withdrawn, Bill wrote, "the anguish and loss of my self-regard and self-confidence really set in. I hardly slept for weeks and kept going by eating compulsively and reading until exhaustion brought sleep."

Why was he unburdening himself now? "Because you have been good to me and have a right to know what I think and feel," he told Holmes. "I am writing too in the hope that my telling this one story will help you to understand more clearly how so many fine people have come to find themselves still loving their country but loathing the military, to which you and other good men have devoted years, lifetimes, of the best service you could give." Bill signed the letter, simply, "Merry Christmas."

Now free to enjoy himself, Bill embarked on a forty-day train trip through Scandinavia, the Soviet Union, and Eastern Europe. At each stop along the way, the bearded, curly-haired Southerner managed to hook up with acquaintances or friends of acquaintances who would show him around, feed him, and put him up for the night. In Oslo, he ran into Father Richard McSorley, who had marched alongside him during the November 15 peace rally in London, and visited an old friend from Hot Springs, Jim Durham.

Once he reached Finland, Bill dropped in unannounced on former Georgetown classmate Richard Shullaw, whose father worked at the American Embassy in Helsinki. The Shullaws had no choice but to invite him for Christmas dinner, but they could not put him up in their modest apartment. They did, however, pay for him to stay at a nearby youth hostel.

On New Year's Eve, 1969, Bill crossed the border into the Soviet Union. Border guards, suspecting that the disheveled young foreigner might be smuggling drugs, ordered a strip search. As soon as he arrived in Moscow, he checked into the prerevolutionary National Hotel on Red Square, where he promptly charmed two middle-aged American businessmen who were there hoping to glean some information on American servicemen missing in North Vietnam.

Clinton tagged along with the two Americans for a week, essentially providing them with a Rhodes Scholar's insight into the Soviet system while they paid for his meals. "Bill stayed around with us," recalled one of the Americans, Charlie Daniels. "He was always hungry and always broke." At one point, Bill introduced them to Anik Alexis, a friend from England who was now studying at Moscow University. With her help, Bill was able to arrange a meeting between Daniels and North Vietnamese officials.

After a full week in Moscow, Bill boarded a train for Prague, where he stayed for several days with the family of his Oxford classmate Jan Kopold. The Kopolds were dissidents who had been imprisoned in the 1950s, and again ran afoul of the Communists when they supported reformer Alexander Dubček. Bill listened intently as the Kopolds gave their chilling account of the 1968 Soviet invasion, when Russian tanks rolled through the streets of Prague.

Carnival was in full swing by the time Bill arrived in Munich, where he and his old friend Rudi Lowe donned costumes and went to several masquerade balls. "He was going back to Oxford," Lowe said, "and it was pretty clear all he wanted to do was party and enjoy himself."

Not that the partying stopped when he returned to England. Now that the draft and the prospect of being shipped to Vietnam no longer hung over his head like the Sword of Damocles, Bill seemed visibly relaxed. He resumed his pattern of juggling several lovers simultaneously, and began inviting as many as a half-dozen women at a time to play sexually charged games of strip poker in his room. "There were usually twice as many women as men," one female participant recalled, "and Bill always ended up being the first one with all his clothes off."

In January 1970, Bill invited Sara Maitland and Mandy Merck to a lecture by the bombastic feminist Germaine Greer. Her controversial book *The Female Eunuch* had not yet been published, and all Clinton knew about Greer, according to Maitland, "was that she was more than six foot tall, had great legs, and was going to talk about sex. Her gist was that middle-class men were terrible at sex and intelligent women would only do it with truck drivers."

Bill wore a bright pink poplin suit to the lecture, and when Greer was finished delivering her lecture he raised his hand with a question. She could not miss him. "About the overrated orgasm," he said. "In case you ever decide to give bourgeois men another chance," he said, "can I give you my phone number?"

"No!" Greer replied in mock outrage once the laughter had died down.

Charm aside, to those who knew him it was clear that Bill saw sex and power as two sides of the same coin. It bothered Cliff Jackson, who remembered the rainy evening when he and Bill were walking back from the gym and talking about the war.

Suddenly Bill burst out laughing. "I heard this great story from a senior guy in Fulbright's office," he told Jackson. "This secretary at the White House walks into the Oval Office, and there is Lyndon on the floor having sex with this girl. Actually, she was on top of him, and a peace sign was dangling between her breasts!"

Clinton repeated the anecdote, which he firmly believed to be true, many times over the years—embellishing it as he went along. In the fall of 1970, Jackson would write Clinton and ask how one went about getting a White House fellowship. "About the White House fellowships," Bill wrote back from Yale, "the best story I know about them is that virtually the only non-conservative who ever got one was a quasi-radical woman who wound up in the White House sleeping with LBJ, who made her wear a peace symbol around her waist whenever they made love. You may go far, Cliff; I doubt you will ever go that far!"

Jackson told journalist Meredith Oakley that he found the story disturbing—not the anecdote so much as the way Bill told it. "The impression I got was that Bill thought it was so neat that Lyndon Johnson could get away with something like that. It was just his reaction to it that made it stand out in my mind. It was like—it's just the power, the idea that Lyndon had the audacity to do something like that right in the Oval Office at the height of the war. It was something above and beyond locker room snickering."

Without ever actually earning an Oxford degree, Bill applied to

Yale Law School and was admitted on the strength of his status as a Rhodes Scholar. He still intended to return home to Arkansas and pursue a political career there—but not quite yet. First, he confided to his Yale-bound buddy Bob Reich, Bill needed the veneer of an Ivy League law degree. He also wanted to add to his list of contacts the names of people who, like himself, would one day emerge as leaders on the national stage. There was an added bonus: Like Oxford, Yale Law School was very selective. But classes were now offered on a pass-fail basis, making graduation a near certainty.

Bill spent his first summer after Oxford working for Operation Pursestrings, a citizens' lobby that backed legislation that, had it passed, would have cut off funding for the war in Southeast Asia. After enrolling at Yale, he moved into a Milford, Connecticut, beach house with three classmates—Dartmouth graduate Donald Pogue, fellow Rhodes Scholar Douglas Eakeley, and William T. Coleman III. Clinton had better things to do than attend classes, however, and was soon helping to run the U.S. Senate campaign of antiwar college professor Joseph D. Duffey.

Volunteers poured in from around the country to campaign for Duffey, who had gained national prominence as chairman of the considerably left-of-center Americans for Democratic Action (ADA). But blue-collar voters were turned off by Duffey and his band of rich-kid carpetbaggers, and liberal Republican Lowell Weicker won the election in a landslide.

Still, Bill emerged victorious. He had continued to hone his skills as a grassroots campaigner, and had made scores of new contacts. None, of course, would be as important as the determined young woman who walked up to him in the law library and brazenly introduced herself.

At the time they met, Bill was already involved with several women on campus. Hillary, conversely, had not seriously dated anyone since leaving Wellesley. She had lots of male friends, but Michael Medved recalled that Hillary "was like a den mother to all the guys . . . She was not a glamorous figure by any stretch of the imagination. She was everybody's best friend."

But, despite his own considerable success disarming members of the opposite sex, Bill Clinton was undeniably intimidated by Hillary

Rodham from the outset—and vice versa. When she first visited the Connecticut beach house, he rehearsed what he and his roommates would say so that the erudite Ms. Rodham would be suitably impressed. He was right to be concerned. "Hillary was awfully cautious at first," said a fellow law student. "She was really sizing him up, and he knew it." By way of convincing Hillary that he was more than just a good ol' boy, Bill invited her out to the beach house to debate the great issues of the day.

By spring, Hillary was a fixture at the Milford house. "It's hard to describe the chemistry," Don Pogue said. "We watched all the other young ladies disappear in a hurry when Hillary appeared on the scene. Hillary had a sharp mind coupled with a traditional Midwestern openness. Bill was the quintessential Southerner, charming and gregarious. It was fun to watch the dance."

They also sparred—affectionately—with Hillary throwing most of the punches. While the other women in his life usually gazed adoringly and batted their eyes as Bill waxed eloquent about the virtues of the South, Hillary stopped him cold. "Come off it, Bill," she would blurt out with a hearty laugh. "We've all heard it before." Another favorite line: "Clinton, cut the crap!"

But there was no doubt that the affection between them—born of a mutual belief that Bill would someday be president—was genuine. Medved was walking home from a movie when he ran into the couple on the street. "It startled me to see the two of them together and so obviously in love," he said, "since Hillary had been so solid, sweet, and substantive and Bill had generally struck me, despite his eating achievements, as such a lightweight. Nevertheless, there they were, basking in each other's admiration, taking pride in their mutual possession."

Hillary pulled Medved aside, he recalled, "and she was so proud to be with Bill Clinton. She was so proud of him . . . It struck me that these two had real physical chemistry. These two people unequivocally had the hots for each other. She was so in love. It was so painfully obvious and he looked like he had just swallowed the canary. He was so pleased with himself. And I remember him leaning back and Hillary taking me aside and talking to me and the whole point of the conversation was, 'Look at this, I'm in love. I am happy and I have got this great guy who is going to change the whole world.' "

There were other reasons she fell for the six-foot-two-inch-tall, 210-pound boy from Arkansas. "He was the one guy," she said, "who wasn't afraid of me." For all the hokum about Hope's prize-winning watermelons, she also found Bill's devotion to Arkansas oddly endearing. "He cared deeply about where he came from, which was unusual," she later said. "He was rooted and most of us were disconnected."

But he doubted that Hillary could ever be happy in Arkansas. "You know," he told her. "I'm really worried about falling in love with you because you're a great person. You could have a great life. If you wanted to run for public office, you could be elected, but I've got to go home. It's just who I am." Recalling those early misgivings, he conceded, "I loved being with her," he recalled, "but I had very ambivalent feelings about getting involved with her."

That reluctance gradually melted away, and that summer they decided to live together. In September 1971 they moved into a $75-dollar-a-month apartment in a Victorian house at 21 Edgewood Avenue, just off the campus. No sooner did they move in than Bill received word that his old Oxford buddy Frank Aller, who had returned home to Spokane only to have draft evasion charges against him dropped, had shot himself in the head anyway. Aller's shocking and inexplicable suicide plunged Bill into a deep depression during which he questioned his own ambition.

"Bill was absolutely grief-stricken," said a classmate of Hillary. "He literally cried on Hillary's shoulder, and she had the strength to pull him out of it." From the moment she made the first move, in fact, it was apparent there would be a reversal of roles in the relationship. "Theirs was a union of brains and sex appeal," a friend observed. "Her brains and his sex appeal."

Although Bill continued to harbor doubts about their future as a couple—particularly whether she would ever be willing to subordinate her own career to his and move to Arkansas—this was not the message he conveyed to Virginia. After Bill paid a brief visit home that fall, Virginia—who at this point had heard a great deal about Hillary but never met her—walked him to his car and sat with him chatting for a while until it was time to go. "Mother," he said, "I want you to pray for me. Pray that it's Hillary. Because I'll tell you this: For me it's Hillary or it's nobody."

The day after Christmas, 1971, the doorbell rang at 236 Wisner Street. Hillary, home in Illinois for the holidays, had invited Bill to join her there. From the instant she saw him standing on her front porch, Dorothy Rodham recalled, she knew "there was an air of seriousness about him."

"Hello, my name is Bill Clinton," he said earnestly.

"That's nice," Hillary's mother replied without smiling.

Having driven straight from Hot Springs without stopping, Bill had hoped for a warm reception. Instead, Dorothy later conceded, "the introductions were rather cold. To tell the truth, I would have preferred that he left. He had come to take my daughter away."

Dorothy called up to her daughter that Bill had arrived, and she watched as he went upstairs to find her. "I knew nothing of him," Dorothy recalled. "But, I don't know why, I trusted him."

Hillary had purposely told her mother very little about Bill, fully expecting him to win over her parents effortlessly. The day after he arrived, Bill noticed that Dorothy was reading a philosophy text for an extension course she was taking at a local college. He asked her which philosopher most intrigued her, and then proceeded to share his opinions. No one in the Rodham house—certainly not Hugh— had expressed the slightest interest in what she was studying. Now this bright young Yale Law School student, a former Rhodes Scholar, was treating her like an intellectual equal. "He was brilliant," she said. "From then on, I loved him."

Still, she was not so charmed that she would allow him to sleep with Hillary under the Rodham roof. During that first weeklong visit with Hillary's family, Bill slept in her brother Tony's room. "My husband and I watched," Dorothy said, "to make sure he stayed in there!"

Like everyone else who encountered them during this period, Dorothy was impressed with the couple's mutual passion for the politics of change. Their conversation, Mrs. Rodham remembered, was "incessant, always the same subjects: Arkansas! American society! They never stopped thinking about it." Whatever the cause, she said, "they were utterly passionate about it."

When she asked him what he planned to do after Yale, Dorothy expected him to say that he was going to join a top law firm in New York or enter government service in Washington. She was not prepared to hear that he intended to return to Arkansas and run for office. "OK," she said. "You'll go back to Arkansas to realize your ideals, but what about my daughter?"

That question would continue to nag Bill as well. "He was really concerned," Bill's mother remembered, "about whether she really would be happy in Arkansas—or would even come."

Yet, back at Yale, they were seen by classmates and professors alike as a formidable, if unlikely, pair. Bill and Hillary joined forces in April 1972 to compete in the Prize Trial, a moot court competition conducted by the Yale Barristers' Union. The Prize Trial was a major production, with New Haven residents and students recruited to serve on the jury and testify as witnesses. A judge of some renown was usually brought in to preside, in this case Abe Fortas, who had recently resigned from the U.S. Supreme Court rather than face possible impeachment on conflict of interest charges.

Hillary, who usually scored higher on law school exams than Bill, organized their case and spent hours drilling him on the finer points of cross-examination. Her most difficult task was getting Clinton, who tended to ramble even when examining a witness, to focus on the task at hand once they stepped into the courtroom.

She had more luck rehearsing her friend Kris Rogers in the role of a "sultry, lying" witness Bill would take apart under cross-examination. "Come *on*, Kris," Hillary would say, "you're supposed to be a tramp, a real slut. *Nobody* is going to believe a word you say."

Rogers remembered that Hillary, who acted out the part of "real slut" with gusto, "had the role down pat. She was just cutting up. She could be a real ham." More important, it marked the first time Hillary and Bill worked in concert to undermine the credibility of a female witness.

Despite Hillary's best efforts, Bill's earnest country lawyer approach failed to sway either the judge or the jury. Hillary stayed cool, but Clinton was visibly outraged when Judge Fortas awarded the prize to someone else; Bill shook his head in frustration and slammed his hand on the prosecution table before his partner could stop him. Once he calmed down, Bill tried to explain his lackluster performance to Hillary. "I just," he told her with a shrug, "had a bad day."

There was no need for Bill to apologize. For their defeat Hillary, unflappable throughout the proceedings, blamed the witnesses, the defendant, the judge, and the jury—"everyone," said her friend, "but the one person who really deserved it—Bill."

To stay close to the man she loved, Hillary extended her three-year law school program to four, earning law school credit for work at Yale's Child Study Center. With Marian Wright Edelman as her mentor, Hillary immersed herself in children's issues. In addition to her work at the Child Study Center during this time, she wrote background papers on the legal rights of minors for the nonprofit Carnegie Council on Children, and worked with the staff of Yale–New Haven Hospital on drafting guidelines for the medical treatment of abused children.

But when Bill departed for Texas in the summer of 1972 to help run George McGovern's ill-fated presidential campaign in that state, Hillary dropped everything to accompany him. Not that he wanted her to. "She's a great person," he confided in one campaign co-worker in Houston, "but I really don't need to be looking over my shoulder all the time."

He need not have worried. Much of the time, they were in separate cities—she registering Hispanic voters in San Antonio, he working the phones out of party headquarters in Austin. Hillary did, however, make a point of dropping in unannounced, then taking her place at a desk that adjoined Bill's. When she was in Austin, she stayed in the cramped apartment Bill shared for a time with fellow McGovern foot soldier (and future Pulitzer Prize–winning author) Taylor Branch.

The result, observed a staff member, was to "put the other attractive young women working on the campaign on notice that Bill Clinton was taken." An exasperated Bill got the message:

"Gol dang," he blurted out one day, "I couldn't do something if I wanted to!"

In truth, he got away with quite a lot. "If anything," said another McGovern volunteer, "I got the distinct impression that the prospect Hillary might show up at any minute made the game that much more exciting."

Bill was certainly not alone. "Sex," said McGovern campaign staffer Bebe Champ, "was always part of the political equation in Texas." The Austin office, staffed by antiwar activists, ex–campus radicals, and commune-dwelling hippies as well as seasoned political professionals, apparently accounted for more than its share of drinking, marijuana consumption, and casual affairs. Even with Hillary hovering about, one veteran of the McGovern campaign in Texas remembered Clinton "sleeping with at least three women in a one-week period"—and nearly getting caught when Hillary made one of her unexpected visits from San Antonio.

That July, Hillary accompanied Bill to the Democratic National Convention. "The wonderful thing about going into a McGovern headquarters," he told an Arkansas journalist, "is that there is no ego-tripping." Yet Bill's old Rhodes Scholar buddy Rick Stearns was now McGovern's deputy campaign manager. Clinton, already a polished pro when it came to trading favors, used this connection to ensure that he would be the candidate's sole contact with the Arkansas delegation.

"Arkansas was Bill's, plain and simple," said another campaign operative. "The phone from the floor to the McGovern nerve center, a trailer parked alongside the convention center, became the delegation's lifeline. Bill obviously intended for everyone in that delegation to know who he was and to become familiar with his voice as the voice of authority."

Rick Stearns ran interference for his friend if someone tried to encroach on his territory. On the one or two occasions when someone had the temerity to contact a delegate on the floor directly, Clinton flew into a rage, revealing for the first time a very different—and disturbing—side to the otherwise charming young politico.

Bill had used the convention not only to establish credibility with the party faithful of his state but to make himself known to the national leadership. Kennedy brother-in-law and veteran political infighter Stephen Smith echoed the sentiments of many top Democrats who saw Clinton in action for the first time. "I was thoroughly impressed," Smith said, "at how well this twenty-five-year-old Yale student moved among the famous and the powerful in the party."

Indeed, Branch had never seen anyone for whom politics came so naturally. "Bill loved the game," he said. "He seemed fully at home in a roomful of county chairmen or a roomful of radicals."

Not long after the convention, Bill accompanied McGovern on a brief campaign swing through Arkansas. It was there, at a fund-raiser in the home of an old friend, that he again encountered Dolly Kyle Browning. With the presidential nominee of his party in the living room, Bill grabbed Dolly in the kitchen and kissed her passionately. McGovern and his wife, Eleanor, stayed at the party for thirty minutes, but Bill and Browning remained for over four hours, offering to stay behind and baby-sit the hosts' children while they went on to another fund-raiser.

With the kids tucked in bed, Bill and Dolly went for a walk in the humid night air. As they strolled across the expansive back-yard, Browning recalled, "I tripped over a chaise longue cushion and he used it as an excuse to grab me." Bill pulled her down onto the cushion, and within a matter of minutes they had shed their clothes and were making love. When they were finished, she turned on a garden hose and let the warm water "flow slowly and gently" over their naked bodies—all the while "thankful," she later wrote, that she this was "a quiet neighborhood without street lights."

Hillary remained in the dark about Bill's dalliance that night with Dolly Kyle Browning. In turn, Browning had no idea Bill had moved in with Hillary.

Despite the fact that Bill and Hillary were living together and sharing the same bed, their colleagues in Texas—unlike their friends back at Yale—did not see them as ideally suited to each other. "I just did not necessarily see them as a permanent couple," said Branch, who also had a hard time imagining them together in Arkansas. "Whereas his purpose was so fixed," he observed, "she was so undecided about what to do."

One who shared that view was Betsey Wright, a tough-talking, chainsmoking, University of Texas activist-turned-Democratic-Party organizer. Wright would eventually become one of Bill Clinton's most trusted advisors and an indefatigable chief of staff during his years in the Arkansas statehouse.

For the time being, however, it was Hillary who captivated her. When asked if she thought Bill had met anybody like Hillary before, Wright later told *Vanity Fair*, "*Nobody* had met anybody like Hillary before."

Indeed, Wright, an ardent feminist who had campaigned for liberal Texan Sissy Farenthold in her unsuccessful quest for the party's gubernatorial nomination, conceded that in 1972 she was "less interested in Bill's political future than Hillary's. I was obsessed with how far Hillary might go, with her mixture of brilliance, ambition, and self-assuredness." Later, she would admit she was "disappointed when they married. I had images in my mind that she could be the first woman president."

No one was more aware of Hillary's potential than Bill. He continued to worry that she would never agree to live in Arkansas, and wondered if he even had the right to ask her to make the sacrifice. In late October 1972, Bill paid a visit to Diane Kincaid, a political science professor at the University of Arkansas in Fayetteville. They had met at the Democratic Convention in Miami, where she was a delegate committed to favorite son Wilbur Mills.

Halfway through lunch, Bill stopped abruptly. "I can't believe," he said, "how much you remind me of the woman I love."

Kincaid was touched. "It was just the sweetest thing," she later said. "He told me I made him lonely for this marvelous woman named Hillary. I think *I* fell in love with him right there."

Still, Kincaid wanted to know why he had not yet asked this Hillary Rodham to marry him.

"My political life will be in Arkansas," he replied, "and this is a woman whose future is limitless. She could be anything she decides to be. I feel so guilty about bringing her here because then it would be my state, my political life, and my future."

Kincaid had never encountered a man who seemed so attuned to "a woman's career plans and future options. It just won my heart."

Bill would often wax poetic about Hillary when he was in the company of attractive young women like Kincaid. "There is something very seductive," agreed a young worker in the McGovern campaign, "about a man who starts behaving like a lovesick puppy. But it's also a challenge." According to the volunteer, Bill tearfully explained how much he missed Hillary one evening, then made love to her atop a desk at campaign headquarters.

Hillary was not unaware of Bill's tendency to stray, and on at least three separate occasions confronted him within earshot of fellow campaign workers. But he invariably fought back, and at the laid-back parties where McGovernites unwound in a blue-white haze of marijuana smoke, the heated exchanges between Hillary and Bill became, in the words of one eyewitness, "our own little floor show."

At one point in late 1972, Hillary announced she was packing up and moving back to New Haven—alone. At the last minute, a friend—San Antonio labor leader Franklin Garcia—interceded on Bill's behalf, convincing Hillary to give him another chance. They returned to Yale as they had left it—together.

As was his custom, in the last few weeks of his last year in law school, Bill made up for almost never attending class by borrowing his friends' notes and cramming. He breezed through finals, as did Hillary, whose fourth year struck her as superfluous.

After graduation in May 1973, Hillary went straight to work as a staff attorney for Marian Wright Edelman's fledgling Children's Defense Fund in Washington, and Bill again pulled strings with his contacts in Fayetteville to land a $25,000-a-year job teaching law at the University of Arkansas. Although they would be living and working a thousand miles apart, Bill and Hillary still considered themselves a couple. When it came time to take her bar exam, as a symbolic gesture Hillary traveled to Arkansas with Bill, and then the two took the exam there—both easily passing on the first try. With an eye on what future impact their living together might have on their political careers, both Rodham and Clinton had fretted over whether to put the same New Haven address on their Arkansas bar exam applications.

That trip to Arkansas, Hillary's first, would also mark her introduction to the rest of the Clinton clan. Virginia's house in Hot Springs was only an hour from the airport, but first Bill wanted to show his state off to the woman he loved. Selling Arkansas was no easy task. A hot, dusty backwater populated by 2.3 million people spread out over an area the size of New York State, Arkansas consistently ranked next-to-last when it came to income, literacy, and standard of living. Only Mississippi was in worse shape.

"We drove eight hours," Hillary later said. "He took me to all these places he thought were beautiful. We went to all the state parks. We went to all the overlooks. And then we'd stop at this favorite barbecue place. Then we'd go down the road and stop at his favorite fried-pie place. My head was reeling because I didn't know what I was going to see or what I was expecting."

After the whirlwind tour, Bill turned and asked Hillary what she thought of his state. "What exactly," she replied bluntly, "do you expect me to say?"

When they finally arrived in Hot Springs, half brother Roger and "Dado" were equally unimpressed with the girl who had apparently stolen Bill's heart. "Think back—to beards, scraggly hair, dirty jeans, tie-dyed T-shirts, clunky sandals," Virginia later said. "Suffice it to say that Bill and Hillary were very much of their time."

Virginia "didn't know what to think when they walked through the door," she recalled. "No makeup. Coke-bottle glasses. Brown hair with no apparent style . . ."

Bill, his mother remembered, shot both his mother and brother a "withering look" before maneuvering them into the kitchen while Hillary unpacked. "Look, I want you to know that I've had it up to here with beauty queens," he said angrily. "I have to have somebody I can talk with. Do you understand that?"

Hillary reacted with icy indifference. "Just think about what she was seeing," Virginia later confessed. "A mahogany brown woman with hot pink lipstick and a skunk stripe in her hair . . . I can understand how offended Hillary must've been—here she was in darkest Arkansas, and the first people she met were acting like they wished she would hop the next plane out."

Thinking back to Bill's admonition the previous year that she pray for him to marry Hillary ("It's Hillary or it's nobody"), Virginia claimed that she did pray. "Of course," she added, "once I got through praying, I would grind my teeth and wish I could sit Hillary on the edge of my tub and give her some makeup lessons." Hillary later observed of her future mother-in-law: "We were utterly different. Like the characters in *Star Trek*, Virginia and I seemed to be from different planets."

On the campus at Fayetteville, Bill proved an instant hit with students—and no wonder. His loosely structured classes were basically free-form discussions that touched on whatever appealed to Bill that day. "Off the cuff" is the way fellow law professor Mort Gitelman described it. Bill was also by the far the most lenient faculty member when it came to grading; he freely dispensed A's and B's. He was also so famously tardy and disorganized that he once "misplaced" the blue book final exams. Freed from the tedium of having to grade the papers, he offered to make the course pass-fail, and then announced that he had passed everyone.

"Bill was a good teacher, he did it so effortlessly, speaking without notes and all," said a former student, Woody Bassett. "But it was pretty clear this was just a stopping-off point for him. Tell you the truth, I'm not sure Bill prepared all that hard."

With his long, curly hair, plaid shirts, corduroy jackets, and jeans, Bill was also "sort of a campus sex symbol," said one of his female students. "There were other faculty members carrying on affairs with students, but we figured he set a new record. I knew three girls—all in the same class—who were sleeping with him. And when they found out about the others, they didn't care."

Nor did he seem concerned about the prospect of getting caught. "Right in front of everyone," said the ex-student, now a leading Little Rock attorney, "he would put his hand around your waist or rub up against you. He always made suggestive remarks—it went way beyond flirting. But it was all so brazen, no one said anything." Did it bother him that one of his student lovers might say something to the administration? "I think that was all part of the game. The risk was what made it that much more exciting."

Such diversions aside, within a few months Bill had grown restless. For months the country had been transfixed by Watergate and the spectacle of the Nixon Administration coming apart at the seams. Now he had a chance to play a role in the unfolding impeachment drama.

In December 1973, the House Judiciary Committee's new chief counsel, John Doar, approached a half dozen of Yale Law's most promising recent graduates to work on the impeachment inquiry staff. Bill Clinton was one. Hillary Rodham was another.

By any measure, it was the most compelling assignment a young attorney straight out of law school could hope for. The fact that it offered them both an opportunity to participate in the toppling of Richard Nixon, whom they both reviled, made the offer that much more tempting. But Bill had already mapped out his political future in Arkansas, and it did not include any detours to the nation's capital.

Hillary, on the other hand, seized the opportunity. She and several others on the staff who had campaigned for George McGovern had never tried to disguise their hatred of Nixon. But now Doar, a well-respected moderate Republican who had been one of the Justice Department's fiercest civil rights prosecutors, demanded at least the appearance of fairness and impartiality.

"She was very scrupulous," recalled another lawyer on the impeachment staff. "Despite her politics, she didn't try to shape things. It was a real sign of character."

While most of her young colleagues were assigned to gather the facts concerning the Watergate burglary and the cover-up, Hillary was given the more mundane job of researching the precedents for impeachment in law. A quarter century later, she would come to fully appreciate the irony of her Watergate assignment: to research what constitutes an impeachable offense.

Hillary did, however, get to listen to some of the infamous Nixon tapes. "I was kind of locked in this soundproof room with big headphones on, listening to the tapes," she later said. "There was one we called 'the Tape of Tapes.' It was Nixon taping himself listening to the tapes, making up his defenses to what he heard on the tapes. So you would hear Nixon talk and then you'd hear very faintly the sound of a taped prior conversation with Nixon and [his aides] Bob Haldeman and John Ehrlichman . . . And you'd hear him say, 'What I meant when I said that was . . .' I mean, it was surreal, unbelievable."

Her schedule was grueling, but to Hillary the work more than compensated for the hours spent poring over case histories. "It was wonderfully exciting," she recalled. "We would work ten, fifteen, twenty hours a day or all night. It didn't matter."

Not so long as Hillary received her daily phone call from Bill. "It was her fix," a colleague said. "She could be very abrupt, even rude under the best of circumstances. We were all under a lot of tension. I mean, Hillary must have said 'shit' and 'fuck' twenty times a day. If Bill didn't call, you didn't want to go near her. If she was walking three feet off the floor and grinning, you knew she'd just spoken to him on the phone."

What impressed everyone was Hillary's oft-expressed belief that her boyfriend would one day be elected to the highest office in the land. "You know," she exclaimed brightly to fellow staffer Tom Bell, "Bill Clinton is going to be President of the United States some day."

One senior member of the impeachment staff, Bernard Nussbaum, was not amused by such predictions. One evening Nussbaum, who had taken Hillary under his wing, was giving her a ride home when she mentioned that Bill was coming to Washington for a visit. "I want you to meet my boyfriend," she told Nussbaum. "He's really good. He's going to be President of the United States."

When he heard this, Nussbaum said, "I went a little crazy. We're under a lot of pressure on the impeachment, and here was somebody telling me her boyfriend is going to be president!"

Bill had, in fact, already taken the first steps toward making his boyhood dream a reality. From his professor's perch at the University of Arkansas Law School, he eyed the Third Congressional District seat occupied by Republican John Hammerschmidt. After four terms, the conservative Republican's seat seemed secure; an unusually large number of retired military personnel lived in the district, and Hammerschmidt sat on the powerful Veterans Affairs Committee.

But Bill, receiving regular reports from Hillary on the tapes and the strength of the impeachment argument, was convinced he could use Watergate to bludgeon Hammerschmidt at the polls. Before he committed himself to a race for Congress, Bill sought advice from one of the district's most knowledgeable politicos, Carl Whillock.

Now a University of Arkansas vice-president, Whillock had been administrative assistant to Congressman Hammerschmidt's Democratic predecessor, James W. Trimble. In typical fashion, Clinton had actually been courting Whillock for months—bending his ear over lunch in the faculty cafeteria, dropping by his house in the evenings to flatter his wife and flirt with his three teenage daughters.

"I could sense this was a man with a future," Whillock recalled. "But I had to be sure. So I told Bill that if he was serious about running for Congress, he should come out with me into the surrounding counties where I could introduce him to some people who could help him."

With Whillock at the wheel, they drove through each of the congressional district's twenty-one counties, dropping in unannounced on dozens of local movers and shakers. In Berryville, they met Methodist minister Victor Nixon and his wife, Freddie. In Harrison, Bill shook hands with J. E. Dunlap, editor of the *Harrison Daily Times*. While Bill sought out the editor of the local newspaper in tiny Mountain Home, Whillock looked for local political kingmaker Hugh Hackler. Whillock found him where he expected to—playing dominoes with his cronies at Roger's Pool Hall.

"I've got a young man who's running for Congress and I want you to support him," Whillock said.

"Can't do that, Carl," he replied. Hackler, it turned out, was already backing Gene Rainwater in the Democratic primary.

"Well, at least sit with him awhile," Whillock said. "He's going to be governor or a senator some day, and you're going to want to be able to say you supported him at the beginning."

The two men ambled over to the Mountain Home drugstore where Bill was supposed to meet them and squeezed into a booth in the back. When Bill walked in twenty minutes late, the sixtyish Hackler eyed him warily. "Trust me," Whillock recalled. "Hugh Hackler hadn't met many people like Bill Clinton, nor did he want to. Yet Bill charmed him in no time flat."

"So you're from Hot Springs?" Hackler asked Clinton.

"Yessir."

"I have a good friend in Hot Springs," Hackler said. "I doubt if you know him. He has a drugstore there. Name is Gabe Crawford."

"Sure, I know Gabe Crawford," Bill replied. "He and my dad are good friends. We visit in his home all the time, and he and his family come over to our house."

A few minutes later, Bill excused himself to go to the bathroom. "You know, Carl," Hackler said. "I'm gonna call my friend and tell him the bad news. I'm a Bill Clinton man now."

(The meeting would stay with Bill. Years later, as he was seeking the presidency, Clinton turned to Whillock and asked, "Remember that day with Hugh Hackler? I thought he was gonna eat me alive.")

Bill's exchange with Hackler was typical of hundreds he would have in the course of his first campaign alone. Indeed, it was difficult to find a person in the district who was not connected to him in one way or another.

Similarly, the young candidate turned on his formidable charm to solicit campaign contributions from old friends and acquaintances. He wrote notes to or called virtually everyone he knew: hometown folks, classmates from Georgetown, Oxford, and Yale, literally hundreds of women he had met—including, by his own estimate, "maybe fifty" former lovers.

The women Bill had dated turned out to be the most generous contributors, but Hillary Rodham was not to be outdone. In March, she wrote out the first sizable check of the campaign, for $400. For serious money, however, Bill turned to a familiar source. Unable to raise any significant funds on his own, he prevailed on Uncle Raymond Clinton, the Hot Springs Buick dealer who had helped him finesse his way out of the draft, to cosign a $10,000 loan from the First National Bank of Hot Springs.

Bill also went to his boyhood friend Vince Foster, who had graduated from the University of Arkansas two years earlier and was already on his way to becoming a partner in Little Rock's prestigious Rose Law Firm. At first Foster "questioned Bill's decision to run," although he conceded it showed "a real can-do attitude." Later, Foster hosted Bill Clinton's first fund-raiser with Arkansas financial heavy hitters inside the paneled conference room of the Rose Law Firm itself.

By March, Bill raised nearly $40,000 for his primary race alone—more than four times the amount raised by any other Democratic contender. But his charisma would prove to be his greatest asset. "I was convinced," Whillock said, "Bill could persuade two out of every three voters to support him if he could have a one-on-one conversation with them."

Toward that end, Bill declared his candidacy on March 22 and then spent eighteen hours a day touring the Third District's back roads—first in a grime-covered green 1970 Gremlin, then in a Chevy pickup with its bed covered in AstroTurf. "The minute he met someone," Whillock said, "Bill established a rapport with that person. Once he heard someone's name, or a story—the smallest detail about a person's life—he filed it away mentally for later use." Another early supporter recalled how Clinton "would walk up to somebody and ask how their son was liking college, or how their trick knee was doing, and of course the person would just be flabbergasted that he remembered such personal things. That was his magic. He knew that this was the most important thing to people—'Hey, he really knows who I am. He must really care.'"

Another close friend, Little Rock businessman Guy Campbell, believed Clinton's effectiveness as a campaigner came down to one essential thing. "Bill connects," Campbell said. "Even if it's just for a moment, he *connects* with the person he's talking to. And he does like to touch. Just look at the way he shakes hands. If you're about his height, he'll put his hand on your elbow. If you're shorter—and most people are—he puts his hand on your shoulder. He always makes intense eye contact. By the time he's finished, everybody in the room thinks he's Bill Clinton's new best friend and confidant."

For the most part, Bill's drivers were plucked from the small army of student volunteers that kept his campaign afloat. On those infrequent occasions when Bill was behind the wheel, his passengers invariably pledged never to let him drive again. The candidate "drove like a madman," said Ron Addington, his friend and campaign advisor.

Bill was guilty of just about every infraction: tailgating, trying to pass over a double line, looking at his passenger instead of the road as he chatted nonstop, weaving onto the shoulder and then veering back toward oncoming traffic, never using his turn signal, and of course speeding—often forty or fifty miles over the posted speed limit. "It was not for the faint of heart," Addington said. "After the first trip, I said never again. From that point on if we were in the car together, I did the driving."

While Bill crisscrossed the district, Hillary managed to find time out from her grueling impeachment schedule in Washington to bombard her boyfriend's Fayetteville headquarters with five and six phone calls a day. Bill had often spoken of Hillary with pride, but now his staff wondered if he knew she was trying to run the campaign by remote control. "She was telling us who to hire," said one campaign staffer, "what changes had to be made in Bill's schedules, what issues he should be focusing on. We knew Hillary was his girlfriend, but she was behaving more like his wife."

To further complicate matters, word filtered back to Hillary that Bill was having a torrid and rather public affair with one of his student volunteers. At eighteen, the girl—a fresh-faced blonde of the "beauty pageant" variety favored by Bill's mother—was nine years his junior.

She had also heard rumors that Dolly Kyle Browning, who had just divorced her first husband, had resurfaced in Bill's life. In February, Bill had brought Dolly Kyle Browning along to a breakfast meeting with potential contributors in Hot Springs. J. William Fulbright had lent his protégé the use of his hotel suite, and when the breakfast meeting was over, Bill and Dolly went to the senator's room for a tryst.

Afterward, as they were dressing to leave, the newly divorced Dolly asked when they might see each other again. By this time Bill, having grown tired of Hillary's possessiveness, had come up with a new name for her. He called Hillary "The Warden."

"I don't know when we can get together again," he told Dolly. "The Warden doesn't let me out too often."

As it happened, Bill and Dolly rendezvoused at hotels and motels around the state several times over the next few weeks. Immediately after officially filing as a candidate on March 22, he picked Dolly up and drove her to Hot Springs for the weekend.

Hillary took action, dispatching her father and younger brother, Tony, down to check up on Bill. They drove down from Park Ridge, Illinois, in Hugh Rodham's Cadillac, arriving unannounced at the Clinton headquarters one morning in mid-April. "Hillary told me I ought to come down here," said the lifelong conservative Republican, "and help you out."

They spent the next several weeks driving around northwest Arkansas, posting dozens of CLINTON FOR CONGRESS signs wherever they could find a willing property owner. The Rodham men's real reason for being in Arkansas had nothing to do with helping out in the campaign. They were there to spy on Bill, and what they learned disturbed Hillary's father.

Beyond Dolly Kyle and the eighteen-year-old student volunteer, Hillary knew nothing of the other women crowding Bill's social calendar until her father angrily informed her. By Hugh Rodham's count, Bill was involved with "five girls—two in Little Rock and three in Fayetteville."

That was scarcely the tip of the iceberg. To their astonishment, Addington and the other campaign workers who followed Bill onto the hustings discovered that Bill was having affairs with, by one count, thirty young women—"one for each of the twenty-one counties plus some spares."

Much of Clinton's success with the opposite sex stemmed from his near-messianic appeal. Michael Glespeny, of Fayetteville's alternative newspaper the *Grapevine*, recognized that "Clinton's workers are influenced by the Dexedrine-like effects of campaigning . . ." Like "members of a cult," he wrote, "the volunteers are extremely reluctant to talk about themselves. They constantly muttered the aspirant's name in hushed tones: 'Bill thinks . . .' 'Bill feels . . .' 'Bill does . . .' "

On one of his rare afternoons at home in Hot Springs, Bill picked up the phone. Hillary was on the other end of the line. "What do you think you are doing to me? To us?" she screamed, her words clearly audible to the workers in the room.

"Hillary, I don't know what you heard but—"

"Don't fuck with me, Bill," she yelled as his face turned crimson. "You are a real shit, do you know that, Bill? Christ, a real SHIT."

"But—"

"You know, Bill, there's a guy here who has been trying to get me to go to bed with him and that is exactly what I'm going to do."

With that, Bill began sobbing. "I'm begging you, Hillary," he cried, "don't go and do something we'll both be sorry for." For the next ten minutes, he pleaded with Hillary to forgive him and begged her not to be unfaithful. She remained silent during Bill's tearful monologue, and when it was over she simply hung up.

Bill's heartfelt plea worked. Two weeks later she joined him in Arkansas for the final push leading up to primary day. On primary day—May 28, 1974—Bill borrowed a wealthy contributor's twin-engine Aero Commander and flew to Little Rock's Adams Field for a last-minute television interview. During the stopover, he also planned to drop by at the campaign headquarters of his mentor Senator Fulbright, who was in a tough primary battle against popular Arkansas Governor Dale Bumpers.

Bill had arranged for a friend to meet them at the airport and drive them to their appointments. As she followed Bill down the stairs onto the tarmac, Hillary could see an attractive blonde in a clingy blue-and-white-knit dress climb out of a car and wave. Bill strode toward her purposefully, and Hillary could see the woman begin to reach out with both arms until he stuck out his hand to shake hers.

"How nice of you to come," he told Dolly Kyle, who detected "fear and confusion in his eyes."

Hillary then sidled up alongside Bill. "Dolly, this is Hillary," Bill said. "Hillary, Dolly." According to Dolly, that would be the first and last time Bill ever mentioned Hillary's name.

"Pleased to meet you," Dolly said brightly, trying to disguise what she later described as her "utter shock" upon viewing the future Mrs. Clinton for the first time. According to Kyle and others in the Clinton campaign, Hillary had shown up that day in an ill-fitting brown dress and sandals, her hair matted with grease and her unshaven legs covered with black hair. As usual, Hillary eschewed both makeup and deodorant—the latter a mistake in light of Arkansas's oppressive heat. To put it bluntly, Kyle said, "Hillary smelled. I had never smelled an odor like that. I was so shocked, I just didn't believe this could really be Hillary. I thought it was one big cosmic joke. This couldn't be the woman I'd heard Bill was serious about. I honestly thought this was an actress he had hired to play Hillary, and that suddenly he'd burst out laughing. After a few minutes, it dawned on me that this was no joke."

Hillary merely glared at Kyle, refusing to take her outstretched hand. When it came time to leave, Dolly got behind the wheel and motioned to Bill to walk around the other side of the car and climb into the front passenger seat. He did, assuming Hillary would get in back. Instead, she ordered Bill to "move over" and slid into the front seat beside him.

Hillary lingered in the shadows, all but ignored by Bill as he made his television appearance. Then, instead of going on to Fulbright headquarters as planned, he ordered Dolly to drive him back to the airport. He had heard reports over the radio that the senator was losing his race against Bumpers. "I don't," Bill said matter-of-factly, "want to be seen with a loser."

On the plane ride back, Hillary again exploded at Bill. "How *dare* you have that woman meet us?" she screamed. "Do you think I'm stupid? Christ!"

Bill sat red-faced and sheepish as she scolded him in full view of the pilot and three staffers. Yet he offered no explanation as to why—on the day of his first real election—he would orchestrate a confrontation between Hillary and Dolly. "When you are totally egocentric, when you think the world revolves around you, you don't think all that much about other people's feelings," Kyle said. "It was expedient for him to have me there to drive him around. It's that simple. I don't think it occurred to Billy that there might be a problem until the moment he saw me standing there. Frankly, it wasn't so much risk-taking as stupidity on his part. But I knew from looking at Hillary that she'd make him pay."

As it happened, Bill handily won the primary, and the subsequent June 11 runoff against his closest competitor, State Senator Gene Rainwater. But the race against Republican incumbent John Hammerschmidt would prove to be far more problematic.

Hillary had returned to Washington and was jubilant when the House Judiciary Committee voted three articles of impeachment against Nixon—based in significant part on her legal legwork. Then, on August 8, 1974, the Watergate saga came to an abrupt and dramatic conclusion when Nixon went on television to tell the American people that he would be resigning the next day.

Now Hillary was free to pursue any of several career opportunities. With her credentials, she could easily land a position with any major Washington law firm. There was also the tug of the children's rights issue; Marian Wright Edelman had made it clear there would always be a place for her at the Children's Defense Fund. Then again, politically savvy people like Betsey Wright were urging her to run for office. "There was never any doubt in my mind," Wright said, "that she had the intellect, the vision, and the guts to get elected to national office." Concurred Hillary's friend Kris Rogers: "We clearly thought she'd probably at least be a senator."

Then there was Arkansas, and Bill. When he finally did ask her to come to Arkansas and marry him, she was loath to give up her feminist principles for a man. "I know this is a really hard choice," Bill conceded, "because I am committed to living in Arkansas."

"Yeah," she agreed, the memory of meeting one of Bill's lovers at the airport still painfully fresh in her mind. "Yeah, Bill. A really hard choice . . ."

Hillary made her trade-offs early on, and I think she steeled herself not to look back.

—*Jan Piercy*

If you're married for more than ten minutes, you're going to have to forgive somebody for something.

—*Hillary*

Hillary loves Bill. And Bill loves Bill. It gives them something in common.

—*Dick Morris*

Her tolerance for some of his behavior just amazes me.

—Betsey Wright

She must feel she is walking though a minefield
every day.

—Gary Wills

What am I supposed to do about these women who
throw themselves at me?

—Bill

4

"HILLARY WAS VERY much in love with Bill but had to reconcile what ambition she might have with marrying him," said a friend from Yale Law School, Carolyn Ellis. "She knew she was going to do things political and go into public service, run for office. I think there was some fear on her part that she would simply be an adjunct to him."

Nor was Hillary entirely sold on the idea of living in Arkansas. "I love Bill," she told Taylor Branch. "I believe in him, but," she added, her eyes rolling to the ceiling, "*Arkansas?* God, before I met Bill I wasn't even sure where it was."

Kris Rogers agreed that "it made absolutely no sense for Hillary to go there. Arkansas felt to all of us, except Bill, like the end of the earth!"

Nor had Bill's relatives gone out of their way to make his Yankee girlfriend feel welcome. "When she came down to Arkansas," Roger conceded, "it was a big cultural clash, personal clash, mental clash, educational clash, to say the least."

That summer Bill again complained to his mother that she had failed to treat Hillary with "the warmth and respect she deserves." That, apparently, had the desired impact on Virginia. While driving back to Hot Springs after visiting relatives in Hope, Bill's mother suddenly realized "that if I didn't do something to mend that fence, I was about to put Bill in the position of having to choose between the two of us. And I thought, God, if you'll let me get back to Hot Springs, I'll spend the rest of my life correcting this, if I can."

Once she got home, Virginia wrote Hillary a letter in which she "poured out my heart to her. I asked for her forgiveness. In my mind, I had made peace with her." Hillary had not responded, but Virginia claimed that did not bother her. "Once I mailed that letter, I began to live again."

That August, however, Virginia returned to her house from work to find her husband dead as a result of complications from diabetes. Only days before he had been manning phones at Clinton headquarters in Fayetteville.

Bill delivered a stirring eulogy, and several days after the funeral, Hillary sent her future mother-in-law a copy from Washington with a note. "I have never known a more generous and stronger woman than you," Hillary wrote to Virginia, who at fifty-one had now buried three husbands. "You're an inspiration to me and so many others. In addition, you're just as good a politician as your son. After he wins, we'll have to decide what position you'll seek. If there's anything I can do for you, please let me know. Be well. Love, Hillary."

It was "a letter that meant the world to me," Virginia later said. Moreover, it constituted Hillary's long-delayed response to Virginia's earlier plea for a truce.

Knowing that Virginia was now willing—in theory, at least—to accept her as a member of the family pushed her in the direction of relocating to Arkansas. But she would continue to wrestle with the question for weeks. "I had to make a decision," she later said. "What was I to do? I could have gone to work for a big law firm in a place like Chicago or New York. I could have gone back to work for the Children's Defense Fund—stayed on that career path for whatever series of motivations I had been moving toward all my life."

But, she added, "I also knew that I had to deal with a whole other side of life—the emotional side. Where we live and where we grow, and when all is said and done, where the most important parts of life take place."

She was swayed, she said, by the fact that "as much as I would have liked to have denied it, there was something very special about Bill and there was something very important between us." On an earlier trip down to Fayetteville, Bill had introduced Hillary to the dean of the University of Arkansas Law School, Wylie H. Davis. Dean Davis had offered her a teaching position, and now she was calling him to see if the offer was still good. "You bet," he answered.

Still, she was not entirely sold on the idea of moving halfway across the country to a place where, she confided to a friend, "I have only one person I can turn to." To remedy that problem, Hillary talked her brothers, Hugh and Tony, into moving to Arkansas and enrolling at the university.

She packed her belongings—several boxes of books, a few clothes, a ten-speed bicycle—and arranged to drive down to Arkansas with her friend Sara Ehrman and with Alan Stone, who had campaigned for McGovern with her in Texas. But even on the eve of her departure from Washington, she expressed misgivings.

Her last night in Washington, Hillary had a farewell dinner of sorts with her impeachment staff colleague Fred Altshuler and two of his friends, both young lawyers embarking on exciting new jobs in the nation's capital. "Hillary seemed to be heading into a future that was less glamorous than ours," Altshuler said. "Here she was, socially committed—and going to Fayetteville." In reality, she "did not seem all that committed to life in Arkansas. Not at all." Altshuler would describe the evening, and Hillary's mood, as "poignant."

The next morning, however, Hillary left Washington as planned. "I had no choice but to follow my heart. Following your heart is never wrong." Nonetheless, as she made the trek southward she still harbored lingering doubts. "My friends and family thought I had lost my mind," Hillary later said, "and I was a little concerned about that as well."

So, too, was Sara Ehrman. Hillary's traveling companion spent most of the trip taking detours so she would have time to talk her friend out of "making a huge mistake. She wanted to get going but I forced her to do a little sightseeing along the way. We stopped at Charlottesville and I made her look at the University of Virginia. We drove up to Monticello and looked around there. We stopped in Abingdon to see the Barter Theater, where I used to take my kids. And every twenty minutes I told her what I thought about her burying herself in Fayetteville."

Ehrman was merciless. "You are crazy," she yelled at Hillary. "You are out of your mind. You're going to this rural remote place—and you'll wind up married to some country lawyer."

Once they finally arrived in Fayetteville, Ehrman's worst fears seemed to have been realized. The university was in the midst of a football rally, and students wearing pig caps ran through the streets screaming *Soo-ee, soo-ee, PIG! Soo-ee, soo-ee, PIG!* "I," recalled Ehrman, "was just appalled."

As soon as she arrived in Arkansas, Hillary hurled herself into Bill's congressional campaign. None too soon, according to several supporters. Hillary brought with her a "much-needed sense of discipline," observed Paul Fray, who had moved to Fayetteville with his wife, Mary Lee, to manage his old friend's campaign. "Organization and sticking to a schedule were not exactly Bill's strong suit."

Nor was "The Boy," as they now referred to Bill, particularly adept at controlling his temper. The loyal foot soldiers who had fanned out from campaign headquarters to hand out leaflets and tack up posters were now astonished to see their leader flying into tantrums, said Fray, "on a more or less regular basis." Typically, Bill would ignore warnings from staff members that he'd be late for his next stop, then blame it on them when he was.

"The rages were pretty amazing," one staffer said. "He'd scream, pound his fist on his desk." One of his favorite ploys was to walk up to an underling, glare at him with nostrils flaring, and then stick his forefinger within inches of the person's face. "Never," Clinton would say, "*never* do that to me again. Do you understand me?"

The tantrums "might have been comical—I mean, with all the ranting and raving it was like something a horribly spoiled child would do. But when the child is six-foot-two and weighs 220 pounds, it isn't funny—it's terrifying."

What he found particularly frustrating was the incumbent's popularity. "I'm sick and tired," Bill blurted out during a staff meeting, "of hearing what a nice guy Hammerschmidt is!" At Hillary's suggestion, the Democratic candidate had hammered away relentlessly at the incumbent's longtime friendship with Richard Nixon. "You've got to saddle him with Watergate," she had told Bill. "Don't be afraid to use it against him."

Conversely, questions began to surface about Bill's own lack of military service and his antiwar activities. Hammerschmidt had served as a bomber pilot during World War II, and was considered one of the Pentagon's staunchest allies. On the few occasions when he allowed himself to be cornered on the subject of why he had not served in Vietnam, Bill merely answered that his draft lottery number never came up.

When he told Fray about the letter to Colonel Eugene Holmes in which he admitted to deceiving the ROTC commander in order to evade the draft—and confessed that he "despised" the military—Fray urged him to get hold of the document and destroy it. "Make it go away," he said, "or you'll end up in a pickle."

By this time, Colonel Holmes had retired. Rather than approach him directly, Bill leaned on allies within the University of Arkansas administration where Holmes had run the ROTC program to persuade the colonel to surrender the original of the letter to Bill.

Within a matter of days, the original was removed from Clinton's ROTC file and burned. But not before Holmes's aide, Lieutenant Clinton Jones, had secretly made a copy.

The damning letter would not surface for years, but there were other rumors swirling about the Clinton campaign in 1974. After defeating Fulbright in the primaries, Dale Bumpers called Paul Fray personally, wanting to know if there was any truth to the story that Bill Clinton liked to partake of drugs along with his young campaign workers.

Bumpers was repeatedly assured that Bill was not a drug user, although the same could not be said for certain members of his staff. Neal McDonald, who coordinated campaign efforts on the Fayetteville campus, as well as the Frays, conceded that drug use was rampant among Bill's army of supporters; at parties that he threw for the rank and file at his home, one of Clinton's key advisors offered up not only marijuana, hashish, cocaine, and a wide variety of pills, but also syringes for hard-core users. Not surprisingly, Bill's brother

Roger, who would later serve time in prison on drug charges, seldom missed one of these affairs.

Then there was the issue of Hillary. Although they had lived together openly in New Haven, any such arrangement would almost certainly cost him votes in Arkansas. So, while Bill continued to live in a cramped cottage in Fayetteville, Hillary set up housekeeping separately in a sprawling glass-and-wood split-level lent to her by Terry Kirkpatrick, an Arkansas lawyer who had served with Hillary on the House impeachment staff.

Beyond that, however, Hillary made few concessions. Bill's mother and Mary Lee Fray tried to convince her to change her appearance—to wear makeup, nail polish, and flouncy dresses, and to ditch the thick glasses for contacts—but she flatly refused. When she walked into her criminal law classroom for the first time, students were taken aback by the sixties radical in their midst.

"There weren't many women in the law school then, and she looked more like a student than a teacher," recalled Woody Bassett, who wound up having Hillary as well as Bill as a law school instructor. "But she was extremely well prepared and much more blunt than Bill, a much more aggressive questioner and much more analytical. A lot of people initially weren't sure how they felt about her because she came on kind of strong."

To be sure, there were those even among Clinton supporters who saw Hillary as belligerent and pushy—and said as much. "She rubs people the wrong way," campaign advisor Doug Wallace wrote in a memo to Clinton, "and boy, did she ever. She managed to antagonize almost the entire staff."

One who shared Wallace's sentiment at the time was Don Tyson, chairman of Springdale, Arkansas-based Tyson Foods and Bill's biggest contributor. "Big Daddy" Tyson, who inherited the company from his father, was one of the most colorful and controversial figures on the Arkansas landscape. Tyson ran his chicken empire from a corporate headquarters where the doorknobs were egg-shaped and a chicken head was carved above the fireplace. (Later, he would have his executive suite redone as a replica of the Oval Office.) He wore the same khaki work uniform with red stitching on the shirt pocket that all Tyson employees wore.

"Ruthless" and "amoral" were two of the most common adjectives used to describe Tyson's business methods. Tyson was one of the state's biggest polluters, the scourge of environmentalists and union organizers alike. Yet none of this seemed to matter to the avowedly reform-minded Clinton. Whenever Bill ran short of cash, he would call up his longtime friend and former Fulbright campaign manager Jim Blair, who also happened to be Tyson's chief legal counsel, and ask to set up a meeting. Then Bill would sit down with Tyson and his cronies at the Gas Lite bar or one of Big Daddy's other smoke-filled hangouts and hammer out a deal.

Tyson would go on to become far and away Bill Clinton's most important financial backer. Yet in 1974 Tyson also felt, Fray recalled, that Hillary "could really screw things up for Bill. He told me she should keep her mouth shut."

Hillary's drab appearance and her brusque manner fueled rumors in both Democratic and Republican circles that she was a lesbian. So persistent was the gossip that Paul Fray finally asked Bill point-blank if Hillary was indeed gay. When Bill simply shrugged, Fray went straight to Hillary.

"There have been all these rumors, Hillary. Is it true?" he asked.

"It's nobody's goddamn business," she snapped back.

Fray pressed on. "Maybe so," he said, "but we can't ignore this—all these rumors are hurting Bill."

Hillary would have none of it. "Fuck this shit!" she yelled, then stormed off.

At the same time, certain church leaders were circulating the rumor that the tall, boyish-looking Clinton, twenty-nine and unmarried, was gay—a notion that struck those who knew Bill as, in one friend's words, "nothing short of hysterical."

To several campaign workers, however, the theory that Hillary was gay or at the very least bisexual helped explain why Bill felt free to openly pursue women throughout the district and beyond. According to the Frays, Hillary did suspect that Bill was seeing other women, but said nothing. Bill, meanwhile, put them in the uncomfortable position of concealing his girlfriends from Hillary—in particular a student who, as it happened, was well liked by the Frays and other campaign staffers.

One day Bill was standing near his teenaged girlfriend's desk bending over papers, reaching down and running his hand over her thigh, when he glanced up to see Hillary's car pull up in front of the building.

"Shit, it's Hillary," he yelled, rushing over to Mary Lee. "Get her out of her," he said, motioning to the young volunteer. "Do it *now*—out the back way. Now go, before Hillary sees her."

From then on, one of the Frays' most important jobs was to keep Hillary from finding out about the women the staff now referred to as Bill's "Special Friends." For Mary Lee, that got to be a full-time job in itself. "It got to be just too damn complicated—there were so many women," Fray said. "So to keep track of who was who we kept a list." The list of Bill's Special Friends grew to include dozens of names—including the wives of some of the district's most upstanding citizens. One of the women on the list, the teenaged daughter of one of Arkansas's leading political figures, was alarmed when someone referred to Hillary as Bill's fiancée. "But *I'm* Bill's fiancée," she protested. "Who is this Hillary?"

Not surprisingly, it was not long before Hillary snapped. One afternoon when he was meeting with Don Tyson, she went through Bill's desk, pulling out his girlfriends' phone numbers and then, in a frenzy, ripping them up.

As much as, if not more than, his flagrant womanizing, Hillary was hurt by Bill's offhand treatment of her. After months spent trying to convince her to follow him to Arkansas, Bill had suddenly turned cold. "I never heard him refer to Hillary as his fiancée," a volunteer said. "Not once." In those instances when she accompanied him to public events, she was "shoved into the background and basically forgotten." And when the state Democratic Convention was held at Hot Springs, no one reserved a room for Hillary.

These and other slights had Hillary wondering if she had made the wrong choice. "She was not happy with the way Bill was treating her—that was pretty obvious," Fray said. Twice, Hillary disappeared for several days to ponder her future, reemerging to discover, she confided to a friend back in Washington, "that Bill hardly noticed I'd been gone."

By September, Hillary had decided to "stay and fight." Literally. To the astonishment of others in the campaign, Bill and Hillary were not reluctant to quarrel—often furiously—in front of others. As the congressional race drew to a close, tensions between the two escalated. "They'd have the biggest damn fights," campaign organizer Ron Addington told journalist Dave Maraniss, "shouting and swearing."

On the way to one campaign appearance, Addington drove with Bill in the front passenger seat and Hillary in the back. A discussion over how hard to attack Hammerschmidt on his Nixon connections mushroomed into what Addington called one of several "battle royals."

"That is what I'm gonna say, Hillary, and that's all there is to it," Bill yelled, pounding his fist against the dash.

"For God's sake, Bill, for once don't be an asshole," she screamed, slapping the back of the seat with her open hand. "If you want to lose this election because you're too chickenshit, then go ahead!"

Expletives flew and the pummeling of the car's interior continued until the car paused at a stoplight. "I'm getting out!" Hillary declared, opening the door.

"Go on," Bill yelled back.

With that, she got out of the car, slammed the door behind her, and stormed off down the street alone.

"It always struck me as odd," another campaign staffer said, "that they got into these passionate fights over politics when she had to know he was screwing around behind her back. That's where she channeled all her rage—she was just too proud to deal with the rest."

On election night, tempers flared again when it became clear that Bill was losing by the narrowest of margins. Paul Fray had already put aside money from local dairy interests that could be used to buy boxes full of thousands of absentee ballots—enough to tip the scales in Clinton's favor.

He persuaded Bill to go along with the scheme, but his wife and Hillary would have none of it. It did not matter to Hillary when Bill screamed, "This is the way things are done down here." Mary

Fray, meantime, knew that if Paul got caught stuffing the ballot box, Bill could not be counted on to back him up.

A pitched battle ensued. Fray ripped a phone out of the wall and tossed it through a window. Hillary grabbed a book and hurled it at Bill, striking him in the side. Glass shattered, and other staff members scurried for cover. Mary Lee Fray, who had grown increasingly critical of Clinton, unleashed the most devastating weapon of all.

"You ought to know that Bill is sleeping with half the district," she told a stunned Hillary. "Do you know what he's been making us do? He's been making us hide his girlfriends from you—and believe me, it hasn't been easy."

"The Boy" wound up losing to Hammerschmidt by only four thousand votes—48.5 percent to the Republican's 51.5 percent. Bill knew that he had not really lost at all; by coming closer to defeating the popular incumbent than anyone ever had or would (Hammerschmidt eventually retired undefeated in 1992), Bill Clinton had become an overnight political sensation. "John Paul Hammerschmidt was considered unbeatable," *Arkansas Gazette* writer Ernest Dumas recalled, "and this guy almost did it. That's what we all wrote about: Bill Clinton—here's the man to watch, the rising star."

There was, however, one thing Bill would have done differently during the campaign to tip the scales in his favor. In the end, he had determined that the rumors of his womanizing had hurt him with hard-core churchgoers. "They wouldn't have voted against me if I was a family man," he said. "If I had announced my engagement to Hillary, it would have made a difference."

For Hillary, the end of the congressional campaign signaled her return to academia. In Fayetteville she taught criminal procedure and trial advocacy, and ran the school's legal aid clinic, where third-year law students handled uncontested cases under Hillary's supervision. She also directed a program in which legal assistance was given to criminals serving sentences at two regional prisons.

Her first legal case involved a rape victim who did not want her own sexual history used against her by the defense. "It was a long-standing historical tradition in the law that women were property and had been expected to accept it," said Ann Henry, another friend of Hillary's who also happened to be a lawyer. "It was like the assumption that anybody wearing hot pants or a miniskirt deserved to be raped."

One afternoon, Hillary called a meeting of like-minded feminists at the Henry home to hammer out plans for the state's first hotline serving victims of rape and domestic abuse. She also was a vocal advocate of state legislation barring testimony concerning a rape victim's sexual history.

Bill, meanwhile, had also returned to his full-time teaching position at Fayetteville. Never was the contrast in their styles more apparent. "Bill was the eternal lounge rat," Woody Bassett said. "When Bill Clinton wasn't in the classroom, he was down in the lounge shooting the breeze with the students." As for Hillary: She was "tough, intelligent, and highly articulate . . . you either liked her or you didn't, but no matter what, you grew to respect her."

As she widened her circle of friends, Hillary gradually became more comfortable with her life in Bill Clinton's beloved Arkansas. On weekends, she played tennis with her friend and fellow transplant Diane Kincaid (who would later wed Jim Blair). But most of her social life revolved around Bill and his small army of admirers.

With the election over, it was no longer necessary—or from his perspective, economical—for Hillary and Bill to maintain separate addresses. She was, after all, living rent-free in the elegant home lent to her by Terry Kirkpatrick. "Bill was a total freeloader," Mary Lee Fray said. "He wasn't about to pay for anything as long as somebody else was willing to."

At this point in his life, Bill needed Hillary, and not just to help him plan his next political move. Pampered by women and friends and friends of friends his entire life, he had not mastered some of life's basic tasks. The brilliant Rhodes Scholar and Yale Law School graduate who had narrowly missed being elected to Congress had no notion of how to balance a checkbook, how to maintain a car in running order, or how to pay his bills. At one point, he called a friend and announced he was coming over to take a bath.

"Why in the hell do you want to come to take a bath?"

"Because they shut off my water," Bill answered.

"Why did they shut off your water?"

"Because I forgot to pay my goddamn utility bill," he shouted into the phone, "that's why!"

Anyone who knew Bill Clinton also quickly learned that he was, in Fray's words, "utterly incapable" of paying his own way. Indeed, Clinton made a point of never carrying cash. Even student volunteers who worked to pay tuition were forewarned that the candidate never carried cash. "If we stopped to get gas," one said, "or to grab a sandwich, even to use a pay phone, there was never any question. At a coffee shop he'd just get up and leave the check on the table. It was understood you'd just take care of it."

Even Bill's friends weren't immune to this treatment. If he and Hillary went out to the movies, no one recalled them paying for their own portion of the check, much less picking up the tab. On those occasions when they went out alone to the movies or a restaurant, it was Hillary who fished through her purse for money to pay. Once when she poked fun at him for "sponging" off everyone else, Bill shrugged. "I read somewhere that Jack Kennedy never paid for anything, either."

In December 1974, Bill moved in with Hillary, and the two law school faculty members were soon behaving like any married couple. They went to movies and to basketball games, played backyard volleyball, and ate barbecue with fellow faculty members and cronies. Every party featured endless political talk and spirited games of charades that lasted into the early morning hours. Both were highly competitive. But where Hillary could dissolve in laughter at a missed clue or a lost turn, Bill, said their friend Ellen Brantley, would "go wild and scream."

As surprisingly comfortable as her life in Fayetteville had become, Hillary still had grave doubts about staying—doubts that grew stronger as friends pressured them to marry. In July 1975, before returning to teach at the University of Arkansas Law School for a second full term, Hillary visited her parents in Park Ridge, then flew east—first to New York, then Boston, then Washington—to confer with her friends.

In the end, the people she trusted most from her days at Wellesley and Yale Law School, and from the Watergate impeachment staff, were split down the middle on whether Hillary should marry Bill and settle permanently in Arkansas. "It nearly didn't happen at all," Hillary later admitted. "Making the decision to get married took time for me . . . I never doubted my love for him, but I knew he was going to build his life in Arkansas."

If anything, Hillary's return to the Northeast left her feeling that she hadn't missed a thing over the past year. "I didn't see anything out there," she said with a shrug, "that was more exciting or challenging than what I had in front of me."

Whatever lingering doubts she may have had evaporated after Bill met her at the airport in Little Rock. Exhausted, she told him she wanted to go straight home. Instead he took a detour.

"You know the house you liked?" he asked.

"What house?" she replied.

"You know, the house on California Street—the pretty redbrick one you said you liked?"

"But, Bill," she objected as they pulled up in front of the dilapidated one-bedroom cottage, "I've never been inside it."

"Well, I thought you liked it," he said. "So I bought it." Bill opened the front door and showed her inside. "Needs some work," he said hopefully, steering her to the one piece of furniture he had purchased on his own: a bed covered with sheets purchased at Wal-Mart. "So," Bill told Hillary, "I guess we'll have to get married now."

Nine weeks later—on the morning of October 11, 1975—Virginia was having breakfast with friends at the Holiday Inn when Bill broke the news to her that the woman he was marrying that day insisted on keeping her maiden name. Virginia looked at him for a moment, and then burst into tears. "Pure shock" was the way Bill's mother later described her reaction. "I had never conceived of such a thing." In a matter of moments, the other women sitting at the table were weeping, too.

Hillary Rodham's soon-to-be mother-in-law had regained her composure by that afternoon, when a handful of family and friends crammed into the living room of the house at 930 California Street for the wedding of Hillary Rodham and Bill Clinton. One of Bill's friends from the congressional campaign, Methodist minister Victor

Nixon, performed the service. In view of Hillary's role in Congress's Watergate inquiry, Hillary later admitted, "We couldn't resist the idea of telling our friends, Nixon performed the ceremony."

Hillary wore a floor-length, Victorian-style dress she bought off the rack at Dillard's department store only the night before. Bill, meanwhile, wore a dark blue suit and silk tie. His brother Roger, already grappling with serious drug and alcohol dependency at age nineteen, was best man. The couple exchanged traditional vows and heirloom rings, then were pelted with rice as they left for an afternoon reception at the home of State Senator Morris Henry and his wife, Ann.

In contrast to the uncharacteristically intimate ceremony, more than three hundred friends representing every stage of the newlyweds' lives—from Park Ridge, Wellesley, Georgetown, Oxford, Yale, Washington, and Fayetteville—gathered at the Henrys' to toast the happy couple.

Over the course of the evening, guests refilled their glasses from a bubbling fountain of champagne, watched the bride and groom cut the seven-tiered wedding cake festooned with yellow roses, then ambled out onto the sprawling grounds to talk about the bright young couple's political future.

"Hillary was thrilled," Ann Henry said. "We all were." She might not have been so thrilled to learn that, on their wedding day, her husband had made passes at several guests. One woman—a member of the Fayetteville contingent who would remain a friend of the Clintons for decades—pushed open a bathroom door and was "totally floored" by what she saw: Bill "passionately kissing a young woman. He was fondling her breasts. I was so shocked I just closed the door quickly and quietly. They never knew I saw them."

No one had made honeymoon plans, but when Dorothy Rodham spotted cut-rate fares to Acapulco that November, she bought six tickets—for the newlyweds, herself and her husband, Hugh, and Hillary's two brothers. Bill's side of the family—Virginia and Roger—was pointedly excluded.

No matter. Bill knew that Acapulco was the vacation spot where a young Senator John F. Kennedy and his beautiful wife, Jacqueline, honeymooned in a pink clifftop villa overlooking the Pacific. Despite his bad back and debilitating Addison's disease, JFK had spent the better part of his honeymoon in 1953 fishing for marlin. But during his ten days in sun-splashed Acapulco, Clinton behaved more like Jackie, writing hundreds of thank-you notes to wedding guests.

When they returned home in November, Arkansas was in an uproar over the new look of Governor David Pryor's flamboyant wife, Barbara. Arkansans were aghast that their First Lady had gone from the standard Southern bouffant to a fashionable frizz. Within a matter of weeks, the Pryors had separated.

The day the Pryor split was announced, Hillary showed up for a dinner party with the same frizzy hairstyle that had caused so much trouble for Barbara Pryor. "It's wrong," she said, ever mindful of her own appearance, "to criticize her for the way she looks. What does that have to do with her brain?"

Bill and Hillary hit the ground running in January 1976. Months earlier, he had weighed his options and come to the conclusion that he would run for Arkansas attorney general. Toward that end, he had his childhood friend Mack McLarty, now chairman of the state Democratic Committee, assign him the job of meeting with party leaders around the state to determine the best way of selecting delegates to the 1976 National Convention.

On March 17, 1976, with his bride of five months standing at his side, Bill Clinton announced his candidacy for attorney general in the capitol rotunda. He had begged Arkansas's Democratic Governor David Pryor to convince the other two primary candidates to drop out of the race, but without success. He would have to defeat Secretary of State George Jernigan and Deputy Attorney General Clarence Cash for the Democratic nomination. Once that was accomplished, however, he could relax. In a state where Democrats outnumbered Republicans by a wide margin, the GOP did not even bother to field a candidate for state attorney general.

During the otherwise lackluster primary campaign for attorney general, a question was raised that would continue to nag Bill Clinton for years. Why, he was asked repeatedly, did his wife insist on being known as Hillary Rodham? His stock reply: "Hillary is a nationally recognized authority on children's legal rights and has every right to keep her name."

But even among their staunchest supporters there was resentment over the name issue. One day their close friend Guy Campbell told Hillary, "Damn it, I just don't understand why on earth you want to keep your maiden name!"

"Well, Guy," Hillary said, batting her eyes, "the real reason is that I just love my daddy so much."

Recalled Campbell, "That was it. From that moment on, she had me."

On May 26, 1976, Bill handily won the three-way race with 55.6 percent of the vote, thereby averting a runoff. With no Republican opponent in the general election, Bill had plenty of time to run Jimmy Carter's Arkansas campaign against incumbent President Gerald R. Ford. Given Carter's Southern roots and his longtime links to some of the richest men in the state, Bill had no trouble dipping into some of Arkansas's deepest pockets for the former Georgia governor. No pockets were deeper than those of Little Rock financier Jackson Stephens, whose investment bond firm was the biggest outside New York. Fortunately for Carter, Stephens had been one of Carter's classmates at Annapolis.

Hillary also went to work on behalf of Carter, but not in Arkansas. In August she took a leave of absence from the University of Arkansas Law School and headed to Indianapolis, where she served as the Democrats' deputy campaign director in Indiana.

Once again, Hillary instantly ran afoul of the locals with her abrasive, take-no-prisoners approach. But there were also those who appreciated her candor. "She didn't sugarcoat," said campaign worker William Geigreich. Agreed another Carter operative, Ruth Hargraves: "She could out-argue anybody, and the last thing you wanted to do . . . was disagree with her. You always knew she was going to win."

Despite Hillary's effort, her candidate failed to carry Indiana. But Jimmy Carter did narrowly win the election, and rewarded both Clintons handsomely once he entered the White House. The new president appointed Hillary to the board of the Legal Services Corporation, and within weeks she had managed to get herself elected chairwoman. For his role in delivering Arkansas to the Democrats, Bill was allowed a major say in dispensing patronage jobs in the state, including several presidential appointments to the federal bench. Clinton and Rodham also found themselves being invited to various functions at the White House, where, true to form, they added to their ever-expanding network of contacts.

Back in Little Rock, where they had moved into a modest single-story brick house in the city's Hillcrest district, Bill and Hillary faced a new challenge: how to supplement his meager $6,000 salary as attorney general.

"Bill made it clear to me," Dolly Kyle recalled, "that there was a big role reversal in their marriage. He was to be the decorative one in the relationship, and she was to be the breadwinner."

Herb Rule, a former legislator who had raised money for Bill Clinton's 1974 congressional race, was in charge of recruiting new lawyers to the Rose Law Firm, Arkansas's most highly regarded firm. When the new attorney general told him Hillary was looking for a position in Little Rock, Rule recalled that he "tracked her down." Less than a month after her husband was sworn into office, Hillary went to work as a Rose associate at a starting salary of $25,000. Within five years, she would be taking home three times that amount.

The new attorney general, meanwhile, was giving his suite of offices in the capitol his personal touch. The place was not much to begin with—Arkansas's top law enforcement official was surrounded by fake walnut paneling, folding metal chairs, and collapsible tables. On the door of his private bathroom, Bill tacked up a full-length pinup of Dolly Parton spilling out of a bikini.

As much as he may have enjoyed the trappings and prestige of his new office, it was well known throughout Arkansas that Bill had no intention of staying in it for long. In May 1977, just five months after taking the oath as attorney general, Bill told a reporter that he had not yet decided whether he was going to run for governor or the U.S. Senate the following year.

In truth, Clinton had his eye on the governorship. But everything hinged on whether the formidable John L. McClellan, who had served in the Senate for thirty-six years, was, at eighty-one, still up to the rigors of running for a seventh term. If McClellan bowed out, Governor Pryor was almost certain to run for the Senate. Bill could either announce for the Senate himself, and oppose Pryor in the Democratic primary, or take the easier road and seek to succeed Pryor as governor.

That summer of 1977, while he bided his time making speeches and forging alliances, Bill continued pursuing other women. The second week in August, Dolly Kyle, who had since moved to Dallas with her husband and earned a law degree, drove to Little Rock and resumed her affair with Bill. The next morning, August 16, she accepted her old beau's invitation to visit him at his new office in the state capitol.

Before driving on to meet her husband in New Orleans—it was their wedding anniversary—Dolly let Bill take the wheel of her new pale green Cadillac El Dorado convertible with cruise control and forest-green leather upholstery. Racing at speeds in excess of one hundred miles an hour, Bill careened from lane to lane, smiling broadly as he sang along with Elvis on the state-of-the-art eight-track tape player. Dolly held her breath; she had almost forgotten how "completely terrifying" it was to be a passenger in a vehicle driven by Bill Clinton. No garden-variety tailgater, Bill liked to drive up to the car in front of him at full speed, forcing the hapless motorist to get out of the way or risk being rear-ended.

After fifteen minutes on the road, Bill turned back. Just short of the exit that would have taken him back to his office, he veered off and, without explanation, drove to a residential area just blocks from the capitol, where they parked in front of a vacant lot. He turned off the ignition and got out of the car. Then, according to Dolly, Bill told her to strip while he methodically removed his clothes, folded them neatly, and placed them on the backseat.

According to Dolly, whose accounts of their quarter-century-long affair would never be contradicted by Bill Clinton, they then proceeded to make love in the front seat of the Cadillac with the top down—twice. Dolly would later see this episode, like so many others, as another striking example of Bill's need to take risks. "He is so arrogant he thinks he'll never be caught," she said. "And then there's a part of him that wants to get caught because he thinks he can lie his way out of anything. Usually, he can."

That afternoon, Bill flew to Fort Smith to deliver a speech. On the way to the hall, the driver told him that Elvis Presley had died at Graceland of an apparent drug overdose. He was forty-two.

Shattered, Bill found the nearest pay phone and called his mother. Virginia worshipped Elvis, and instilled in her eldest son a reverence for the King that bordered on the fanatic. From the time he was eight, Bill had delighted his mother by delivering flawless interpretations of "Hound Dog" and "Heartbreak Hotel," complete with upcurled lip and churning hips. Bill still knew every lyric to every Elvis song. Once he got through to her, Virginia had already heard the news on the radio and was so distraught she could not speak. "It was like suffering a death in the family," she later said, "as if I'd lost my own son."

Indeed, this was something else the two honey-voiced Southern charmers had in common. Bill's deep affection for Virginia mirrored Elvis's own fabled devotion to his mother. Like his mother, Bill Clinton wept at the news that Elvis had died.

Three days later, Hillary threw a thirty-first birthday party for Bill. It was his first as an elected official of the state of Arkansas, but now that seemed of little consequence. He was still grieving for Presley—and the passage of an era. "Bill sort of identified with Elvis," Hillary said. "In a way he was an early role model. He was deeply hurt by Elvis's death. It really upset him. That's all he would talk about for days."

Not long after, there was also news concerning that other sacred icon of his youth—John F. Kennedy—that would have a profound impact on Bill's behavior. In her autobiography, *My Life*, Judith Campbell Exner confirmed that she had conducted a torrid affair with JFK in the White House while simultaneously carrying on with Frank Sinatra and Chicago mob boss Sam Giancana.

The book touched off a flurry of stories about President Kennedy's frenzied sex life—from his affair with Marilyn Monroe to the parade of women smuggled into the White House by the Secret Service right under Jackie's nose.

Bill's identification with Jack Kennedy had intensified over the years since that near-mystical meeting in 1963. Now Exner's book, which he devoured in a single sitting, only validated Bill's theory that great men had great sexual appetites. If he was to emulate his idol and rule over a second Camelot, then the revelations concerning Kennedy's sexual exploits—fraught as they were with danger— did more than merely validate Bill's perilous sexual behavior. They prodded him to push the limits that much further.

He did just that—with a vengeance. While Hillary was working her way toward partner at the Rose Law Firm, Bill chalked up what by one aide's tally was "at least two or three one-night stands a week." Several affairs begun during this period would have lasting ramifications.

One of these was with twenty-two-year-old Susan McDougal, the comely wife of his friend James McDougal, who at thirty-nine was seventeen years her senior. Once a teenaged political prodigy, the flamboyant, hard-drinking McDougal was running Senator Fulbright's Little Rock office when Bill had first met him in 1968. McDougal, whose taste for the high life earned him the sobriquet "Diamond Jim," was an accomplished yarn-spinner best known in Democratic circles for his dead-on impersonation of FDR.

Susan was a student in McDougal's political science class at Arkansas's Ouachita University when they began dating in 1974. A year later, Bill met Susan when McDougal invited him to speak to his class. Clinton sent McDougal a thank-you note: "I really liked that pretty girl."

The political science professor and his attractive pupil had been married a year when Bill encountered her again in Tennessee in the fall of 1977. The occasion was a Democratic fund-raising gala at a restaurant called Justine's, a veritable Memphis landmark.

At the gala, Arkansas's boyish attorney general, his hair spilling over his collar and ears, spotted Susan McDougal across the room. She was wearing a slinky black gown with a provocative flesh-colored top and rhinestones across the bodice. Her long, straight auburn hair cascaded over her shoulders.

Bill scanned the room to make sure Hillary was not in the vicinity, then crept up behind Susan, slipping his arm around her waist. She grabbed his hand, then looked up at him. Her surprise, said a friend of Susan who witnessed the event, "turned to adoration. You could feel the electricity between them."

According to friends, Bill's affair with Susan McDougal would purportedly continue off and on for fifteen years, and end with her serving time in prison for contempt rather than divulge the details of the Clintons' involvement in a questionable land deal called Whitewater. Another attractive woman he began sleeping with that year would not prove to be so loyal.

Unable to make ends meet as a singer, Gennifer Flowers had managed to land a job as a cub reporter for KARK-TV, NBC's Little Rock affiliate, in 1977. She was on assignment in the capitol when she first encountered Bill that fall. A statuesque brunette (she would later bleach her hair white-blond) who at twenty-seven fit the beauty queen mold favored by Virginia, Gennifer (real name: Eura Gean) was taken aback when Bill walked up to her, ran his eyes up and down her body, and blurted, "Where did they find *you*?"

A month later, she left KARK to pursue her singing career full-time, and he began showing up at her performances. Their affair began that October, and would last until 1989. "I was consumed by Bill Clinton," she later recalled. She allowed that, while she loved him, he never "looked me in the eye and said 'I love you.' " So why did she fall for him? "I cared so much about him. I figured thirty minutes of wonderful was better than a lifetime of mediocre."

When she was singing at a local nightclub, Flowers would look directly at him while she performed love songs. "I'd look at him while I was singing 'Since I Fell for You.' He knew what I meant." Bill and Gennifer trysted on a near-weekly basis for the next twelve years, nearly always at her condominium apartment in Little Rock's Quapaw Tower complex.

Later, as governor, Bill would sometimes jog over from the capitol. But most often his limousine would take him, and his driver would wait downstairs. "We had trouble with his car being parked out front," said Quapaw Tower manager John Kauffman, who personally saw Clinton enter the building (ten to twenty times). "He'd arrive late in the evening and park in the unloading zone." Then, according to Kauffman, Clinton "would get out, go into the complex, and stay anywhere from one to four hours. On at least three occasions, my security guard had to tell the chauffeur to park in the lot like everyone else."

Even though he was now unquestionably the most recognized figure in the state, Bill insisted that the blinds be left open as he and Flowers made love on the floor or on the living room couch—in full view of downtown Little Rock. In fact, Flowers said, "we used every spot in that apartment . . . We made love everywhere—on the floor, in bed, in the shower, in the kitchen, on the cabinet, the sink."

Periodically, they even made love in the bedroom. Flowers's boudoir, said her friend and sometime roommate Lauren Kirk, "was made for sex. King-sized bed. Black satin sheets. Black satin spread. Zebra drapes and a canopy. She had candles and room fragrances. She went to the scent shop for those aromatic rings you stick on lamp shades so they'll emit a fragrance. She put on special bedtime makeup, mascara and everything, and gorgeous negligees."

The consummate politician even in bed, Clinton always made a point of complimenting his lovers on their appearance, their talents, their achievements. He also inquired about their problems, their doubts, and their fears. Early in their relationship, after one of the lovemaking sessions, he picked up a hairbrush and began stroking Flowers's hair. "It was like therapy," she recalled. From then on, it became a shared ritual.

"What he can do to you is play your soul like a finely tuned Stradivarius," Flowers said. "He seduces your mind as well as your body." Just as he had a pet name for Dolly Kyle, Bill dreamed one up for Gennifer. He called her "Pookie." She called him "Baby."

At about the time Bill started seeing Gennifer Flowers, Senator John McClellan died suddenly. With the Senate race now wide open, the attorney general had an important choice to make—and quickly. Within a matter of days, Bill met with fledgling New York–based political consultant Dick Morris to determine whether he should run for governor or senator in 1978. Morris would later say he "had never met a Southerner who talked fast. The accent was there, but he talked as rapidly as any New Yorker."

Bill listened as Morris outlined new polling techniques he had pioneered. According to Morris, voters no longer responded to a candidate's image as much as they responded to his stand on specific issues.

"Kennedy won on image," Bill protested, citing the figure after whom he continued to pattern both his personal and political life.

But Morris argued that the American people were more sophisticated than they had been in the 1950s and 1960s. "They want to know where you stand on the issues," he said. "That's really all that matters."

Bill told Morris that he preferred to run for the Senate in 1978, primarily because the term of an Arkansas governor was only two years compared to a senator's six-year term. But Morris's polls showed that while Bill might win the Senate race, he was a virtual shoo-in for governor.

It was not enough for Bill to be elected governor, however. Pryor's chief opponent in the primary would almost certainly be Jim Guy Tucker, the handsome, charismatic young congressman who had preceded Bill as attorney general. Clinton told Morris that he saw Tucker as his main rival "in the long run. We can't let him win."

Meanwhile, on December 19, 1977, Gennifer Flowers visited her Little Rock gynecologist, Dr. K. M. Kreth, and complained that her period was late. A urine test at the Clinical Laboratory of Little Rock confirmed what Flowers suspected: She had become pregnant by Bill Clinton.

Bill remained blithely oblivious to the possible consequences of not wearing a condom. And Gennifer could only speculate that in the heat of passion, she had either forgotten to wear her diaphragm "or it just slipped."

She told Bill about the pregnancy and her decision to have an abortion. The procedure was performed in late January, and on February 6 she returned to Dr. Kreth for what is described in her medical records as a "post-abortion exam." The following month, she visited Dr. Kreth again.

In March 1978, while Gennifer Flowers recuperated from the abortion procedure, Bill Clinton announced his candidacy for governor while his wife, mother, and brother looked proudly on. He wanted to be governor, he said, "because a governor can do more for more people than any other office. Any office," he added, "except the President."

That spring of 1978, Clinton worried little about his primary battle. Instead, he spent hours with Dick Morris devising a strategy that would help David Pryor crush Jim Guy Tucker—the one person Bill saw as a viable rival and, as such, a threat to his political future.

At Rose, Hillary's career flourished even as Bill moved ever closer to his ultimate goal. In Arkansas, it was of little concern that the wife of the attorney general—not to mention the next governor— was practicing at a firm whose powerful clients had extensive dealings with Little Rock.

From agriculture to banking to real estate, manufacturing, and the retail industry, Rose represented the most powerful interests in the region. As such, it hired not only the most talented legal guns but those with the best connections. Over the years, Rose numbered state supreme court justices, legislators, congressmen, even a former U.S. senator among its partners. But even by these standards, Hillary Rodham was, in Rule's words, "a prize catch." Another former partner was more blunt in his assessment of Hillary's role at the firm: "Hillary was this huge political asset—pure and simple."

From the start, there were those who complained loudly. To have the attorney general's wife (and by extension her husband) reap the benefits from a law firm that represented clients before the state, they charged, constituted a flagrant conflict of interest. But in a state where, according to one journalist, "everyone's in bed with everyone else—literally and figuratively," the criticism eventually died down.

Despite its omnipotence, even the Rose Law Firm could not offer Hillary all the challenges she sought. At Rose, Hillary was able to move effortlessly between family and corporate law, but to try her hand at criminal law she had to search for an associate outside the firm. She approached William R. Wilson Jr., one of the state's more flamboyant trial attorneys, and asked if she could help him "represent accused citizens" in her spare time.

Hillary's first criminal client was "Tiny," a three-hundred-pound man accused of aggravated assault against the woman he lived with. When Hillary was introduced to her client, she refused to use the demeaning moniker, and was the only person involved in the proceedings who insisted on calling him by his real name. "It was obvious how pleased he was, just having been shown that human sensitivity," Wilson said of the man's reaction to Hillary.

Moreover, Wilson was almost certain the assault case would go to trial. Instead Hillary, exploiting a technicality, managed to get the case dismissed during the preliminary hearing for lack of probable cause. "She had celestial fire," declared Wilson, who in 1993 would be appointed by President Clinton to the federal bench. "And she had a steel-trap mind."

For Hillary, the case seemed a radical departure from her highly publicized efforts on behalf of rape victims. To compound the irony, Hillary had no way of knowing that even as she was busy getting charges dismissed against a man accused of assaulting his girlfriend—and taking special care not to bruise the overweight man's feelings—Bill was in the process of committing an act that would ultimately result in an even more damning accusation.

Of all the hundreds of admiring female volunteers who campaigned for the dashing, mesmeric Bill Clinton during that first race for governor, thirty-five-year-old Juanita Hickey was a standout. A registered nurse who had worked at several nursing homes around the state, Hickey had decided to start her own care facility in 1973.

Five years later, Hickey invited candidate Clinton to drop by her nursing home, Brownwood Manor in Van Buren, on his campaign swing through her part of the state. "I thought he was great," Juanita said, "that as governor he was going to be good for Arkansas." On first meeting him, she was impressed with "his smile, his warmth. He was a very charismatic man, very intelligent—I *liked* him."

Bill was obviously struck by the attractive blonde, and invited Juanita to drop into the Clinton campaign headquarters the next time she was in Little Rock. Juanita, then about to leave her husband for another man, was delighted. She had signed up for a meeting of the American College of Nursing Home Administrators the following week, and told Clinton that she would love to take him up on his offer.

"Wonderful," he replied, taking her hand. "Wonderful."

On April 25, 1978, Juanita and her friend Norma Kelsey, a nurse, arrived at Little Rock's Camelot Hotel. At around 9 A.M., she called Clinton headquarters and was surprised at her reception. Not only had Bill been expecting her call, but she was given his home phone number and told to dial him there.

"Juanita," he said, "why don't I just meet you for coffee at your hotel?" A little before ten, however, he called back with second thoughts. "Can we meet in your hotel room instead?" he asked. "It's so noisy in the coffee shop, and there are reporters there . . ."

"I was a little uneasy," Juanita later admitted. "But I felt a real friendship toward this man." Besides, "this was the attorney general . . ."

Excited that she would be playing host to such a distinguished visitor, Juanita ordered a pot of coffee from room service and "placed it with some flowers on a little table by the window. It was very pretty."

When he arrived at her room, Bill shook her hand and she led him to the table by the window. They looked out at the Arkansas River, and he pointed to a small structure—the Pulaski County Jail. "It's ugly, isn't it?" he asked. "When I'm governor, I'm going to renovate it. It'll look beautiful."

With that, scarcely five minutes after he entered the room, Bill slipped his arm around Juanita's waist, turned her around, and started kissing her.

"No!" Juanita protested, pushing him away. "Please don't do that."

Bill looked nonplussed. "Didn't you know," he asked, "why I was coming up here?"

"I can't," Juanita insisted.

"But we're both married people," he said, implying that sex between them would be free of emotional entanglements.

"Yes, I am married—but I'm in love with someone else," she tried to explain, hoping to persuade Bill that she had no interest in him. The "someone else" was the man she had been having an affair with for over a year, David Broaddrick. Juanita would marry Broaddrick two years later.

Bill ignored Juanita's protests and kissed her again. Then, without warning, he bit her top lip. Hard. She tried to pull away, but he would not release her.

Biting down on her lip even harder, Bill forced Juanita onto the bed. "I was very frightened," she said. "I tried to get away from him."

"Please don't!" she yelled, still struggling. But every time she tried to get up, he pressed down on her right shoulder and bit harder on Juanita's lip.

"He was just a different person then," Juanita would later recall, "a vicious, awful person." Without letting go of her lip, he unzipped his pants, pulled up her skirt, and tore a hole in her panty hose. Then, according to Juanita, Bill Clinton forcibly, painfully, raped her.

When he was finished, Bill got up and straightened himself while Juanita lay frozen on the bed. She was too distraught to notice that Bill, as was his practice, had not used a condom.

"Don't worry," he reassured her. "You won't get pregnant. I'm sterile. I had mumps when I was a teenager."

"As though that was the thing on my mind," she later said. "I wasn't thinking about pregnancy, or about anything. I felt paralyzed and was starting to cry."

Then, in a scene that would be indelibly etched in Juanita's memory, Bill Clinton put on his sunglasses, looked at her swollen, bleeding lip, and said, "You better put some ice on that." Then he turned around and left.

Juanita had told Norma Kelsey that she was meeting Clinton. When she returned to their room from the seminar, Norma found her friend on the bed in a state of shock, her panty hose ripped at the crotch, her mouth purple from all the biting, her lips swollen to twice their normal size.

"I can't believe what happened," Juanita said, rocking back and forth. For several minutes, this was her mantra: "I can't believe what happened. I can't believe what happened. I can't believe what happened . . ."

Norma applied ice to Juanita's lip, and instead of attending the conference the two women left for home immediately. They would stop for more ice on the way to Van Buren, but Juanita would not seek any medical attention. "There was internal pain, of course, from being violated," she later said. "I wanted this to all go away. I wanted to go home."

She also chose not to report the rape. "I didn't think," she said, "anyone would believe me in the world."

As they drove away from Little Rock, Juanita scourged herself for allowing Clinton to come up to her room. But she also kept asking, "How can a man like this be governor of a state?" At the time, it never entered her mind that he might someday be President.

When she got back home, she told her lover David Broaddrick that she had been struck in the mouth by a revolving door at the hotel. He did not believe her. Two days later, she told Broaddrick the truth. "I've been raped," she wept, "by Bill Clinton."

At the time she would also confide details of the assault to several friends, including Susan Lewis, Louise Maw, and Jean Darden. But she was too ashamed and humiliated to report it to the authorities. "I was also frightened," she conceded. "This was the attorney general, and now I knew what he was capable of."

But less than three weeks after the attack, Juanita Broaddrick went ahead with plans to attend a Clinton fund-raiser at the home of her friend Dr. Chris Wells. "I can't explain why I went," she later said. "I was still sort of in denial, a state of shock. I didn't know what to think, what to do."

When the Clintons arrived at the fund-raiser, Clinton studiously avoided Juanita. His wife was another matter. "Hillary sought me out, and when somebody told her where I was, she came straight for me and cornered me and grabbed my hand very forcefully."

"I want you to know how grateful we are for all you've done for Bill," Hillary said, her eyes boring into Juanita's. "We are so grateful for all you've done for Bill, *and all you'll keep doing*." Broaddrick tried to pull away, but Hillary held on to her hand for a few more seconds until, said Juanita, "she was satisfied her point had been made. She was looking me straight in the eye and I understood perfectly what she saying. I knew *exactly* what she meant—that I was to keep my mouth shut. That meant that *she knew* almost from the beginning—that he must have confessed at least something to her. But apparently it was something she was willing to overlook.

1.

Billy Blythe, here at four, never knew his father, who was killed in a freak accident before Billy was born. His possessive grandmother threatened to sue for custody when Billy's mother married Roger Clinton, an abusive alcoholic, in 1950.

2.

Eleven-year-old Hillary *(seated at the lower right)*, with her sixth grade class at Eugene Field Elementary School in Park Ridge, Illinois. Her mother, Dorothy Rodham, told her someday she could become the first female Supreme Court Justice.

3.

At fourteen Billy played saxophone in the Hot Springs High School band. Soon the outgoing Virginia (pictured below with Billy and his half brother, Roger, in 1959) was taking the underage "Bubba," as she called Billy, to nightclubs as her "date."

4.

5.

6.

A self-proclaimed "Goldwater Girl," Hillary spars for the camera before debating LBJ Democrat and Maine South High School classmate
Ellen Press Murdoch on the eve of the 1964 presidential elections.

A defining moment: a sixteen-year-old President-to-be meets the President at the White House in 1963. Eventually, Bill would come to resent the fact that the Washington press did not "protect" him the way it did JFK.

7.

8.   While Hillary campaigned for George McGovern in Texas in 1972, a
mop-topped Bill met the candidate and Arkansas Democratic Party
Chairman Joe Purcell at the Little Rock airport.

Hillary, looking over the shoulder of Bernie Nussbaum during House Watergate hearings in 1974, sent her father and brother down to Arkansas to keep tabs on Bill when she heard her fiancé had been dating other women.

9.

The newlyweds strike a happy pose after their October 11, 1975, wedding. Virginia Clinton wept when Bill told her Hillary was keeping her maiden name.

10.

11.

"Diamonds and Denim" was the theme of the Clintons' 1979 inaugural ball kicking off his first term as Governor of Arkansas. Six weeks later, Bill and Hillary were guests at a Carter White House dinner honoring the nation's governors.

12.

13.

After a difficult labor, Chelsea Victoria was delivered by cesarean section
on February 27, 1980. Chelsea's birth, Hillary later said,
"transformed our lives."

Hillary, widely blamed for Bill's being turned out of office in 1980 after one term, took the Clinton name, underwent a makeover—and helped him recapture the Arkansas Governor's Mansion in 1982.

14.

Hillary and Chelsea at about the time the four-year-old started asking why her mother left each day for work. "Ah," Hillary said, "there's the guilt that strikes your heart."

15.

Chelsea watches Daddy vote in the 1986 elections that returned him to office for a fourth two-year term as governor. It was about this time Hillary and Bill began politically "drilling" Chelsea at the dinner table, at times reducing her to tears.

16.

17.

Vince Foster and his wife, Lisa, out with the Clintons in 1986. Whenever Bill left, said the guards at the Governor's Mansion, Foster showed up "like clockwork" to spend time with Hillary— and often did not leave until the next morning.

Hillary, warned that Bill's womanizing would destroy his career if he ran for president in the wake of the Gary Hart scandal, wipes away a tear as Bill announces he will not make a run for the White House in 1988.

18.

19.

Chelsea, eleven, with her parents when her father was inaugurated for a fifth term as governor in 1991. He ran promising that he would fill out his term and not seek higher office.

20.   On the hustings in New Hampshire during the 1992 primary season, a weary
Bill and Hillary stop for coffee at Blake's Restaurant in Manchester.

Admitting to
"problems in our
marriage," Hillary
stood by her man
during the pivotal *60
Minutes* interview—
and turned the tide
in Bill's favor.

21.

22.

In the bar in Macy's near Madison Square Garden, site of the 1992 Democratic National Convention, the Clintons watch the delegate count on television—and cheer when Ohio puts Bill over the top. *(below):* Savoring the moment of triumph.

23.

24.

25.

The President-elect and Mrs. Clinton take a bike ride along the beach in Hilton Head, South Carolina. Hillary was already in charge of where and when the press would be allowed to cover them.

A tender moment between father and twelve-year-old daughter at the Little Rock airport in January 1993 as they prepare to leave for their new life in the White House. Her parents comforted a shattered Chelsea when she became the butt of cruel jokes on TV's *Saturday Night Live*.

26.

After being sworn in, Bill hugs the two most important people in his life. Later, in a sparkling blue lace gown, Hillary danced with her husband for the first time as the First Lady and the President.

29.

Super Bowl Sunday in the White House theater. With Texas Governor Ann Richards on one side and New York Governor Mario Cuomo on the other, Bill, Chelsea, and the First Cat Socks watch the 1993 game between Dallas and Buffalo.

Comforted by Vince Foster *(on her left)*, Hillary listens to Bill after she arrives in Little Rock for her father's funeral on April 8, 1993.

30.

31. Film of a teenage Clinton meeting her husband so impressed Jackie Onassis that she invited the Clintons to cruise with her off Martha's Vineyard in August 1993. Privately, Jackie urged Hillary to stand her ground and offered tips on raising Chelsea.

The Women—a sampler: Bill first denied, then admitted to his extramarital affair with Gennifer Flowers *(bottom)*. Miss America 1981 Elizabeth Ward *(below left)* first denied, then admitted to her affair with Bill. He also reportedly sneaked away from the Governor's Mansion to spend time with Miss Arkansas 1980 Lencola Sullivan *(wearing crown)*, although she denied it. Clinton business partner Jim McDougal was convinced his wife, Susan *(right)*, was having an affair with Bill.

When Hillary returned from the bedside of her dying father, she was furious that Barbra Streisand had spent the night at the White House with Bill. He often tinkered with his traveling schedule to rendezvous with Sharon Stone *(above)* and Eleanor Mondale *(left)* in California.

Then–Arkansas Attorney General Clinton posed in 1978 with Juanita Broaddrick *(top left)* at the nursing home she owned. Bill never directly denied her charge that he raped her later that year. Paula Jones's sexual harassment suit set in motion events that eventually led to his impeachment. Longtime Clinton friend Kathleen Willey *(left)* said he groped her outside the Oval Office the day her husband shot himself.

On Christmas Eve, 1994, father and daughter do some last-minute shopping at a Washington bookstore. "Chelsea," said a friend, "is the one thing he loves most in the world."

Chelsea and her mom wore traditional Islamic scarves when they visited a mosque in Pakistan during their two-week tour of South Asia in 1995.

43.

The First Family goes white-water rafting on the Snake River during
their two-week Wyoming vacation in August 1995.

Hillary's wrap snags on the
ramp of the presidential
helicopter as the First Family
heads for Hilton Head on
New Year's Eve, 1995.
Only a few hours earlier,
Bill had trysted with
Monica Lewinsky in his
Oval Office study.

44.

For a second time, the Clintons—poised, confident, and immaculately turned out—march down Pennsylvania Avenue at the start of the January 20, 1997, Inaugural Parade.

45.

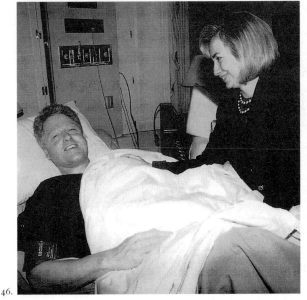

After stumbling at golfer Greg Norman's Florida home, Bill underwent surgery on his right knee on March 14, 1997. He was still on crutches two weeks later when he had his final sexual encounter with Monica Lewinsky.

46.

47. In a strange life-imitates-art moment, Bill and Hillary don masks and glare at each other during a state visit to Mexico in May 1997.

"A part of us," an emotional Bill told Chelsea's graduating class at Washington's Sidwell Friends School, "longs to hold you once more."

48.

With their Secret Service detail in tow, Bill and Chelsea jog along a bike path on Martha's Vineyard in August 1997. The large scar from his surgery was plainly visible on his right knee.

49.

Freedom! A continent away from Beltway pressures, Chelsea rejoices as she walks with her parents across the Stanford campus on her first day of school in September 1997.

Bill and Hillary share a few stolen moments dancing on the beach in St. Thomas on January 4, 1998. In a matter of days their world would start to unravel.

The Monica Lewinsky scandal exploded onto the front pages in January 1998. At left, Monica with the President on November 17, 1995—the day they had a sexual encounter while he chatted on the phone with Alabama Congressman Sonny Callahan. A year later, he stopped at a ceremony to give her a hug.

52.

53.

54.

Dressed in sunny yellow, Hillary whispered a few words of encouragement in her husband's ear, then nodded in agreement as he made his famous finger-wagging denial that he had ever had sexual relations with "that woman" Monica Lewinsky.

55.

56.

While scandal rages back home, the Clintons visit the terra-cotta warriors near
Xi'an during their nine-day trip to China in late June 1998.

Bill once again employed a finger to scold prosecutors during his videotaped August 17, 1998, grand jury testimony. A furious Hillary had, in the words of a friend, "blasted him" for his actions.

57.

58.

Clasping hands, with House Minority Leader Dick Gephardt and Vice President Al Gore beside them, a defiant Bill and Hillary walk out to meet congressional supporters after the December 19, 1998, House vote to impeach.

59.

The strain was evident on January 28, 1999, when Bill and Hillary attended
a memorial service for Florida Governor Lawton Chiles at the
height of the Senate impeachment trial.

I was so upset I went out into the hallway and became sick to my stomach."

Later, Juanita learned from a friend who had met the Clintons' plane that "I was the only thing Bill and Hillary talked about during the twenty-minute ride in from the airport. She kept saying, 'Bill, now be sure and point Juanita out.' My friend thought it was very strange that Bill and Hillary Clinton were so concerned about me."

Not long after, Bill handily won the primary with 60 percent of the vote. But more important, the secret campaign he and Dick Morris concocted to undermine Jim Guy Tucker had worked. Pryor won the Democratic nomination for U.S. Senate, effectively removing Tucker as Bill's only real competition for the title of Arkansas's reigning Golden Boy.

That August, confident that he would win, Bill and Hillary dined with Jim and Susan McDougal at Little Rock's Black-Eyed Pea restaurant. Over steaks, McDougal outlined the terms of "a real sweet real estate deal" that he wanted to "cut you and Hillary in on."

The deal McDougal laid out before his friend involved the purchase of 230 subdividable acres on a bluff overlooking the White River—a prime spot, McDougal contended, for vacation and retirement homes. The Clintons and the McDougals could form a partnership to buy the land for only $202,000 and, he hastened to add, they would not even have to put up their own money for the down payment.

The Clintons had not seen the land and would never even visit it, but Susan McDougal was ecstatic over the possibilities. "Bill had no business sense, so he couldn't have cared less," McDougal said, "but Hillary paid very close attention to the details. She was interested, and she was the one we talked to."

The two couples formed the Whitewater Development Corporation, and took out a $20,000 loan from the Union National Bank for the down payment. They financed the $182,000 balance with a loan from Citizens Bank and Trust of Flippin, whose president, James N. Patterson, just happened to be one of those they were purchasing the land from.

Despite Susan McDougal's enthusiasm, the lots would not sell, interest rates would skyrocket, and everyone would eventually lose money on the deal. In the meantime, however, Whitewater merely whetted Hillary's appetite for the acquisition of wealth—an instinct she had long suppressed.

Jim Blair, who counted Tyson and a number of other agribusiness giants among his clients, had been one of the Clintons' closest friends in Fayetteville. He would later wed Diane Kincaid, the University of Arkansas political science professor who had known both Rodham and Clinton since 1972, and the Blairs would become perhaps the closest of all their Arkansas friends.

Blair had made a fortune investing in cattle futures through the Refco brokerage house, and convinced Hillary it was a fast and sure way to turn a tidy profit. "I was on a streak," Blair said, "a streak that I thought was very successful, and I wanted to share this with my close friends, as I did."

Hillary was all too aware that Bill, who had always floated above the petty concerns of earning money and trying to manage it, had tacitly assigned her the role of breadwinner. On October 11, 1978, just two months after Clinton and Rodham entered into the Whitewater deal, Hillary took the plunge into the commodities market. Blair turned her over to his longtime trader at Refco, Robert L. "Red" Bone.

A bluff, poker-playing Tyson crony, Red Bone would be disciplined by market authorities for, among other things, "serious and repeated violations" of various trading procedures. From the outset, the normal rules did not seem to apply to Hillary, who was allowed to buy ten cattle futures with an investment of just $1,000 when the minimum required purchase was $12,000.

For the next nine months, Hillary played the market aggressively, sometimes making several trades a day. With margin calls that can bankrupt an investor in a matter of seconds, commodities trading is a risky business at best. But Hillary need not have worried. While other investors were routinely told to pay their margin, Hillary never was. Blair was such a big Refco client, and responsible for bringing so many high rollers to the table, that neither he nor any of his friends was pressed to pay up.

Thus, while at various times Bill and Hillary would have seen their assets and salaries wiped out had they been required to play by the rules, she kept on trading. When she cashed out the following July, Hillary had miraculously parlayed her single $1,000 investment into a cool $100,000. After a careful analysis of Rodham's trades, the *Journal of Economics and Statistics* concluded that the chances of her accomplishing this feat without special help from her well-placed friends were less than one in 250 million.

Hillary's insistence on sticking with her maiden name—as well as her Coke-bottle glasses and chilly Northern demeanor—still rubbed many Arkansas voters the wrong way. But it was not enough to keep her husband from racking up 63 percent of the vote against his little-known Republican opponent Lynn Lowe. At thirty-two, Bill Clinton was the youngest governor elected in the United States in four decades.

At 9:30 that election night in November 1978, Bill emerged to greet the well-wishers who had gathered in the ballroom of the Camelot Hotel, the same Little Rock hotel where six months earlier he allegedly attacked Juanita Hickey. "The election," he told his cheering supporters, "is fundamentally a tribute to the decency and judgment and hope of the people of Arkansas . . . I will try to be worthy of the enormous trust you have placed in me this evening."

Juanita, sitting in the living room of her home in Van Buren, turned off the television and cried. And in the ballroom of the Camelot Hotel, Hillary—almost as innocent of her husband's secret life as the people of Arkansas—looked on with pride.

There's nobody in the world who hasn't done things
they weren't embarrassed about. Aren't they ever
allowed to be in the past?

> —*Bill*,
> in 1987

Just tell Chelsea that Mommy loves her.

> —message phoned
> to Chelsea's school
> whenever Hillary was
> on the road

Hillary is intensely human and sensitive and feels every slap and aches with every blow. Her stoic exterior masks enormous pain.

—*Dick Morris*

What's important to us is that we've always dealt with each other. We haven't run away or walked away.

—*Hillary*

Well, everybody needs sex, don't they?

—*Bill*

5

"I T'S REALLY SOMETHIN', ain't it?" Governor Clinton said, checking to make sure Hillary was out of sight before reaching under the table to squeeze the buxom redhead's thigh. The new governor had chosen "Diamonds and Denim" as the theme of his inaugural gala—another defining moment in Bill's life that would transpire inside the Camelot Hotel.

Hillary, meanwhile, was dancing with her friend and cattle futures benefactor Jim Blair. Later that year, Bill, in his capacity as governor, would pronounce Blair and Diane Kincaid husband and wife; Hillary would stand up for them both as the couple's "Best Person."

This night, however, Hillary was a waltzing advertisement for Bill's beloved Arkansas. Patterned after Hillary's off-the-rack wedding dress by Arkansas designer Connie Fails, her dusty rose velvet gown was trimmed with Victorian beads and antique lace donated by several Arkansas *grandes dames*. From her neck hung the Kahn diamond, a dazzling 4.25-carat canary-yellow gem that had actually been mined in Arkansas. When an *Arkansas Democrat* photographer came into view, the new governor swept his wife up in his arms and, as she beamed at him through her thick glasses, whirled her across the dance floor.

For Bill, the gala was both celebration and reunion—again, friends and colleagues from the various incarnations of Rodham and Clinton gathered in Little Rock to share what many of them viewed as a generational passing of the torch. Kincaid spoke for everyone when she described the evening in a single word: "Thrilling."

Before long, however, it would become painfully evident that many of the qualities that helped him get elected—his willingness to talk with anyone who managed to collar him, his desire to please people by telling them what they wanted to hear, his disregard for schedules if they got in the way of making another convert—now worked against him.

The open and easy management style that had served Bill well as a campaigner undermined his authority. For example, instead of a chief of staff his office was run by a triumvirate of unshaven liberal tyros known as the "Children's Crusade"—an arrangement that quickly led to dissension in the ranks.

Nor was Governor Clinton any more inclined than Candidate Clinton to be punctual. Routinely showing up two or more hours late for important meetings, he quickly alienated key business, labor, and legislative leaders. And Bill's famously short attention span—he snapped "What else?" whenever he grew impatient during a briefing—sabotaged efforts to actually implement some of the grandiose reforms outlined in his ambitious agenda. The result: The governor's inexperienced, too-liberal staff was branded in the press and even by members of Bill's own party as both ineffectual and incompetent.

During his first term, Clinton himself would make a series of political missteps—most notably pushing an increase in car licensing fees that incensed motorists. To make matters worse, not long after he declared that anyone who exceeded the state's fifty-five-mile-per-hour speed limit would be ticketed, the governor's limousine was clocked by reporters going eighty miles an hour on the way to a library dedication. Asked about the incident at a press conference, Clinton shook his fist and angrily denounced the press for "trying to make me look bad."

But much of what transpired in Arkansas during 1979 and 1980 was beyond his control. There was a serious downturn in the national economy. A series of twisters tore through the region, truckers went on strike, and the Ku Klux Klan held its national rally in Little Rock.

These paled in comparison to the decision made by Bill's friend

President Jimmy Carter to relocate some twenty thousand Cuban refugees to Fort Chaffee, near Fort Smith, Arkansas, for processing. "You're fucking me!" Bill screamed at Carter's chief of staff over the phone when the decision was made. That was as far as the protests went—Bill was not willing to jeopardize his standing with the Democratic Party's national leadership, and his own future on the national stage, by publicly defying the President. Bill paid the price when rioting erupted among the younger Cuban males protesting their lengthy confinement. More than one thousand broke out of the camp and began marching toward town, forcing him to call out the National Guard.

Through it all, *Arkansas Gazette* political cartoonist George Fisher could not resist depicting the state's callow new chief executive as a baby in a bonnet or a toddler pedaling a tricycle. There was also the growing perception that Bill was cowed by his overbearing wife, who, even his friends pointed out, was doing him political damage by remaining Hillary Rodham. "People thought even his wife didn't like him enough to take his name," journalist Meredith Oakley said. "She didn't shave her legs. She was a ball-busting feminist."

Inevitably, the stark contrast between Hillary and the Southern belles who had preceded her as First Lady led to a resurgence of the unfounded rumors that she was gay. "Some of the women she was close to were tough-as-nails types," said a top woman fund-raiser for the Democrats in Arkansas. "They wore unflattering, boxy business suits, let their hair go gray, and swore like sailors. But mostly these were people she had known for years, and she liked them because they were as smart and as ambitious as she was." Did Hillary know about the persistent gay gossip? "Hillary knew *everything* that was said about her and Bill, but she just laughed it off. Once she joked, 'When I look at what's available in the man department, I'm surprised more women aren't gay.' She thought the whole gay thing was just too silly for her to waste her time on."

During the 1978 campaign, Hillary had sidestepped the issue of her name. But after moving into the Governor's Mansion, she finally addressed the issue. "I had made speeches in the name of Hillary Rodham. I had taught law under that name. I was, after all, twenty-eight when I married, and I was fairly well-established." As for her decision to continue practicing law at Rose: "We realized that being a governor's wife could be a full-time job," she allowed. "But I need to maintain my interests and my commitments. I need my own identity, too."

In essence, it was left to Bill to convince the people of Arkansas that his wife was just plain folks. "It depresses her when she thinks it's hurting me," he said in Hillary's defense. "But she's a lawyer and she doesn't want to go into the courtroom as somebody's wife. If people knew how old-fashioned she is in every conceivable way, they probably wouldn't say these things about her."

Clinton went on to insist that Hillary was not the hard-nosed Yankee she had been made out to be. "She's just a hard-working, no-nonsense, no-frills intelligent girl," Bill said, "who has done well, *who doesn't see any sense to extramarital sex*, who doesn't care much for drink, who's witty and sharp but without being a stick in the mud. She's just great."

Hillary did, in fact, say she felt right at home in the governor's official residence, a two-story redbrick Georgian-style mansion set behind a fountain and circular drive on six acres. Encircled by the restored nineteenth-century houses that made up Little Rock's historic Quapaw Quarter, the Governor's Mansion housed an eclectic collection of furnishings, from an eighteenth-century sideboard to a silver service that had been used by the officers of the battleship *Arkansas* to a two-hundred-year-old crystal chandelier that had been imported from Paris.

To be sure, Bill and Hillary did seem during those first months in the Governor's Mansion to be as happy as they had ever been. One of the state troopers who often acted as Clinton's driver remembered "him and Hillary sitting in the backseat, eating fried chicken and throwing the trash on the floor—me and the other trooper were both starving to death—and they sat back there eating and laughing and smooching like newlyweds."

In late July 1979, Hillary told Bill she was pregnant. The prospective father was overjoyed. Despite his claim according to Juanita Broaddrick that a case of the mumps had rendered him sterile, Bill and Hillary had been trying to conceive for more than two years.

In fact, they were on the verge of consulting a fertility specialist when Hillary's doctor telephoned with the happy news.

Bill wanted to announce the coming blessed event immediately—it would help, Dick Morris had pointed out, to bolster their standing in the polls. But Hillary preferred to err on the side of caution, and waited until September to make the official announcement.

"Hillary did everything she could to bring her child into the world under the best circumstances," Hillary's longtime friend Rose Crane said. "Hillary once told me that what she wanted more than anything was a great big Tab over crushed ice—but she was afraid that it might not be the best thing for the baby." Hillary was determined, however, not to let pregnancy interfere with her schedule—or stand in the way of her being named a partner at Rose Law. But work on a particularly tough child custody case—not to mention her duties as First Lady—took its toll. Clinton and Rodham had prepared themselves for natural childbirth, and Bill was ready to coach her through the delivery. Instead, almost as soon as he returned home from a trip to Washington, Hillary went into labor three weeks early.

Hillary was rushed to Little Rock's Baptist Medical Center, where she endured four more hours of labor at the hospital before doctors reached a decision. Because of the baby's position in the womb, they would perform a cesarean. Natural childbirth or no, Bill insisted on being present when his child was born. "We had a little discussion about it," Hillary recalled. "He was the governor but they were worried that as a father he would pass out or fall flat and cause more of a commotion than a help. Eventually, they were convinced that he wouldn't."

On February 27, 1980, a nurse handed Bill Clinton his six-pound, one-and-three-quarter-ounce newborn daughter. He held her gingerly, as do most nervous first-time fathers. But when it was time to pass her back to the nurse, he refused. Instead, he walked around the room cradling her in his arms. It was, their friend Diane Blair said of the moment, "like he'd invented fatherhood."

The baby had arrived on William Blythe's birthday, an irony not lost on the son Blythe never got to see. "I think for a long time, because his father died before he was born, Bill didn't believe he'd ever live to be a parent," Hillary explained. "That was something almost beyond his imagination." He told her once that seeing his child "was more than my father got to do."

They had decided on the name Chelsea Victoria a year earlier, on a ten-day vacation to England they took before he was sworn in as governor. "We were trying to have a child, something we were working on," Hillary said of the trip. "It was this glorious morning. We were going to brunch and we were walking through Chelsea—you know, the flower pots were out and everything. Bill started singing, 'It's a Chelsea Morning.' Remember that old song? Judy Collins's song?" ("Chelsea Morning" actually described not London's but New York's Chelsea district, and was written and popularized by Joni Mitchell, then a resident of the Chelsea Hotel. However, Collins also recorded her own hit version of the song.)

After the difficult delivery, Hillary was told by her doctors that both she and Chelsea were perfectly healthy. But they also warned her that another pregnancy wasn't worth the added risk. Hillary would later confess to feeling "sad" that Chelsea would never have a sibling, but Bill seemed unaffected by the news. It was miracle enough, Bill figured, that he had lived to see one child born.

For three days, Bill and Hillary shared a suite at the hospital while Chelsea shuttled back and forth between them and the nursery. As with any new parent, there were moments of panic. While breast-feeding, Hillary summoned the nurse when milk started streaming out of Chelsea's nose.

"What's wrong? What did I do?"

"Well," the nurse said calmly, propping the baby up. "Maybe if you hold her up a little higher that won't happen."

Not long after, Hillary became the first woman partner in the 160-year history of the Rose Law Firm. With Bill still earning only $25,000 per year, this was an important step toward providing her family with some degree of financial security. "Now," she said, breathing a sigh of relief, "I can do for Chelsea a little of what my mother did for me."

While Hillary took a four-month paid leave of absence to bond with their baby, Bill dealt with the various crises—from natural disasters to the Fort Chaffee mess that threatened to cut short his political career. Neither the pleasures of parenthood nor the pressures of his office were enough to dampen Bill's libido, however.

Even before Chelsea's birth, Clinton had decided that he was not going to let his new job interfere with his extramarital exploits. At this time, Susan McDougal was making a name for herself appearing in television commercials for their real estate business. The ads featured Susan, clad in tight shorts, cowboy boots, and a clingy shirt, leading a white Arabian horse through a meadow.

Dubbed "Hot Pants" by the press, Susan became a fixture in the governor's office. "She would make a grand entrance every time she dropped by," remembered Clinton aide Randy White. "She liked to flaunt herself with low-cut blouses and miniskirts," another staffer said. "She acted liked she owned the place with 'Bill this' and 'Bill that.' She'd disappear into his private office for two hours—or they'd go out for lunch and not come back. We got the message loud and clear, and he did nothing to make us think otherwise."

"Hot Pants" was not alone. "As soon as Hillary was out of town," said a junior member of his staff, "he was lining up girls to come on over and play." Barely one month after taking the oath of office, Clinton called "Pretty Girl" Dolly Kyle to let her know "The Warden" was on a speaking engagement in Washington. He asked Dolly if she would like to come to the Governor's Mansion for "a game of hearts."

Following Bill's very specific instructions, she drove her Cadillac convertible to within five hundred feet of the Governor's Mansion, flashed her brights twice, and watched as the mansion's gates swung open.

When she got inside, Dolly was surprised to see several men sitting at a card table actually playing hearts. It was a moment before she realized that each card in Bill's personal deck was decorated with the portrait of an American President.

That night, Bill merely introduced Dolly to his tight circle of friends, most of whom had heard him talk about her for years. No mention was made of Hillary. In fact, Bill had never once uttered the name to Dolly. It was always "The Warden."

"He didn't talk about Hillary," Dolly said. "She was not an issue when it came to dealing with me, or any other woman for that matter. She is not a factor—not a factor in his emotional life, anyway. They made a deal a long time ago. That's pretty obvious. She does not figure in his thinking *at all*."

The day after Dolly showed up at the Governor's Mansion to play cards, Bill invited her out again. This time he took her to a cocktail party at the home of a friend, and then for a drive through Little Rock in his official limousine. With a state trooper at the wheel, they stretched out in the backseat, holding each other, until the stretch Lincoln pulled up in front of the capitol. Then, with his arm around her and the trooper trailing thirty feet behind them, they strolled in the moonlight.

"Billy never made the slightest attempt to conceal me from his friends or his staff or anyone," she said. "I thought he was taking a lot of chances, but he never thought so. He was just so sure of himself, so totally self-involved he didn't even consider the possibility that he could actually get caught."

Dolly claimed that only once did she see a flash of his fabled temper. "The minute he started I let him know in no uncertain terms that I wouldn't put up with it," she said. "I told him, 'You may get away with treating other people like that, but don't you even *think* of talking that way to me.' He backed off right away. Billy will push you as far as you will let him push you."

At the time, Dolly was unaware of Bill's alleged sexual assault on Juanita Hickey Broaddrick. But she would later hear the story of his attack on her—and similar attacks on other women. "Do I believe Billy is capable of rape? Absolutely," she said. "There is a very cruel side to Billy. He is willing to destroy anyone—man or woman—who gets in his way. That was part of his nature then, but I never saw it until later."

There were those few, however, who realized at the time what "Billy" was capable of. At the height of his reelection campaign in 1980, Bill spotted Juanita and David Broaddrick at a party and greeted them warmly. Suddenly, in full view of the assembled guests, Juanita's husband grabbed Bill's hand hard, yanked Bill toward him, and warned him, "Stay away from my wife and stay away from Brownwood Manor—or I'll kill you."

Bill, startled for a moment and aware that all eyes in the room were on them, tried to pass the incident off as some sort of joke. But Broaddrick would not release Clinton's hand from his viselike grip. Guests looked on in amazement as Bill, turning crimson and laughing nervously, struggled and eventually freed himself.

In 1980, it was not enough that Juanita Broaddrick and all the other women in Bill's life were keeping what Gennifer Flowers called "our little secret." Bill's political career was unraveling any-way—in large part, those close to him would say, because an in-explicable malaise had set in following the birth of Chelsea.

"Bill Clinton was not the same person psychologically in 1980," insisted his chief of staff, Rudy Moore. He was distant, distracted—though by what no one could say with certainty. He was simply not "fully engaged" in the way he needed to be to overcome the political obstacles strewn in his path. At the time, Moore speculated this sud-den shift in mood might have stemmed from "something personal, perhaps in his relationship with Hillary, but he was ambivalent and preoccupied." So preoccupied, in fact, that he spent hours at a time playing a pinball machine in the basement of the Governor's Mansion rather than attending to the political fight at hand.

To make matters worse, Hillary was not paying attention to the campaign. Ordinarily, he went on, she "was a perfect balance to Bill, who tended to trust everybody and sometimes to be hopelessly optimistic. She saw the dark side of events, and she could see that certain programs and ideas wouldn't work."

When it came time for a reality check, Hillary did not mince words—or soften her language—at staff meetings she attended. "Bill, don't be such a fucking Pollyanna!" she said during one such session. "Some of these people you think are your friends *aren't*."

But Hillary the political infighter was nowhere to be seen. "Hil-lary had her baby, the law practice, and a lot of things going on," Moore observed, "and Bill's political instincts took a temporary va-cation. I literally begged him to make some changes in the cam-paign. I brought it up all the time."

In this case, perhaps neither Hillary nor Bill took their Republican opponent seriously. Frank White, a garrulous savings and loan executive who had never before sought elective office, had actually switched parties in 1980 just to run against Clinton.

White's most effective weapon was a television spot showing footage of Cuban refugees rioting at Fort Chaffee. Convinced that no one could possibly hold him accountable, Bill did not counterattack. Within a matter of days after the first spot was aired, Clinton plummeted ten full points in the polls.

With only one week remaining in the campaign, Hillary suddenly awoke to the realization that they might be turned out of office. In 1979, after Dick Morris had helped him win the governorship, Clinton concluded the New Yorker's style was "undignified" and fired him. Now Hillary picked up the phone herself and called Morris's wife, Eileen. "We need Dick down here right away," Hillary pleaded. "Bill's losing the race badly."

But it was too late. When Frank White won by a 31,000-vote margin, no one was more surprised than White. He called it "a victory for the Lord." Clinton, meanwhile, holed up in the Governor's Mansion watching the returns on television and speaking to no one. It was an emotion-filled evening, as both Bill and Hillary alternately railed at their enemies and choked back tears. Shortly before midnight he made an appearance in the ballroom of Camelot Hotel, where supporters wept openly as he solemnly delivered a concession speech that lasted less than five minutes.

The next morning, some three hundred friends and supporters gathered on the lawn behind the Governor's Mansion to hear Bill give the first of several farewell speeches, each more poignant than the last. "They all," journalist Meredith Oakley said of the hastily assembled throng that morning of defeat, "looked a little shell-shocked." While women and men alike wept, Bill's hirsute half-brother Roger, now looking every inch the rock star he was trying to be, waved his hands in the air and shouted, "We'll be back!"

Later, with Hillary and ten-month-old Chelsea at his side, he bade a similarly melodramatic farewell to a joint session of the state legislature. "Remember me," he said, his eyes welling with tears, "as one who reached for all he could for Arkansas."

When he wasn't waxing poetic in public, however, Bill was inveighing against those he felt cost him the election. Chief among these was Jimmy Carter, who had also gone down to defeat to Ronald Reagan—although not before saddling Clinton with the whole Fort Chaffee mess. "Your boss fucked me," he told one senior member of the White House staff. "Don't expect me to forget it."

In a masterpiece of understatement, his old friend Mack McLarty would use one word again and again to describe Bill's state of mind following his 1980 reelection defeat: "Blue. He was just feeling kinda . . . blue." The atmosphere at the Governor's Mansion during this awkward lame-duck period remained tense as Bill played the election over again and again in his mind. Said his old friend Carolyn Staley: "He was truly unhappy, truly depressed, down."

That Christmas season, Hillary looked for ways to bolster her husband's spirits. One evening he was brooding in the living room when a group of carolers appeared outside the mansion singing "O Come, All Ye Faithful"—a group of Bill's classmates, it turned out, from Hot Springs High. As the carolers streamed inside, Bill settled into a wing chair and sobbed. "You guys are wonderful," he said, tears streaming down his face. "God, I love you guys."

Bill did not stay mellow for long. On New Year's Day, 1981, he downed several drinks and then called respected AP reporter Bill Simmons. "[Jim Guy] Tucker warned me to watch out for you," he screamed at the dumbfounded journalist. "He said you gotta watch out for Simmons, he'll fuck you." At that point, Clinton slammed down the receiver.

Clinton would spend nearly all of 1981 "wallowing," as Hillary later put it, in self-pity and regret. Wherever he went—in restaurants, at the homes of friends, in the locker room at the country club, on the street—Bill apologized to people for losing touch with them and asked what he might have done differently. "We'd go out and there'd be these confessionals in the supermarket aisles," Hillary recalled. "People would come up to Bill and say they voted against him but they were sorry he lost, and he'd say he understood and he was sorry for not listening to them better."

For the first time, he invited a group of clergymen to come to the mansion and pray for him—a gambit he would employ repeat-edly in the coming years. This orgy of recrimination became so unseemly that even Bill's harshest critics worried about his mental state. "He apologized so often and with such remorse," said the *Arkansas Democrat*'s John Robert Starr, "that even I begged him to stop."

The blizzard of mea culpas was, in fact, merely the first step in Bill's master plan to be reelected. Only ten days after his defeat, he called Betsey Wright, their old friend from the McGovern cam-paign, and asked her to come to Little Rock to get his career back on track. The blunt-speaking Wright, a five-pack-a-day chain-smoker, had spent the last few years working for a women's political action group in Washington. Although she had always felt Hillary was the one with the real political potential, the idea of resurrecting Bill's career intrigued her.

Less than a week later, Wright was living at the Governor's Man-sion, rifling through the basement cabinets that held the key to his political rebirth. Here were the ten thousand index cards that re-corded the names, addresses, and phone numbers of every person he had ever met—starting with the date and place of their first meeting and the places, dates, and circumstances of every subsequent encounter.

The same day Bill phoned Wright, Hillary called Dick Morris in New York. "Bill needs you right now," she told him, "and you've got to help him see how he can get his political career back on track." When he arrived in Little Rock, Morris found Bill in "this state of confusion. I knew it would be futile to talk him out of his depression."

Nevertheless, Clinton was scarcely without options. He was of-fered the chairmanship of the Democratic National Committee, as well as positions with several top law firms in Washington and New York. Instead, with an eye on regaining the statehouse, he signed on instead with the Little Rock law firm of Wright, Lindsey & Jennings.

At his cramped law office in Little Rock's Worthen Bank Build-ing, he seemed, in the words of Dick Morris, "a lost and pathetic figure. He was clearly not a happy man." Hillary, meantime, flourished at Rose, where she and fellow law partner Vincent Foster, married and the father of three, were fast becoming close friends.

Foster, who had also grown up in Hope and knew both Bill and Mack McLarty, met Hillary in 1976 when he was in Fayetteville recruiting on the law school campus. First in his class at Fayetteville, Foster had joined Rose after graduating, and promptly earned a reputation as the firm's most upstanding partner. Tall, lanky, and square-jawed, Foster was, according to colleague Thomas Mars, "the Clint Eastwood of the legal profession in Arkansas. He was superorganized and meticulous." On first meeting him years later, presidential aide George Stephanopoulos would draw his own parallel with a Hollywood star. Foster reminded him of "Gregory Peck as Atticus Finch in *To Kill a Mockingbird*."

Among Rose partners, Foster was regarded as the least attuned politically. Yet Hillary was drawn to him, she would later say, because "Vince is a great listener." Said a friend: "Hillary did not need advice from Vince Foster about how she and Bill were going to get back in the Governor's Mansion. But she did need a sympathetic ear—someone to talk to about the pain she was going through because of Bill's depressed state of mind."

Indeed, Bill's dark mood was taking its toll at home. In January the family had moved out of the Governor's Mansion and into a yellow turn-of-the-century house in Little Rock's affluent Hillcrest section. Their new home boasted a wraparound porch, four bedrooms, and a paneled library with floor-to-ceiling bookshelves. In keeping with his compulsive nature, he went on a buying binge, filling the house with tacky *objets* and bulky furniture.

The live-in nurse who had taken care of Chelsea at the Governor's Mansion came along to their new address, and they also employed a full-time maid. Still, since they no longer shared the burden of public office, they were seeing more of each other than they had in years—and the strain began to show.

"They fought all the time," a longtime friend of Hillary's said. "Unbelievable screaming matches. Basically, she was fed up with his moping around and feeling sorry for himself, and he was angry that she wasn't showing him more sympathy."

Nor, apparently, were they particularly conscious of the effect it was all having on Chelsea. One visitor was waiting downstairs when suddenly the sounds of shouting reverberated down the hall. "You could have heard them screaming at each other if you were standing across the street," she said. "He has this booming voice, which didn't surprise me. But if anything hers is louder. After a couple of minutes of this, I could hear Chelsea burst out crying."

Even in those moments of calm at the house, the undercurrent of hostility was unmistakable. Another friend stopped by one day and found Bill on the floor of his study playing with his one-year-old daughter while Hillary poured coffee in the kitchen. Chelsea giggled as he clapped and sang a children's tune to her—only with lyrics of his own making. "I want a *divo-oo-orce*," he sang, "I want a *divo-oo-orce*."

Ever since his humiliating election defeat, Bill had sought solace in the arms of several women—only now that he no longer had a chauffeured government limousine at his disposal, he was forced to drive himself to each assignation. At one point, Dolly Kyle tried to get him to overcome his depression by gauging exactly what he wanted out of life. She posed the question: If he could have a perfect day, how would it begin?

First, he told her that he would put on his favorite articles of clothing: a flannel shirt and Levi's. Then he would have breakfast with the most important person in his life: "Chelsea."

Sadly, had Hillary been asked the question, she would have answered "Bill." For all her considerable maternal instincts, Mrs. Clinton still made Mr. Clinton her top priority. "She idolizes him," said an attorney friend from her Watergate days. "Sure, sometimes she wants to hit him over the head with a rolling pin, and who could blame her? But there is this dreamy schoolgirl side to her that few people know about. And *that* Hillary, the core Hillary, adores Bill. It goes beyond what most women feel about their husbands. With Hillary, it's more like hero worship."

As a teenager, Jacqueline Bouvier expressed her desire to be "part of a great man's life." When she cast her lot with a charismatic young senator from Massachusetts, she was willing to overlook even his more egregious faults for a chance to be a part of history. Hillary had made the same silent bargain with herself, and like Jackie, secretly hoped she could fill the emotional void that propelled him from one adulterous affair to another.

Neither woman, of course, succeeded. At a time when the press conspired to keep the secret of JFK's rampant womanizing, Jackie Kennedy was allowed to suffer in dignified silence. Not so Hillary, who knew that Bill's fevered bed-hopping could trigger a scandal that would cost them everything.

If they were going to get Bill's career back on track, Hillary had to know what weapons—if any—Bill had handed the opposition. Bill's affairs wounded her personally, but they would also have practical political consequences.

In early 1982, Hillary hired a former FBI agent and private investigator named Ivan Duda to investigate her husband. "She wanted me to get the dirt on Bill," Duda said, "to find out who he was fooling around with. But her purpose in having me find out about those women was not so she could confront Bill with the hurt attitude of 'How could you do this to me?' Instead, it was damage control, pure and simple."

Duda's dossier on Bill focused on those women the governor was seeing with some degree of frequency. "I came up with eight women," the investigator said. Gennifer Flowers was at the top of the list, but that was not the name that Hillary found most upsetting. "What really ticked her off," Duda said, "was that one of them was an employee at the Rose Law Firm . . ."

Duda claimed his report "enabled Hillary to go to Bill and work out arrangements for keeping those women quiet—by offering them jobs, promotions, contracts to better positions, or whatever it took to keep everything hush-hush.

"Hillary's main job as a wife," Duda added, "is to protect Bill from himself—to pretend, playact, deny, lie, and cover his rear end."

Whatever the tensions between them, Bill and Hillary pulled together for the 1982 gubernatorial campaign. This time, they heeded Morris's advice and kicked off the campaign with a thirty-second televised apology for hiking car license fees during his first term.

"When I was a boy growing up," Clinton said into the camera, "my daddy never had to whip me twice for the same thing." The folksy ad lib, aimed squarely at those voters who turned him out of office for perceived arrogance, hit its mark.

At their official press conference kicking off the 1982 campaign on February 27—Chelsea's second birthday—Bill and Hillary made it clear that they were willing to do more than just apologize. They had made the changes in their appearance that Morris told them would help placate conservative-minded Arkansans. For his part, Bill had shorn his once-unruly locks; voters were now getting a look at his ears for the first time. His new staff reflected the change. Gone were the bearded, shaggy leaders of the Children's Crusade, replaced with a buttoned-down battalion of experienced politicos.

It was Hillary, however, who had obviously undergone the most dramatic transformation. "I don't vest my identity in my hair or my clothes," she had once objected. "I view that just as what you have to do to get up in the morning and go out in the world."

Now, however, the people of Arkansas were getting a look at a whole new Hillary. Her dark, heretofore untamed hair had also been cut, styled into a flip, and lightened. She dispensed with the thick, oversized glasses that often gave her a saucer-eyed look of perpetual surprise, and replaced them with contacts.

"Oh, my God!" her friend Guy Campbell joked. "Hillary, you actually resemble a beautiful woman!"

"Guy, you son of a bitch," Hillary laughed back. "You are the only person who could get away with a crack like that."

There was more. After years of fighting to keep her name, the candidate's wife announced that while she would continue to practice law as Hillary Rodham, the rest of the time she was to be referred to as "Mrs. Bill Clinton."

Reporters, not quite sure what this really meant, asked why she had suddenly decided to change her name. "I don't have to change my name," she snapped back. "I've been Mrs. Bill Clinton, I keep the professional name Hillary Rodham in my law practice, but now I'm going to be taking a leave of absence from the law firm to campaign full-time for Bill and I'll be Mrs. Bill Clinton. I suspect people will be getting tired of hearing from Mrs. Bill Clinton." Tellingly, she was still registered to vote under the name Hillary Rodham.

The decision had not been made lightly. "I joked one time," Hillary said later, "that probably the only man in Arkansas who didn't ask me to change my name was my husband—who said, 'This is your decision and you do exactly what you want.' And so I did. I just decided that it was not an issue that was that big to me when it came right down to it."

But according to others inside the Clinton camp, Bill had pleaded with Hillary to change her name. Whenever he was asked to approach her about something, Bill's standard not-altogether-tongue-in-cheek reply was "Shit, I can't even get her to use my last name!"

It was only after a concerted campaign to change her mind that Hillary finally acquiesced. "It became a kind of growing concern among his supporters, who came to see me in droves," she recalled, "or called me on the phone and related story after story, and said, 'We really wish you would think about this' . . . After thinking about it a lot and seeking guidance, I became Hillary Rodham Clinton."

She tried to convince even her close friends that it really was not much of a sacrifice. "So I gave it up," she said. "It meant more to them than it did to me." But even Clinton advisors who had fought for the name change knew Hillary was relinquishing what she regarded as an important symbol of her independence. "I teared up," Betsey Wright said. "I had a lump in my throat."

Implicit in Hillary's agreement to reinvent herself was a quid pro quo. In his rematch with incumbent Frank White, Clinton was going to have to take off the gloves and get tough. He did not need convincing. If he lost this time, Bill conceded, "it will be the end of my political life." Remembering his failure to respond to White's attacks in the first campaign, Bill was now spoiling for a fight. By way of explaining his new philosophy, Bill offered the following dictum: "When someone is beating you over the head with a hammer, don't sit there and take it. Take out a meat cleaver and cut off their hand."

Often it was Hillary, ever the stern taskmaster, who made certain Bill wielded the cleaver. Part coach and part policeman, she often lashed out at her husband for his celebrated lack of discipline. Frank White, a teetotaler, had tried to portray Clinton's staff as a motley crew of long-haired substance abusers. So when, on the campaign plane returning to Little Rock, Bill went along with the staff's plans to get together at a local watering hole, Hillary exploded. For the remainder of the flight, aides tried to avert their eyes from the sight of Hillary screaming at her red-faced husband as he seemed to sink further and further into his seat. "How could you be so stupid?" she yelled. "For Christ's sake, Bill. I can't believe you!"

Still, the new strategy worked. Clinton swept back into office with 60 percent of the vote. Once again, political cartoonist George Fisher depicted Bill as a toddler—only this time riding a Sherman tank instead a tricycle.

This time the inaugural ball was held at the State House Convention Center, where the band struck up a rousing rendition of "Happy Days Are Here Again" as Governor and Mrs. Clinton made their entrance. Then they held each other close as they danced to the melancholy strains of "You'll Never Know."

That week, the Clintons moved out of their turn-of-the-century yellow house in Hillcrest and back into the Georgian-style Governor's Mansion—their home, as it would turn out, for the next decade. With her new hairdo, contacts, and a Donna Reed wardrobe of pastel dresses, prim blouses, and tailored skirts, Hillary now looked the way Arkansans expected a First Lady to look.

Ironically, since she was no longer perceived as a raging feminist, there were no objections when Bill appointed her to spearhead educational reform as head of his Education Standards Committee. She attacked the issue with characteristic zeal, urging the state's residents not to settle for schools that consistently ranked forty-ninth in the United States, just ahead of another Southern state. Hillary let it be known that Arkansas's unofficial motto—"Thank God for Mississippi"—no longer struck either her or her husband as particularly amusing.

As she undertook this and other daunting political tasks for Bill, it was still understood that Hillary—not her $35,000-a-year governor husband—would still be the family's principal breadwinner. "It was something we knew was inevitable if we were going to be in public life in Arkansas, because salaries were the lowest in the country," she said. "It does weigh heavily. I think from time to time it was a pretty substantial burden on me personally. But in the balance of our marriage, it was something I was glad to do."

The burden was eased considerably by the fact that—as would continue to be the case for many years—the Clintons rarely had to pay for anything. In Little Rock, they had housekeepers, maids, cooks, chauffeurs, and full-time child care. Inmates from state prisons were put to work doing the landscaping at the mansion, as well as at the Little Rock condominium the Clintons later purchased for Hillary's parents. (Bill was so accustomed to having everything taken care of that, according to his bodyguards, by the time he was elected President he still could not master the task of making a pot of coffee using an automatic coffeemaker.)

Such mundane tasks aside, no one could accuse either Clinton of being lazy. While Hillary was juggling her various roles as working wife, mother, and her husband's political keeper, Bill also kept himself busy. His return to office in 1983 triggered a frenzy of sexual activity that would continue unabated for nine years and involve, by Clinton's own account, "hundreds and hundreds" of women. "You know why people go into politics, don't you?" he asked a female friend one night. "It's because of their unsatisfied sexual desire."

The friend was taken aback. "It was completely out of the blue," she said, "and I remember thinking, 'Hmm, that's a very odd thing to say.'"

By using the state troopers assigned to drive him as virtual procurers, Clinton was able to juggle as many as a dozen simultaneous affairs *and* several one-night stands per week. Many were young college girls—often the daughters of party officials and contributors. "There were all those young girls who genuinely thought that a governor was in love with them," one of the Clintons' closest confidants observed. "When you're nineteen or twenty and the *governor* is hitting on you, it is easy to lose your bearings. None of these young women would ever come forward because they'd been victimized once, and they did not want to be victimized again." Troopers Roger Perry and Larry Patterson later testified that they were ordered by Clinton to approach women and obtain their addresses and phone numbers, make hotel arrangements, drive the governor to his various trysting spots, and then stand guard. Sometimes they loaned him their own state cars so he could drive himself to rendezvous points. On other occasions, they ferried Bill from one bar or nightclub to another as he trolled for female "constituents." In exchange, the troopers conceded, Bill let the troopers have "residuals"—women Clinton was no longer interested in.

On numerous occasions, the troopers sneaked women into the Governor's Mansion while Chelsea and Hillary were asleep. Perry and Patterson said it was their job to stand at the bottom of the staircase leading to the family quarters and alert him if Hillary stirred awake.

Although Perry and Patterson were roughly the same age as Clinton, his obscenity-laced conversations with them rarely went beyond sports talk and vulgar sexual remarks. "He just wanted us to think of him as another good ol' boy at heart," Perry said.

Another trooper, Larry Douglass Brown, occupied a special place in the Clinton household. A native of rural Pine Bluff and a particular favorite of the governor's, "L.D." was also engaged to Chelsea's nanny Becky McCoy (whose mother, Ann McCoy, was, in turn, the mansion's administrator). Bill took the earnest young man under his wing, lending him copies of his favorite historical biographies, discussing political matters with him, offering him career advice. Ultimately, Clinton would even use his influence in Washington to make it possible for Brown to join the Central Intelligence Agency.

Brown would later say in sworn deposition that, during his stint at the Governor's Mansion between 1983 and 1985, one of his principal assignments was to solicit women for his boss—by his count, "over a hundred at least." Bill rated them on a scale of one to ten, and called the women he found most appealing "ripe peaches." According to Brown, Clinton was constantly grading women: "every—pretty much every—woman that we would see—eight, nine, ten, seven, six, whatever." Bill Clinton, he concluded, "thinks women were meant to be chased, dominated, and conquered."

Ironically, Brown and the other guards would also testify that Robyn Dickey, who preceded Ann McCoy as mansion administrator, confessed to having an affair with Clinton. (Dickey, who later denied the affair, would eventually be named chief of protocol at the Pentagon—but not before spending time as an aide at the White

House, where her famous presidential back rubs earned her the nickname "Thumbs.")

Brown would also testify under oath that Susan "Hot Pants" McDougal was among those Clinton trysted with when Hillary was out of town. "Bill told me he had a sexual relationship with Susan," said Brown, who drove Clinton to McDougal's condominium on "numerous" occasions.

Jim McDougal's suspicions about his wife's relationship with Clinton had been confirmed in 1982 when, because of a crossed phone line, he suddenly found himself eavesdropping on a clandestine conversation between his wife and his friend.

"Susan and Bill Clinton were talking—an intimate conversation filled with giggles and sexual innuendo," McDougal recalled. "I was left with no doubt that they were carrying on an affair."

That same day, McDougal asked Susan point-blank if she was having an affair with Bill Clinton. "Rather than lying clumsily," he said, "Susan acknowledged her relationship with Bill."

Although she would deny that she had had an ongoing affair with Bill, he was careful not to issue any such denials. Years later, when as President he was about to testify in a Whitewater-related case, he told Dick Morris that he was worried that the affair would become public.

"I'm worried. What happens," Bill asked Morris, "if they ask me under oath whether I had sex with Susan McDougal or not?"

Morris did not bother to ask whether it was true; he assumed the President would not be worried about answering the question truthfully if the answer were no.

"If you had sex with her, admit it," Morris told Clinton. "Tell the truth . . . The one thing, sir, I beg you, is don't commit perjury, because then nobody can help you."

Clinton, as it happened, was never asked if he had had sex with McDougal.

In the mid-1980s, however, McDougal scarcely had a monopoly on Bill's affections. He was now also seeing Gennifer Flowers more frequently. On one occasion, Bill's behavior left Gennifer "shaken." They were in bed together when suddenly Bill leaped up, backed himself against the wall, and then broke down weeping. He stood there for a few moments, crying into his hands, unable or unwilling to tell Flowers what was wrong. Then he returned to bed and resumed where he had left off.

"I didn't know why and he wouldn't tell me," she said of the bizarre incident. "I couldn't tell if he felt guilty, if maybe he felt some deep emotion with me he realized he'd never get anywhere else, or what."

If it was a sign of guilt—or merely mounting anxiety over the possibility of getting caught—Bill's behavior grew increasingly reckless throughout the 1980s. At one point he invited Flowers to sing at the Governor's Mansion during a party. When he tried to lure Gennifer into the bathroom for sex during one of her breaks, she pointed out that Hillary had just brushed right past her without saying a word.

"Come on, Bill, she *knows* what's going on, for God's sake," Gennifer said.

"Oh," he said within earshot of several guests, "you mean 'Hilla the Hun'?"

When she got home, Flowers complained to her roommate Lauren Kirk about being pointedly snubbed by Hillary. "That tight-ass bitch," Flowers said. "She cut me dead!"

"Well, no wonder," Kirk answered. "What do you expect? You're sleeping with her husband."

"Yeah," Gennifer laughed, "and I'll keep on doing it." Flowers's bravado masked a belief that someday he would leave Hillary for her. "I guess deep in my heart I hoped he'd marry me one day," she later said. "I used to have this fantasy: If Bill got into the White House and was a great President, then maybe nobody would care if he was divorced. I wanted to believe so badly that what I shared with Bill was different, special . . ."

Whether or not Bill regarded his relationship with Flowers as "special," Hillary did know about it. When Bill's wife walked into the room one afternoon just as he was finishing up a furtive phone conversation, she blithely asked, "How's Gennifer doing?" Before Bill could stammer a response, she stormed out of the room.

Despite his insistence to Virginia that he had "had it up to here with beauty queens," Bill was juggling affairs with at least three in the mid-1980s. A native of tiny Booneville, Elizabeth Ward was twenty-one when she entered the Miss Arkansas pageant wearing a dress made of peach tablecloth material that she had hand-embroidered with rhinestones. She won, and the next year was crowned Miss America.

Ward married her high school sweetheart and moved to Manhattan to study acting. In 1983 she made a trip home to Arkansas to attend a benefit, and it was there that she ran into Bill Clinton. He offered her a lift to Quapaw Tower, where she was staying, and they flirted in the back of the limousine. "He's a very charming, handsome man," she later said.

Three days later, Elizabeth Ward Gracen met Clinton at her apartment at Quapaw Tower—the same building where Flowers resided—and they slept together. But Gracen's friend Judy Stokes would testify under oath that there was more to the story—that Gracen had tearfully told her that Bill Clinton had forced her to have sex in the back of a limousine. Stokes's testimony was disputed by Gracen, though it seemed to echo portions of Juanita Broaddrick's harrowing account of being sexually assaulted by then–Attorney General Clinton in a Little Rock hotel room. Whether it took place in the back of a limousine or in an apartment, Gracen did concede that the sex they had was rough—and that at one point Bill bit down on her lip hard enough to make it bleed.

Bill phoned Gracen in New York, trying to convince her to continue their affair. "I told him I was very uncomfortable," she recalled. "I never spoke to him about it again.

"I made a very bad error in judgment. You think you can get away with these things, but they always come back down the road . . . I was very young, but I always knew what I was doing. It's behavior that I wouldn't recommend to any young women, no matter what degree of glamour or glitter there seems to be at first."

At the same time he was seducing the former Miss America, Bill was also pursuing African-American beauty Lencola Sullivan, Gracen's predecessor as Miss Arkansas and fourth runner-up in the Miss America pageant. Clinton and Sullivan met while she was working as a reporter for KARK-TV, the same station where Flowers was briefly employed.

When he ran for reelection in 1984, Little Rock was rife with rumors about Clinton and Sullivan. His advisors warned him that, at least in Arkansas, an interracial romance could cost him the election. Overnight, Sullivan left town for New York. When she returned to her hometown of Morrilton four years later, Sullivan arrived with her new boyfriend, singer Stevie Wonder.

According to a sworn affidavit filed by onetime Clinton aide Larry Nichols, Bill was also carrying on an affair with Deborah Mathis, another attractive young African-American woman and a former columnist for the *Arkansas Gazette*. When Flowers finally heard the rumors in 1990, she called Mathis, who worked at KARK when she did, and asked her about them. "It's garbage," Mathis shot back. But Flowers was not convinced. She remembered that Bill, who was aware the two women had known each other, had specifically instructed her not to tell Mathis—as opposed to any other journalist—about their affair.

"When I heard the rumors that Bill had been with other women, I was devastated," Flowers said. "I didn't believe it. He'd always told me I was the only one, and I believed him. Not once did he ever hint he was seeing someone else."

Bill called Gennifer to reassure her that the rumors were false, and even joked that "one fella told me I had good taste." When pressed, Bill vehemently denied everything. "It's a pack of lies," he said, recalling the time he had told Flowers he had "retired" from wholesale philandering. "And now I'm glad I have, because they've scoured the waterfront. I have talked to Elizabeth Ward maybe three times in my whole life . . . I don't know how she made the grade. At least Lencola Sullivan is a friend of mine. I've never slept with her, but she does come to see me, so I can see why . . ."

As he had done and would continue to do throughout his career, Bill parsed every syllable very carefully. He had, in fact, only spoken to Ward "maybe three times in my whole life." And he may well not have "slept" with Lencola Sullivan. Yet for the time being, Flowers would admit, "I believed his explanation. He had told me what I wanted to hear."

None of them knew about yet *another* former beauty queen, Miss Arkansas of 1958, Sally Perdue, whose affair with Bill Clinton began in 1983. As with the others, troopers Patterson, Perry, and Brown would drop Clinton off in front of her Little Rock apartment complex and wait outside while he spent between one and four hours inside. For the most part, Perdue later said, he behaved "like any other good ol' boy"—perhaps with a few small exceptions. She recalled one particular evening when Bill arrived carrying his saxophone. Later, she claimed, he borrowed one of her black negligees, slipped it over his head, and paraded around her apartment playing the sax.

Their relationship flourished until Perdue announced one day that she was thinking of running for mayor of the Arkansas town of Pine Bluff.

"You'd . . . you'd better not run for mayor," he objected.

"And why not?"

"I'm warning you," he said angrily. "You're not running for anything." From there, the dispute escalated, and when it was over, so was the affair. "I don't think," she told one British journalist, "he wanted me to be an independent thinker at that point." More likely, he wanted to keep his sex life and his political life separate—and at all costs keep from provoking Hillary. "She had given up her own ambitions for public office to promote his career," a former member of his staff observed. "If she thought he was helping some other woman run for office, that would have been the end of the marriage." (Perdue did run for mayor, and lost.)

Troopers Patterson and Perry would also testify under oath that they stood guard while women performed oral sex on Bill in parked cars outside the mansion—often while Hillary was at home. Late one evening a clerk he picked up at a department store appeared at the mansion in a yellow and black pickup truck. Bill climbed into the front seat, and then she parked behind the mansion. Patterson, meantime, aimed one of the mansion's remote-controlled security cameras through the windshield and watched on the twenty-seven-inch video screen in the guardhouse.

At about this time, Bill took up jogging, ostensibly to control his weight. It soon became apparent, however, that he had an unrealistic view of what that exercise could accomplish. Often, he would jog right into a local McDonald's, where he would reward himself with two Big Macs and a large order of fries. "This running thing is great," he would say. "You can jog a few minutes and then eat anything you want!"

There were additional benefits, however. Bill quickly discovered that his jogs could provide cover for his amorous liaisons during the day. Clinton's routine seldom varied: He would emerge from the Governor's Mansion in shorts, T-shirt, and baseball cap, then start jogging down the street with a state police car trailing him. After about half a block—as soon as he was out of sight of the mansion—he jumped into the car and went straight to a hotel or apartment complex for a prearranged assignation. An hour later, he would get back into the car, be dropped a block or so from the mansion, and run back. "He'd be huffing and puffing like he was really winded," said one of Clinton's secretaries. "Which I'm sure he was."

"There had been a number of times," Larry Patterson would later testify under oath, "when Bill Clinton told me, 'The lady in the red dress,' or 'The lady in the green dress,' whatever, or color of hair or distinguishing characteristics. 'Would you get me her name and phone number? She has that come-hither look.'"

Patterson also stood by and watched while one woman—the department store salesclerk—performed oral sex on him one evening in the parking lot of Chelsea's school, Booker Elementary. According to Patterson, Clinton was fully aware that he had an audience and "seemed perfectly fine with it . . . He claimed that there was nothing wrong with what he was doing—that he had studied the Bible carefully and oral sex was not really sex. As far as he was concerned, he was not cheating on Hillary because oral sex was technically not considered adultery."

On August 31, 1984, one of the music world's most celebrated practitioners of this particular art, rock groupie "Sweet, Sweet Connie" Hamzy, was stretched out next to the pool at Little Rock's Riverfront Hilton when she realized that several men were staring at her from a hotel window. By this time Hamzy, who had been immortalized in the Grand Funk Railroad classic "We're an American Band," had numbered among her conquests scores of rock luminaries, including Mick Fleetwood, Huey Lewis, Don Henley, and Keith Moon.

A man in a blue suit emerged and said, "Hi, I work for Governor Clinton. The governor would like to meet you."

"You're kidding," Hamzy replied. "But," she said, pointing down at her "teensy-weensy" purple bikini, "I can't meet the governor. I don't have any clothes on."

"I'm sure that's fine with him." The aide laughed. "That's why he wants to meet you."

Connie walked inside and saw Clinton standing in a hallway with one of the troopers and an aide. The three men left as soon they brought Hamzy inside.

"You looked so good lying out there by the pool," Bill said, "that I just had to meet you. You really made my day."

"Thank you, Governor. You know, we actually met once before, a few years ago, backstage at an Olivia Newton-John concert—"

"Look," he said, interrupting her. "I'd love to get with you. Where can we go? Do you have a room here?"

"No, I live nearby and just sneak in to use the pool once in a while. But," she added, reaching out to touch his crotch, "I hear you're pretty wild. I'd love to get with you, too."

Clinton grabbed her hand and led her down the hall, opening the door to each meeting room and then shutting it once he saw it was occupied. "Where can we go?" he said, the tension in his voice mounting. "Where can we go? Are any of the rooms open? *Where can we go?*"

Hamzy suggested that Bill get an aide to book them a room under an assumed name. "I don't really have time for that," he replied, suggesting instead that they sneak into one of the main-floor banquet rooms.

So again they walked down yet another hallway, she said, "fondling each other and trying every doorknob." Finally, he came to one that was unlocked. "It was the laundry room," she said. "He didn't think we should go in there because people were inside."

"How can I get in touch with you?" he asked.

"I'm in the book," Hamzy said.

Then, as he walked off, Clinton turned and asked how long she would be at the pool.

"All afternoon," she said, reaching up to kiss him. "Come back by."

Then, according to Hamzy, Bill "smiled, got in the car with his guard and aides, and left." Years later, to counter Clinton's denials that the episode happened the way she recounted it, Hamzy submitted to a polygraph examination—and passed.

The Hamzy encounter merely underscored the frantic, random nature of Bill's sexual adventures. That summer of 1984, after speaking at a party fund-raiser in Mississippi, Bill asked an attractive twenty-four-year-old blond congressional campaign worker named Karen Hinton to join him, writer Willie Morris, and several others for dinner. Bill managed to sit next to Hinton, and after chatting with her for half an hour, wrote something on a napkin and slipped it to her. When she unfolded it, she saw that Bill had scrawled his room number at the Holiday Inn, followed by "?"

Hinton's reaction? "I felt," she said, "a bit humiliated." So did many others who, like Hinton, were not remotely interested in taking the married young governor up on his offer.

And even though there were plenty of women who did, it soon became obvious to the state troopers who guarded him that the various long-running affairs and spur-of-the-moment one-night stands were not enough. Bill reportedly began seeking out the services of prostitutes.

In 1983, twenty-four-year-old Bobbie Ann Williams and several other African-American hookers were plying their trade on Spring Street not far from the Governor's Mansion when Bill jogged into view. He stopped to talk to them, but then continued on his way. Three days later, he stopped again—this time pulling Williams behind a thick hedge, where she performed oral sex. "He talked the whole time I was doing it," she said. "Then after he was done, he pulled up his pants and ran off jogging."

Two weeks later, Williams told a tabloid, Clinton arranged to pick up Williams and two of her friends in one of his white Lincolns. With Bill and the three prostitutes in the back of the car, they barreled down John Barrow Road headed for a small house in a secluded spot on the edge of Hot Springs.

Williams would describe the secluded house—a green wood-shingled cabin that belonged to Bill's mother—in minute detail. The property, ringed by a chain-link fence, was nestled on the bank of a lake and boasted a thirty-foot dock. Inside, the walnut-paneled living room featured a small fireplace and oversized leather furniture. Bill's awards and trophies were everywhere, along with photographs dating from his childhood.

That night, according to Williams, one of the troopers stood outside smoking cigarettes while Bill and his guests walked in the door, shed their clothes, and headed for the bedroom. "Bill—we called him Bill from the start—smiled and flopped down on his back on the bed, just laying there, stretched out and naked . . . We all three crawled into bed with him and started playing around . . ."

Confronted with the story, Virginia Kelley (by now she had married husband number four, Richard Kelley) claimed that her son "never comes to this house." But her next-door neighbors, Effie Kirby and Darlene Lewis, disagreed. "Bill uses his mom's place to get away from the stress that he's under," Kirby said. The neighbors had even become friends with Clinton's drivers, including Captain Raymond L. "Buddy" Young, supervisor of Clinton's security detail. Young and the others often passed the time chatting with Kirby and Lewis while Bill "unwound" inside.

Williams was still working on the stretch of Spring Street known as "Hooker's Row" in 1984 when she met Bill on the street and told him she was four months pregnant. Clinton "just laughed," Williams recalled. "He was rubbing my big belly and said, 'Girl, that can't be my baby.'"

Throughout her pregnancy, Williams told her family that the baby she was expecting was Bill Clinton's. But no one believed her—until Williams gave birth to her son Danny at Little Rock's University Hospital in 1985. "He was white," Williams's sister, Lucille Bolton, said of the infant. "That's when I started believing my sister. And as Danny got older, he started to look more and more like the governor."

Danny was only a few months old when his mother went to jail on drug and prostitution charges. Bolton then became his court-appointed guardian, and Danny went to live with his aunt in a run-down section of Little Rock.

Incensed that Clinton would allow his putative son to grow up in grinding poverty, Bolton would finally go to the Governor's Mansion in 1991 to meet with Clinton's aides. "They took my name and address and asked me some questions about the boy, then I never heard another word from them."

What Bolton did not know was that the governor's inner circle—well aware of what one called Clinton's "sexual rampage" through Little Rock—had already heard rumblings that he had fathered a black child. They broached the subject with Bill, who angrily denied that he had ever even met anyone named Lucille Bolton. Technically, he was telling the truth: He hadn't met Bolton. The woman who claimed to be the mother of his son was not Bolton, but Bobbie Ann Williams.

"It was an open secret around Little Rock," one of Clinton's bodyguards maintained. "But the attitude was: 'She's a black hooker on drugs with a criminal record. Who's going to believe a word she says?'"

But Bobbie Ann Williams and Lucille Bolton were given lie detector tests by two separate independent investigators. In both cases, the results indicated the women were telling the truth about Clinton's encounters with Williams as well as the meeting with his advisors.

Moreover, Bobbie Ann's husband, Dan Williams, went so far as to drive up beside the governor while he was jogging and confront him about the little boy. According to Dan Williams, Clinton reached into the pocket of his running shorts, pulled out a roll of bills—presumably cash intended to pay for sex that day—and tossed it through the car window into the front seat, all without breaking stride.

Neither Bill Clinton nor any of his spokesmen would actually publicly deny Bobbie Ann Williams's oft-repeated claim that he had paid for sex with her, or that Clinton fathered her son. But the story gained momentum, in part because local African-American activist Robert "Say" McIntosh had taken up Williams's cause and the allegations were detailed in a tabloid. At a closed-door meeting with Democrats in Chicago, an exasperated Clinton finally protested, "Listen, I don't have a black baby!" But Bill also refused to supply the blood sample that would, presumably, prove his claim that he was not the little boy's father.

In January 1999, the *Star* would make headlines when it obtained DNA samples from Bobbie Ann and Danny Williams and compared them to the analysis of Bill Clinton's DNA published in the Starr Report. No match, the *Star*'s editors claimed. But other DNA experts countered that it would have been "impossible" to make any definitive comparison based solely on the information provided in the Starr Report. Danny, meanwhile, would continue to grow up sleeping on the floor of his aunt's cramped apartment.

No sooner did one rumor flicker out than another burst into flame. Yet—to both the surprise and delight of his inner circle—throughout the 1980s neither Clinton's political opponents nor the Arkansas press made any concerted effort to investigate. Bill even found the time to taunt the woman he had allegedly raped at the Camelot Hotel in 1978. When Juanita Broaddrick's Brownwood Manor was judged the best nursing home in the state in 1984, the governor sent her an official congratulatory letter. At the bottom, he scrawled in his own hand, "I admire you very much." Broaddrick later said the note "sent a shiver down my spine. I didn't know what to think, what he meant by it . . ."

To gain sympathy with his lovers, by the mid-1980s Bill was now claiming his wife had cut him off sexually. In 1984, Dolly Kyle claimed, "Bill told me his sex life with Hillary was over. But that does not mean Hillary wasn't sleeping with him. I took it to mean that he wasn't *enjoying* sex with Hillary. It just wasn't any fun for him anymore, if it ever really was . . ."

If the physical relationship between Bill and Hillary was now in a dormant state, all indications are that this was more his choice than hers. Frequently the Clintons forgot that there were cameras and microphones planted all over the mansion. One day Larry Patterson was in the guardhouse and was listening on an audio monitor as Bill and Hillary quarreled in the kitchen. "I need to be fucked," Hillary said quite distinctly, "more than twice a year."

Her anger and frustration aside, her friends insisted that Hillary remained very much in love with Bill during this time. "Bill and I have always loved each other," she said. "Just because a marriage isn't perfect doesn't mean you walk away from it." Yet, as they entered their second decade as a married couple, Hillary wondered how much longer the cheating and deception could go on. According to journalist Connie Bruck, Hillary was "devastated and humiliated by his behavior during this period, but determined not to leave the marriage in which she had invested so deeply."

That did not mean, however, that she was willing to suppress her rage and accept the status quo. Once she awoke shortly after 1 A.M., turned on the light on the bedstead, and then called down to the guardhouse in search of her husband. According to the troopers, the governor had left no specific instructions on what to say if Hillary asked where he was.

Flustered, Trooper Roger Perry reached for an answer. "The governor," he said, "has gone out for a drive, Mrs. Clinton."

"The sorry damn son of a bitch!" she screamed.

Perry frantically began dialing the numbers of Clinton's various girlfriends until he finally reached him.

"Oh, God, God, God," Bill said. "What did you tell her?"

"That you were out for a drive. You'd better get here right away."

Bill pulled up in his white car, got out, and gingerly pushed open the aluminum screen door leading to the kitchen. He was startled to see Hillary standing there, leaning against the kitchen counter in her robe and slippers, fuming.

"Where the FUCK HAVE YOU BEEN?" Hillary could be heard screaming.

Bill stammered back something inaudible to the troopers standing outside.

"Goddamn it, Bill, HOW LONG DO YOU EXPECT ME TO PUT UP WITH THIS SHIT?"

With that, Bill shouted back, and for the next fifteen minutes they hurled obscenity-laced invectives at each other while the stunned troopers and household staffers listened. Their words were punctuated by the sound of drawers slamming shut, fists pounding on the kitchen table, and smashing glass and crockery.

Once they stormed off in other directions, Perry walked in to survey the damage. A cupboard door had been ripped off its hinges.

Food had spilled out of the refrigerator and onto the floor, and there were shards of glass and shattered dishes everywhere.

At one point during the mayhem, eight-year-old Chelsea could be seen peering out her bedroom door with frightened eyes. For all their undeniable devotion to Chelsea, Bill and Hillary's formidable tempers often blinded them to the fact that their daughter was within earshot. Chelsea would later confide to friends that her parents' pitched battles often left her feeling anxious and fearful. "They yell at each other a lot," she told one. "And that made me worry that they were going to get a divorce. But then my mom told me not to worry—that all parents fight sometimes, and that it doesn't mean they don't still love each other."

Fortunately for Chelsea, most of the skirmishes—which over the course of the Clinton marriage occurred several times a week—occurred either when she was at school or when her parents were together on the road. Often their quarrels took place in the back of the limousine. "They would start throwing things," one trooper said. "Styrofoam cups, books, papers, pens, keys—anything they could get their hands on. And if they weren't throwing something at each other, they were throwing something at us—or at nobody in particular."

Once the car pulled up to their destination, "they would straighten themselves, then be all smiles as they got of the car holding each other's hand. No one would believe that a minute earlier it looked like they were going to murder each other."

There were other times when they simply gave each other the silent treatment. Once State Trooper Roger Perry drove them for two hours "and they never said a word to each other." Perry also contradicted accounts by others who claimed the Clintons could be affectionate. In his seven years on the security detail, Perry said, he "never saw them embrace. I never saw them kiss. I never saw them throw a softball or talk about family dinners. Everybody wanted to see the caring family. But I never saw it."

Nearly everyone saw at least one battle, however. One morning, the mansion staff stood by while Hillary erupted over something Bill had been quoted as saying in the *Arkansas Gazette*. "I came into the mansion," Larry Patterson said, "and he was standing at the top of the stairs and she was standing at the bottom screaming . . . She was calling him motherfucker and everything else."

At the root of her anger was jealousy. She was often forced to endure the indignity of having Bill make passes at women at public events, sometimes in her presence. "Come on, Bill," she would often say, "put your dick up. You can't fuck her here."

Patterson walked into the kitchen where the cook, who had never been known to say anything negative about Hillary in the past, now shook her head. Sometimes, she said, "the devil's in that woman."

To be sure, Clinton was even more volatile; he could still be counted on to terrorize aides and advisors on a more or less regular basis. Once he hurled an apple from the backseat of his car and it splattered on the windshield. More than once he overturned a table or swept everything off a desk with one motion of his hand. While Perry looked on, he became so enraged during a cell phone conversation that he smashed the phone to pieces on the sidewalk. Years later, Clinton advisor George Stephanopoulos would say he occasionally felt as if one of his key roles was to be yelled at by Bill first thing in the morning—a ritual that for his boss seemed to have a cathartic effect.

In confrontations with Hillary, however, his behavior was altogether different. She always initiated their fights—no one could ever recall witnessing an exchange where he fired the first shot. And while he often shouted back, it was not with the full force and fury that marked his verbal attacks on underlings.

It was also not uncommon for Bill to essentially remain silent while his wife berated him. "She could scream and scream at him and he would just sit there turning bright pink, absorbing it," said one staffer. "It was tough to watch." Most of those who worked at the Governor's Mansion agreed with Trooper Larry Gleghorn, who began guarding the Clintons during their first term in office: "He was afraid of her."

Perhaps with some reason, since she was by far the more physical when it came to sparring. "She was a thrower—big time," said a member of Clinton's 1984 campaign staff. At least twice in the presence of aides, she hurled a pen at him when he failed to respond to a question. Another time, a stapler. On yet another occasion, a briefing book.

Files, paper clips, and yellow legal pads were often thrown in the air or sent flying across the room in the heat of anger. Sometimes, without warning, Hillary would take aim squarely at Bill's head. "God, Bill," she said after beaning him with a Styrofoam coffee cup from across the room, "what lousy reflexes."

Indeed, Hillary admitted on various occasions to friends like Diane Blair and Carolyn Staley that she couldn't "see the point of being married if you can't mix it up a little . . . Politics is conflict, and so is marriage."

She also argued that it was better to confront problems head-on rather than allow them to fester. "There are a lot of big and little things that come up in a marriage that if you don't deal with them right then and there, they can sink you."

Yet the more she struggled to stay afloat by confronting Bill's infidelity, the more his lies and evasiveness threatened to pull them under. Their many fights notwithstanding, Hillary was frustrated in her attempts to get at the truth. "If he doesn't want you to know something," Dick Morris later said, "you'll never get it out of him."

Understandably, Hillary lashed out at the most convenient targets—the good ol' boy state troopers she suspected of pimping for her husband. She became livid when she caught them smoking in the cars or on the grounds of the Governor's Mansion, chided them for being overweight, and snapped at them when they wore cowboy boots. "Jesus Christ," one trooper recalled her yelling, "when will you shit-kickers ever learn that cowboy boots ARE NOT PART OF THE UNIFORM!"

From her husband, she had picked up the habit of blasting the troopers when they reminded her she was running late for an appointment ("Fuck off! You don't tell *me* when to go") and then blaming them when they arrived at their destination an hour late. L. D. Brown, Patterson, Perry, and the others often heard both Bill and Hillary complain bitterly about having to deal with "rednecks," clearly lumping them into that category. "But Hillary," Patterson said, "really meant it." Said Trooper Gleghorn: "She was a bitch day in and day out."

Hillary's recurring complaint centered on what she saw as an unwarranted invasion of her privacy. She did not want the state troopers shadowing her, and told them so in no uncertain terms. "We all got used to her screaming, 'Just get the hell away from me,'" said one trooper who claimed that once, out of sheer frustration, she tried to kick him.

Gleghorn, concerned that Hillary was preventing the troopers from guarding the governor and his family, asked Bill to intercede.

"You'll have to fight your own battles with her," the governor responded, and then watched as Gleghorn confronted his wife.

"As far as I'm concerned," the trooper told Hillary, "you're the property of the state of Arkansas, and we're going to do our job and protect you."

"Man, I was sure she was going to rip his head off," Clinton later said. But instead of blasting Gleghorn for impertinence, she simply listened impassively, then calmly walked away.

Gleghorn and the other troopers kept an eye on not only the immediate members of the First Family, but also on the governor's aspiring rock star brother. Beginning in the mid-1970s, Roger Clinton had begun using cocaine, and quickly became addicted. By 1984 he was snorting the drug some sixteen times a day, and dealing drugs to support his four-gram-a-day habit.

Although Bill was actively worried about the possible political fallout from his brother's activities, there were lingering questions in Little Rock circles concerning the governor's own drug use. Sharlene Wilson, a Little Rock bartender and convicted drug dealer, testified under oath to a federal grand jury that she had sold cocaine to Roger on several occasions at the nightclub where she worked. She stated that, in full view of other guests, Roger handed cocaine to his brother and then watched as Bill snorted it. Governor Clinton, Wilson claimed, "would often snort cocaine."

Several others agreed. Jane Parks, the manager of a Little Rock apartment complex where Roger lived briefly in 1984, said she saw Bill drop by often. Standing in the hallway outside apartment B107, Parks said she could hear the brothers' distinctive voices as they talked about the pot they were smoking and the cocaine they shared.

Even Bill's on-again, off-again lover Sally Perdue said that during their 1983 affair the governor offered her joints from a cigarette case and cocaine from a plasticine bag that he poured out onto the coffee table in her Little Rock living room. "He had all the equipment laid out," Perdue said, "like a real pro."

Roger Clinton himself unintentionally offered damning evidence of his brother's drug use. Narcotics officers in Hot Springs claimed that during their undercover investigation into Roger's drug dealing in 1984, a hidden video camera recorded him telling a supplier, "Got to get some for my brother. He's got a nose like a vacuum cleaner."

Beyond the question of whether Bill was a recreational user of marijuana and cocaine, his links to Roger's biggest customer, high-flying investment banker and racehorse owner Dan Lasater, were of deep concern to enemies and allies alike. Lasater, who openly served cocaine at his lavish parties for Arkansas's movers and shakers, was Roger's biggest customer. The financier had also lent Roger $8,000 to pay off drug debts after Roger told Lasater that cocaine dealers were "threatening him, his mother, and brother." At Bill's urging, Lasater also hired Roger to work on his thousand-acre horse farm near Ocala, Florida.

But Roger was not nearly as indebted to Lasater as his brother was. The financier was one of Clinton's principal fund-raisers and a major contributor to all his campaigns. In turn, Bill, who was a guest at several of those parties at which cocaine was served, per-sonally intervened to make certain that Lasater's brokerage firm was selected to underwrite $637 million worth of state bond offerings—a role that meant more than $1.7 million in fees between 1983 and 1986.

In the summer of 1984 Governor Bill Clinton was informed that his brother was suspected of dealing drugs, and that state and local narcotics officers were secretly videotaping Roger in the act of using and selling cocaine. Bill's first impulse was to intervene in some manner, or at the very least warn his brother and thereby sabotage the sting operation.

Hillary would have none of it. Bill was now riding an unprece-dented wave of popularity; a voting public unaware of his private life was about to elect Clinton to a third term. "But if you interfere with this investigation, Bill," she told him, "our enemies will use it against us—and we'll lose everything." Besides, Hillary argued, this way Roger might get the professional help he needed to kick his addiction.

Persuaded by Hillary that rescuing his brother was not an option, Bill informed State Police Colonel Tommy Goodwin he would not interfere with the investigation. "Just go ahead and handle it," the governor wrote, "like you would any other case."

Although it may have been one of the worst-kept "secret" sting operations in history, Bill and Hillary both spoke with Roger on numerous occasions during that period without ever warning him. Neither did they tell Virginia Kelley, knowing full well that she would have alerted Roger to the danger.

The videotapes, shot in the apartment of one of his regular customers, showed Roger snorting cocaine as he bragged about the power and influence of "Big Brother" and how the Clinton name would enable him to live the millionaire's lifestyle he felt he so richly deserved. "We're closer than any brothers you've ever known," Roger said between hits of cocaine. "See, I didn't have a father growing up and he was like a father to me growing up, all my life, so that's why we've always been so close. There isn't anything in the world he wouldn't do for me . . ."

When he was arrested on August 2, 1984, Roger denied everything until he was shown the incontrovertible evidence on the videotapes. Told of the imminent arrest, Bill, visibly shaken, held a hastily called press conference. "My brother," he said, "has apparently become involved in drugs, a curse which has reached epidemic proportions and has plagued the lives of millions of families in our nation, including many in our state."

Then he and Hillary traveled to Hot Springs for a family strategy session. Virginia would later recall that Roger was so upset over the shame he had brought upon his beloved brother and mother that he threatened suicide.

"I caused it!" Roger cried. "I can end it!"

Bill sprang from his chair, grabbed his brother, and shook him. "How dare you think that way!" he shouted.

On August 14, 1984, Roger Clinton would plead not guilty to

six counts of drug dealing and conspiracy. Three months later and only seventy-two hours after his brother was reelected governor by a margin of two to one, Roger changed his plea to guilty on the conspiracy charge and a single count of distribution.

Virginia, who now referred to Roger as "a fourteen-year-old in a twenty-eight-year-old's body," sat alongside Bill and Hillary in the federal courtroom in Little Rock as Roger heard his sentence: two years at the federal prison at Fort Worth, Texas. It could have been worse. Federal prosecutor Asa Hutchinson (who would later be one of the Republican "managers" prosecuting Clinton in his 1999 impeachment trial before the U.S. Senate), agreed to the deal only if Roger agreed to testify in other drug cases. His testimony led to the conviction of Dan Lasater, among others, who would serve a six-month prison term on drug charges.

As his brother was led away in handcuffs, Bill took advantage of the moment to make a statement on the courthouse steps. "I feel more deeply committed than ever before," the governor said, "to do everything I can to fight illegal drugs in our state."

At the same time as their wrenching family drama played out behind the scenes, Bill and Hillary collected one honor after another. The National Association of Social Workers named Hillary "Public Citizen of the Year," the *Arkansas Democrat* crowned her its "Woman of the Year," and *Esquire* magazine named them both among the 272 "best of the new generation."

If anything, Roger's arrest worked to Bill's political advantage. Not only did he show himself to be a concerned older brother, but by not interfering Bill also sent an important message to drug traffickers—that no one, not even the governor's brother, was above the law.

Beneath it all, insisted Betsey Wright, there was genuine pain. "It was like every worst nightmare you ever had come true," she said, adding that other crises the Clintons had faced were "a piece of cake compared to the pain they went through over Roger Clinton's drug arrest and addiction. That's because it was real, it was true, it was personal, and it was someone they loved."

For Hillary, the crisis provided an opportunity to confront not just Bill but all the Clintons on an emotional level. In the weeks leading up to Roger's sentencing, he was ordered by the court to undergo therapy for his drug problem. At the request of his counselor, Karen Ballard, Bill, Hillary, and Virginia joined in the sessions.

"That was incredibly cathartic for them," Hillary's friend Kris Rogers recalled. "Hillary was really one of the first to open up and talk about what she saw as some of the vulnerabilities of that family. She's very good at capturing what's going on in people's hearts and minds, sometimes saying it for them better than they can themselves. I think she does that for Bill a lot."

Not that the Clintons—Virginia in particular—readily agreed with Hillary's assessment of them. Virginia was willing to concede that to survive Roger's drunken outbursts she steeped herself in denial, creating something of a fantasy world in which she could function. The same could be said of both her sons. But Virginia bristled when Hillary suggested that her gambling might also be symptomatic of more deep-seated psychological troubles.

Still, Kris Rogers insisted that Hillary regarded this period of self-analysis as "one of the real watersheds for them. I think it made her feel closer to Bill."

Even blunt-spoken Hillary dared not broach the subject of her in-laws' other addiction. Flirtatious, fun-loving Virginia was a nightclub-hopping good-time girl, and none of the men that came in and out of their lives could be called models of sexual probity.

It was hard to determine what impact, if any, all the soul-searching was having on Roger Clinton. Even as he awaited his sentencing, Bill's little brother brought a string of girls to the Governor's Mansion to snort cocaine.

Bill had often spoken of the impact William Blythe's early death had had on him—how it led him to live his own life at a frenetic pace, as if he were in a race against time. But he had never examined the ways in which his stepfather had shaped his psyche, or sought to determine how the family's history of alcoholism and domestic violence was still influencing his behavior.

In typical Clinton fashion, he pored over a dozen books on alcoholism and its effects on families. "Bill," Wright said, "became very introspective, did a lot of reading about co-dependence." What intrigued him most was the idea that the children of alcoholics, faced with conflict and chaos at home, often do whatever they can to avoid it as adults.

Employing the appropriate pop-psyche jargon, Bill told the *Washington Post*, "People say my number one weakness is that I'm conflict-averse. I think part of that is I'm always trying to work things out because that's the role I played for a long time."

Hillary, of course, did not shy away from conflict; she thrived on it. During Bill's try for a fourth term as governor in 1986, she was a lightning rod for criticism—much of it directed at what many perceived to be blatant conflicts of interest stemming from her work at the Rose Law Firm.

Worried that she was not bringing enough business into the firm, she went to her Whitewater Development partners Jim and Susan McDougal and asked them to put her on retainer representing the thrift they owned, Madison Guaranty Savings and Loan. Among other things, she represented Madison in dealings with the state securities commissioner. (Hillary's famous billing records, which would vanish and mysteriously reappear on her desk in the White House years later, would indicate the extent of her involvement with the failed savings and loan.)

Hillary also saw nothing wrong with representing the Federal Deposit Insurance Corporation in trying to recover funds from major Clinton campaign contributor Dan Lasater after the collapse of another savings and loan, this one in Illinois. Under terms of the settlement worked out by Hillary, their friend Lasater, who had been sent to prison on drug charges after Roger Clinton turned state's evidence, paid only 8 percent of what the government originally asked for.

When these and other apparent conflicts were pointed out by Clinton's perennial GOP opponent Frank White, Bill slammed him for stooping to attack the state's First Lady. "Remember, Frank," Bill shot back, "you're running for governor, not First Lady."

The 1986 election year also marked the start of Chelsea's political indoctrination. At age six she was now old enough to comprehend at least some of the things being said about her parents, and they wanted her to be prepared. Thus began the nightly drills at the dinner table, with Mom and Dad casting themselves as the Clintons' enemies. While they hurled angry insults at the little girl, Chelsea honed her defensive skills, and toughened up in the process.

The drills were not something the Clintons relished, particularly since they saw so little of their daughter. From the very beginning, they had grappled with the same feelings of guilt that vex all working parents. But each tried to be a presence in Chelsea's life. When Chelsea was a toddler, Hillary would spread a quilt in the backyard of the Governor's Mansion so she and her daughter could, as she recalled, "just stare up at the sky and watch the clouds roll by."

When she was four, Chelsea was asked what she wanted to give Hillary for Mother's Day and answered, "life insurance." The little girl believed, Hillary explained, that "life insurance" would keep her mother from ever dying. "This tiny little child wanted me to live forever," Hillary later wrote. "Isn't that what being alive is all about—being loved like that?"

From the beginning, Hillary was intent on nurturing Chelsea's sense of independence and her language skills. When she was on the road, she wrote her daughter letters, and insisted that Chelsea write her back. "She was precocious," Carolyn Yeldell Staley later recalled. Instead of telling Staley that she had to go to the doctor to get some shots, Chelsea announced she was going to get her "immunizations."

As a toddler, Chelsea was not allowed to wear the shoes with Velcro straps that Virginia bought her until she learned to tie her shoes. "I loved the look of accomplishment on her face," Hillary said, "when she showed us all what she could do for herself." When Chelsea made her mother a plastic bead necklace as part of a school project, Hillary proudly wore it to several high-profile functions. "Chelsea made it for me," she boasted, fingering the brightly colored beads. "I think it's the prettiest piece of jewelry I've ever owned."

"When Chelsea was four or five," Hillary recalled, "she went through a stage of asking, 'Why do you have to go to work?' Ah, there's the guilt that strikes your heart. I don't know any mother who doesn't have pangs about leaving. There are times when a child badly wants more of you. I took Chelsea to the office when I could. She went to Bill's, too. There was a corner in his office that was hers, with crayons and paper where she could do coloring. I took work home a lot and did it after she was in bed."

Each year on the first day of school, Hillary invariably burst into tears. It got to be so embarrassing that when she was nine, Chelsea asked Hillary not to bring her to the first day of school anymore.

Chelsea's first-grade teacher, Sadie Mitchell, remembered that Hillary gave her all the numbers where both she and the governor could be reached. She also took Chelsea on field trips and came to school to help with science experiments or read stories to Chelsea's class.

Predictably, Bill's interest, though genuine, was invariably for public consumption. He always kept a child's desk in his office (though she rarely used it), and announced the times when he had dropped Chelsea off at school in the mornings—a job that almost always fell to one of the state troopers. Whenever the family was seen in public, it was Bill who insisted on being seen holding their daughter's hand.

Despite their best efforts, the peripatetic Clintons saw precious little of Chelsea. From the mid-1980s on, Hillary was a veritable blur of activity as she raced from one speech or committee meeting or fund-raiser to another. Bill, of course, saw even less of Chelsea—and the situation worsened in 1986 when he was elected chairman of the National Governors' Association shortly after his fortieth birthday. The NGA was an obvious springboard to the national stage, and as such consumed ever-increasing amounts of his free time.

When asked what her father did, seven-year-old Chelsea replied, "He gives speeches, drinks coffee, and talks on the telephone." It was a line Bill could always count on to get a laugh. But the reality behind it was anything but funny. Bill had essentially grown up without a strong father figure in his own life, and he did not want to be viewed as another absent dad.

Bill beamed with pride whenever he spoke of Chelsea, and was quick to whip out his wallet and pass around the latest snapshots of the little girl with the big smile. They held hands whenever they were together, and the nanny sometimes caught father and daughter roughhousing on the living room floor.

Still, he deferred to Hillary when it came to Chelsea's health. Elaine Weiss of the American Bar Association was in the room in 1987 when Hillary took an urgent call from Little Rock. "Well, I don't know, Bill," Hillary barked. "Did you feel her forehead? I don't know if she has a fever. I'm in *Chicago*."

Bill did frequently complain of how little time he got to spend with his cherished only child. "He never mentioned Hillary, but he was always talking about Chelsea," said Dolly Kyle Browning, who in 1986 spent the Fourth of July cavorting with Bill in a Little Rock hotel room. "I mean, the time Billy spent with me and all these other women was time he could have been spending with Chelsea."

Bill's absence from Chelsea's life was of no particular concern to Hillary. In 1987 she was urging him to take on the added burden of a national campaign. It was finally time, she told Bill, for him to announce his intention to seek the presidency in 1988.

Bill's political godmother, Betsey Wright, was less certain about the timing. But at Hillary's urging, Clinton scouts were sent to test the political waters in Iowa, New Hampshire, Oregon, California, and the Super Tuesday primary states. In April 1987 he made his first foray into New Hampshire. The reception was so warm and the crowds so enthusiastic he was convinced he could place second behind native New Englander Paul Tsongas and then go on to rack up victories in the Southern states.

Later, as he sat on the porch steps of the Governor's Mansion weighing whether or not to run, Chelsea came up and tugged on his sleeve. "Daddy," she said, "are we going to Disney World this summer?"

"Gee, Chelsea," he said, putting his arm around the little girl. "Daddy might run for President. And if I do that, then I'm gonna be awfully busy. I might not have the time to go on vacation this summer."

Chelsea thought for a moment, then smiled. "Well," she said, "then Mom and I will go without you."

■

Of course she's in the loop. She *is* the loop.

—*Ron Brown,*
on Hillary

Call my dad—my mom's too busy.

—*Chelsea,* when
a school nurse
sought permission
to give her an aspirin

■

That man would lie down and kill himself before he would let her leave him. There have been other temptations, but Hillary is the love of his life.

—*Betsey Wright*

Billy won't tell the truth even when it will help him.

—*Dolly Kyle Browning*

I told you—I'm retired.

—*Bill*,
whenever asked by
friends whether he
was still womanizing

6

H E WAS AN adulterer and a liar, they were saying. And worse: a fool. In the face of rumors that he had been unfaithful to his wife, the charismatic young Democratic front-runner with the Kennedy smile angrily denied the gossip, and to prove he was innocent dared the press to shadow his every move.

The *Miami Herald* did just that, and in a matter of days reported that a young woman other than the candidate's wife had spent the weekend at his home. Confronted with photographs of himself and a young blonde named Donna Rice cavorting aboard the aptly named yacht *Monkey Business*, Gary Hart announced on May 7, 1987, that he was withdrawing from the race.

It was no small irony that with Hart out of the picture, more pressure was put on Bill Clinton to run—despite the fact that, in the words of one Clinton advisor, "Bill made Hart look like Billy Graham." To further compound the irony, Hillary, backed by Dick Morris, was pushing hardest for Bill to fulfill his dream and run for the presidency. Since Arkansas law had been changed to make the gubernatorial term four years instead of only two, Bill's current term wouldn't end until 1990. Even if he lost this time, he'd still be governor and positioned to make a second try in 1992. Hillary had been clearly energized by the prospect of Bill's becoming the youngest president in history—younger even than his idol JFK. "Now, Bill," she had whispered in his ear at a staff meeting. "*Now.*"

Only ten days after Hart's withdrawal, Bill sought advice from another source: his childhood friend and lover Dolly Kyle Browning. During yet another tryst, this time at the Hyatt Hotel at Dallas–Fort Worth Airport, Dolly broached the subject of her own sexual addiction—and Bill's—for the first time.

"At first Billy denied it," she recalled. "He just didn't see how a person could be 'addicted' to sex. But then when I asked why he felt compelled to have sex, if sometimes he wanted to get away from his partner right after having sex, if his extramarital sex was affecting his sex life with 'The Warden,' if sex was in any way jeopardizing his career—then he understood."

Not surprisingly, it was that last question concerning the impact on his career that Bill found most intriguing. When he told Dolly that he was being pressured to run for president, she cautioned him that a run against Republican Vice-President George Bush could be "suicide." She added, "There's entirely too much trash in your recent past."

"Like what?" he answered without hesitating.

"Bill, please," she said. "Be serious. Look where you are right now . . . Get real."

Then, suddenly, Bill became emotional. He began crying. "He brought up incidents," Dolly later recalled. "He asked me questions."

"There is temptation on every corner— How do you expect me to pass it up?" he asked, tears streaming down his cheeks. "I can't even walk down the street without someone literally trying to pick me up."

Dolly was unnerved by Bill's response, and suggested they change the subject. But he wanted to go on. "I can take it if you can," he said.

In fact, according to Dick Morris, the political demise of Gary Hart had filled Bill with "a tremendous terror." That spring and early summer, Clinton contacted a number of friends and political contacts throughout the country and casually brought up sex as a campaign issue. What, he wanted to know, was the American public willing to tolerate? Was adultery, if proven, an insurmountable obstacle to getting elected? Or would it be sufficient to simply say one had caused pain in his marriage?

At one point, he even grilled *Arkansas Gazette* editor John Robert Starr—the man who popularized the term "Slick Willie"—on the "Gary Hart Factor."

"Well, you haven't done anything like that, have you?" Starr asked Bill.

"Yes, I have."

Starr was stunned. "You mean," he said, "since you've been married to Hillary?"

"Yes," Bill replied. "Do you want to know about it?"

"*It*," Starr thought. "Do you want to know about *it*? And I," he recalled, "to my eternal regret, said no. I just didn't want to know."

While Hillary clearly knew Bill had been unfaithful, she could not have comprehended the sheer magnitude of his infidelity. Forging ahead, she bought a condo for the Rodhams in Little Rock so Chelsea's grandparents would be there for her while her mommy and daddy were on the road.

But Betsey Wright was not so sanguine about Bill's chances for surviving a presidential run in 1988. She conducted an investigation of her own, ferreting out the names of the women Bill was alleged to have been involved with, as well as where and when some of the liaisons took place.

Once she had assembled a dossier on Bill's rumored affairs, Wright sat him down in her living room. Before they went over each name, she begged him to tell her the whole truth—"I've got to know the *truth*, Bill"—about his relationship with each woman. There were at least a dozen women on the list, including Gennifer Flowers, Dolly Kyle Browning, Juanita Broaddrick, Susan McDougal, Sally Perdue, Lencola Sullivan, Deborah Mathis, and former Miss America Elizabeth Ward Gracen. He did not tell Wright about the countless one-night stands, the hookers, or the violent assault on Juanita Broaddrick.

They then ran down the list a second time, to determine which of the women he had had affairs with might talk to the press, either for money or out of a desire for revenge. The meeting took four hours. When it was over, Wright concluded that he should not run—if for no other reason than to spare his wife and daughter.

Convincing Bill was one thing. But when Hillary discovered Betsey Wright had talked her husband out of running that year, she accused the governor's chief of staff of overstepping her bounds. The two women quarreled bitterly over whether Bill should enter the race; on one occasion, passersby watched in amazement as Hillary stood screaming at Wright in a parking lot. Another time, Wright stormed out of the Governor's Mansion with an enraged Hillary in hot pursuit.

Out of loyalty to Bill—and a genuine desire not to hurt Hillary—Wright did not reveal all she knew. But when it became evident that Hillary was on the verge of convincing him to go ahead with his plans to run, Wright told her that "the same thing that happened to Hart will happen to Bill if he runs."

Hillary continued to press her for details, but Wright would only say that Bill had in fact been "seeing" other women—*lots* of other women. "Hillary," she said, "he *admitted* it."

But what Wright did not know was that five years earlier Hillary had hired private investigator Ivan Duda to trail her husband. Back then, on the eve of Bill's 1982 comeback election as governor, Duda had come up with a list of eight women he had been sneaking away to meet at all hours of the day and night. Hillary ignored most of the names; she did not believe Duda had come up with enough hard evidence to prove that Bill had had affairs with six of the women. Of the eight, she accepted the fact that Bill was probably sleeping with Dolly Kyle Browning and Gennifer Flowers.

"You'd hardly describe either Hillary or Betsey as naive," another Clinton staffer observed. "Of course Betsey took for granted that Hillary knew about Bill's cheating. But she wasn't sure how much she knew, or how she would react."

Wright could not, in fact, have anticipated Hillary's response. Rather than expressing anger at her husband, she looked at Wright and asked, "Who is going to find out? These women are all trash. Nobody is going to believe them."

But Wright stood her ground, insisting that the risk was too great in the wake of the Gary Hart *Monkey Business* scandal. By his own conduct, Bill had simply made himself too vulnerable. "Now is not the time," Wright said. "The climate is all wrong. Bush is too strong. Bill has got to wait until next time . . ."

On July 15, the ballroom at Little Rock's Excelsior Hotel was filled with reporters, camera crews, and political supporters waiting to hear Arkansas Governor Bill Clinton announce his candidacy for president. Instead Bill walked to the podium and, with Hillary at his side fighting back tears, dropped a bombshell.

"I need some family time, I need some personal time," he explained. "Politicians are people too. I think sometimes we forget it, but they really are. The only thing I or any other candidate has to offer in running for president is what's inside. That's what sets people on fire and gets their confidence and their votes, whether they live in Wisconsin or Montana or New York. That part of my life needs renewal. The other, even more important reason for my decision is the certain impact that this campaign would have had on our daughter. The only way I could have won . . . would be to go on the road full-time from now until the end, and to have Hillary do the same thing.

"I've seen a lot of kids grow up under these pressures and a long, long time ago I made a promise to myself that if I was ever lucky enough to have a child, she would never grow up wondering who her father was."

Hillary wiped away a tear, and he went on. "Our daughter is seven. She is the most important person in the world to us, and our most important responsibility. In order to wage a winning campaign, both Hillary and I would have to leave her for long periods of time. That would not be good for her, or for us. My head said go, and my heart said, 'It isn't right for you now.' Deep down inside, I knew it was not the right time for me."

Like other friends of the Clintons, the *Arkansas Times*'s Max Brantley seemed willing to believe that Bill had suddenly abandoned his lifelong dream so he could spend more time with his family. "It was shocking," Brantley said of the abrupt and unexpected about-face. "And it was very moving . . . It seemed a selfless kind of decision."

Hillary, aware that even the slightest hint that Bill had been scared off would doom any future run for the White House, did her best to make it appear as if she had goaded Bill into staying out of the 1988 race. "I want to go to supper with my husband," she said. "I want to go to the movies. I want to go on vacation with my family. I want my husband back."

Bill conceded that it had been a painful decision. "It hurt so bad," he told one journalist, "to walk away from it." He let the family-before-politics facade slip for a moment while watching one of Chelsea's softball games. "You know," he said to his friend Max Brantley as he stared into the distance, "is there a point in a person's life, a political person's life, when the things you've done in the past are forgotten?"

While her husband waxed remorseful in private, Hillary fumed. It was not so much that her husband had been unfaithful—this had always been a painful but bearable part of their life together—but that, for the time being at least, his adultery had cost them their dream.

As she approached her fortieth birthday, Hillary took stock of her life with Bill. "She felt totally humiliated and betrayed," said a friend who got to know the Clintons during Bill's first term as governor. "There had always been this barrier that came down between her and the rest of the world when it came to the marriage. As far as I know, she really didn't discuss Bill's girlfriends with anybody. But when they had to pull out of the race in 1988, she was forced to face up to his womanizing for the first time and it hurt her very deeply."

Immediately following the surprise July 15 announcement, the fights between Bill and Hillary escalated in number and intensity. For the first time, Hillary was learning that her husband was sleeping not with just one or two women but perhaps a dozen or more. And she, better than anyone, knew of his steadfast refusal to wear a condom.

"Well, of course," said a lawyer friend, "she must have been terrified at the prospect of contracting venereal disease, or AIDS. That he would gamble with her health like that just added to the overall sense of betrayal. It's hard to imagine what Bill was thinking . . ." Not long after, Hillary demanded that her husband be tested for HIV.

She had reason to be concerned that her husband might contract a deadly sexually transmitted disease. He had, after all, contracted one already. According to someone who claims to have seen Clinton's medical records, he has a sexually transmitted disease—a fact that could have harmed his presidential prospects only if Clinton's complete medical history were made public. Over the years, advisors would urge their vibrant young candidate to release his medical records as proof of his excellent health, only to have Clinton mysteriously dismiss the idea out of hand.

"I'm sure there are *thousands* of women across the country who would be relieved to see those medical records," Dolly Kyle Browning said, "and determine once and for all if they had any communicable diseases."

When the results of his HIV test came back negative, Hillary breathed a sigh of relief. So did Bill, whose dual addiction to risk-taking and denial blinded him to the possibility that he could become infected with the AIDS virus or another sexually transmitted disease.

But Hillary would not easily forgive her husband. At one point when two Clinton staff members were waiting in the living room of the Governor's Mansion, the sounds of shouting and slamming doors reverberated upstairs. Above the din, Hillary's voice could be heard clearly: "I am only staying, you bastard, FOR CHELSEA'S SAKE!"

Indeed, several of the Clintons' closest friends believe that, had it not been for Chelsea, Bill and Hillary would have divorced in 1987. "It's been tough on Hillary," said Dorothy Rodham, admitting to a friend that the marriage was "in serious trouble. She's taking it really hard. But I know she'll do whatever she thinks is best for Chelsea."

Bill would later tell a confidant that he, too, was thinking of divorcing—and leaving politics—after he turned forty. More accurately, it was his own decision in 1987 not to go after the presidency—a decision preordained by his own libidinous behavior—that prompted him to reevaluate his life. "If I had to become a gas station attendant to live an honest life and be able to look myself in the mirror and be happy with who I am," he said somewhat disingenuously, "that's what I was prepared to do."

At this point, Bill, too, decided to remain in the marriage for the sake of Chelsea. He also began proudly checking off the days on his calendar when he had been "good" and not cheated on Hillary.

Hillary was fond of quoting John F. Kennedy's famous bit of advice concerning the handling of one's enemies. "Don't get mad," JFK said, "get even." There were ways to accomplish this short of divorce, and one was to have an affair of her own.

Ever since Hillary joined the Rose Law Firm back in 1977, she and Vince Foster had behaved, said a secretary at the firm, "like two people in love." She would saunter over to his office every afternoon to snack on the pistachio nuts he kept in his desk drawer. "She wanted him to keep them in his office," said their fellow law partner Amy Stewart, "so she wouldn't get fat."

Over the years, friends, legal colleagues, and assorted aides and staffers would witness Vince and Hillary's unfolding affair. L. D. Brown, Larry Patterson, and the other state troopers assigned to guard the Clintons claimed that whenever Bill left the mansion, Foster showed up "like clockwork" to comfort Hillary. Often, he would not depart the mansion until the next morning.

"Hillary and Vince were *deeply* in love," Brown said. "I saw them, locked in each other's arms, deep-kissing, nuzzling—you have it." Gradually the encounters became so public that Hillary's friends wondered if she wasn't trying to send Bill a message. The troopers said they witnessed the couple embracing and stealing furtive kisses—at functions when they thought no one was looking, even stopped at a traffic light.

Foster was often seen fondling Hillary in public—even at her own birthday party with Bill very much in attendance. During the party, held at a Little Rock restaurant called Alouette, Patterson was seated at the bar when Hillary and her Rose Law Firm colleague Carolyn Huber meandered out to the bar to talk in private.

On the way to the rest room, Foster "came up behind Hillary and squeezed her rear end with both his hands," Patterson said. "Then he winked and gave me the 'OK' sign. On the way back, Huber was turned away, and Vince put his hand over one of Hillary's breasts and made the same 'OK' sign to me."

"Oh, Vince," Hillary giggled. "Oh, Vince . . ."

Another time, Brown said he was "amazed" at the scene when he followed the Clintons, Vince and Lisa Foster and their friends Mike and Beth Coulter out of a restaurant one evening. "Vince was squeezing Hillary's behind and kissing her and and then winking at me," Brown said. "And right in front of *them*, Bill and Beth had their hands all over each other."

As the Hillary-Vince affair heated up even further in 1987, Hillary had the troopers drive her and Foster to a secluded cabin the Rose Law Firm kept at the mountain resort town of Heber Springs. They would often not emerge, Brown and the others reported, for hours. "There are some things you have to get outside your marriage," she confessed to Brown, "that you can't get in it."

"Everybody knew about Hillary and Vince," Jim McDougal later said. "But Bill was not really in a position to object, now was he?"

A year later Bill and Hillary "boxed off" their marital troubles, as they had so many times before, and prepared for Bill to take his first major step into the national arena. Clinton had enthusiastically endorsed Michael Dukakis for President, and now that the former Massachusetts governor had the nomination sewn up, Bill had been invited to give the coveted prime-time nominating speech at the Democratic National Convention in Atlanta.

The once-in-a-political-lifetime opportunity turned out to be an unmitigated disaster. To begin with, the Dukakis camp made dozens of copious additions to the text, turning it into an unwieldy, bland mess. Then, when Bill delivered the speech, the house lights were never dimmed and Dukakis's floor whips ordered delegates to cheer every time the candidate's name was uttered. The fact that no one could hear Bill did not deter him. Delegates shouted, "Get the hook," and booed. The anchors on all three networks complained bitterly—but Bill droned on for thirty-three agonizing minutes.

Betsey Wright flew home to Little Rock early, convinced that Bill's calamitous convention speech had destroyed her boss's career. In the middle of a hastily called staff meeting, Wright broke down.

But the Clintons' Hollywood friends, television producers Harry

Thomason and Linda Bloodworth-Thomason, saw a way to capitalize on the situation. They went to Johnny Carson, who had been poking fun at Bill's abysmal performance every night in his monologues, and suggested he book the hapless Arkansas governor.

After eight days and countless one-liners ("He went over about as big as the Velcro condom," "The U.S. Surgeon General has just approved Clinton as an over-the-counter sleep aid"), Bill made his *Tonight Show* debut. Poking fun at himself, Clinton instantly won over Carson and his huge audience. By the time bandleader Doc Severinsen invited him to perform a shaky rendition of "Summertime" on the saxophone, Bill had resurrected his career overnight. "On the mellow notes of his saxophone," journalist John Starr wrote, "Bill 'The Phoenix' Clinton rose from the political ashes on national television Thursday night."

Still, there was lingering bitterness toward the Dukakis camp for allowing the debacle to occur in the first place. From this point on, Bill referred to his party's 1988 standard-bearer as "that little Greek motherfucker."

By 1990 Bill had occupied the Arkansas statehouse for ten of the past dozen years. He was, in the words of Dick Morris, "bored and restless"—and eager to devote himself to running full-time for the presidency over the next two years.

Hillary, meantime, was working full tilt to promote her family's fortunes. In addition to her work at Rose, where many of the clients did business with the state, she now sat on the boards of retail giant Wal-Mart and the national yogurt chain TCBY. (Although he never earned more than $35,000 a year as governor, and her law firm salary had only recently topped $100,000, somehow the Clintons would manage to report a net worth of $931,000 in cash and bonds by 1992.)

Bill was reluctant to run for governor a sixth time, but Morris made a convincing argument. What if he lost to George Bush in 1992? Bill would be out of office altogether, Morris pointed out, and his political career could "fade away" as he waited for a second shot at the White House in 1996.

"Better make up your mind, Bill," an impatient Hillary joked. "If you don't run, I will." In fact, rumors were rampant that Hillary might run for governor instead of her husband—speculation they both encouraged.

"She'd make a wonderful governor," Bill said when asked about the rumors. "I'm not going to speak for her, that's not my business." But if she did want to run? "Then that would have a big impact on my own decision."

Pushed by Morris to seek a sixth term, Bill surprised everyone—including a visibly disappointed Hillary—by announcing he would indeed run. This time, she decided to take an even more active role than usual in her husband's primary campaign against Rockefeller Foundation policy analyst Tom McRae.

At a McRae press conference in the capitol, Clinton's rival was criticizing the governor's record while occasionally pointing to a cartoon of a nude Bill Clinton, hands placed discreetly over his crotch. The caption read: THE EMPEROR HAS NO CLOTHES.

Suddenly Hillary, wearing a Clinton button on her lapel, appeared out of nowhere ("I just dropped in to pick some things up") and blasted McRae. "Do you really want an answer, Tom?" she shouted. "Get off it, Tom . . . Give me a break!"

While she claimed she had just happened upon the press conference, Hillary had suggested staging the confrontation a day earlier during a strategy session. "If I take him on," she said, "it will get a lot of publicity, but it won't necessarily signal a deep concern about the race by you. It will just be your wife expressing her anger at attacks on her husband."

The debate between the governor's wife and his challenger became, as Hillary predicted, front-page news in Arkansas. Over the next few weeks she repeatedly denied that the confrontation had, for all intents and purposes, been masterfully staged—right down to the notes she just happened to be carrying in her pocket and referred to constantly during her "impromptu" debate with McRae. "Bill Clinton lacks not only fire in the belly," Meredith Oakley said, "but steel in the spine . . . He always sends Hillary out to do his dirty work."

For all the hoopla, Hillary's clever ruse was not enough to tip the scales back in Bill's favor; for a time it looked as if Clinton might not even win his party's nomination for governor. It was at this point that Clinton had one of his more celebrated meltdowns. "You got me into this race," he screamed at Morris. "You've forgotten me, you've dismissed me, you don't care about me! You've turned your back on me! I don't get shit from you anymore! You're screwing me! You're screwing me!"

"I don't have to take your shit!" Morris replied, and as he stormed toward the door Clinton charged him. What happened next is open to debate. According to Morris, Clinton grabbed him from behind, and Morris slid to the floor. Another witness, campaign manager Gloria Cabe, claimed Clinton punched Morris, and sent him hurtling toward the floor.

Even before Hillary helped Morris to his feet, Bill was pleading, "Don't go, I'm sorry. Don't go, don't go." Morris stormed outside, with Hillary in hot pursuit.

"Please forgive him," Hillary said. "He's under so much pressure. He didn't mean it. He's very sorry. He's overtired . . . He values you. He needs you . . ."

Morris did stay on, and Clinton went on to win both the primary and the general election handily. But it would not be the last time he was exposed to Bill's "mind-blowing temper tantrums"—so extreme that Morris soon coined his own nickname for Bill: "The Monster."

During the 1990 campaign for governor, Clinton was asked during a debate if he intended to serve out his term as governor. "You bet," he replied.

On May 8, 1991, Bill Clinton gave a speech to the Governors Quality Conference at Little Rock's Excelsior Hotel. As he stood outside the ballroom where he was about to speak, the governor noticed a young woman manning the reception desk. Her name was Paula Corbin (she would soon marry and become Paula Jones), a twenty-four-year-old secretary who only two months earlier had been hired by the Arkansas Industrial Development Commission at a yearly salary of $10,270. Paula, along with her friend and coworker Pam Blackard, were handing out name tags and literature when she looked over and saw Clinton answering reporters' questions. "I looked up," she said, "and caught him staring at me."

A few minutes later, trooper Danny Ferguson walked over to the table, leaned across to Paula, and said, "The governor said you make his knees knock."

A short time later, around 2:30 that afternoon, Ferguson returned and slipped her a piece of paper with a room number written on it. "The governor would like to meet you up in his room and talk to you."

"Do you think I should?" she asked Blackard, who had been sitting next to her the entire time.

"Find out what he wants," Blackard said, "and come right back."

Paula went upstairs to meet Clinton, she later explained, because she "was brought up to trust people, and especially of that stature— you know, a governor. Besides, it was an honor." She also hoped the meeting might lead to a better-paying job.

When she got to the governor's business suite, which had a sofa but no bed, they made small talk for a few minutes. Jones said Bill then took her hand and pulled her toward him. She withdrew, and stepped back a few feet.

But, as he had done with Broaddrick, Bill Clinton pressed on. "He started pulling me forward and tried to kiss me," she recalled, "and I backed up, and you know, I stood back."

"I love the way your hair flows down your back," Bill said, running his hand up her thigh. "I love your curves." Then he bent down and tried to kiss her again.

"What are you doing?" Paula objected, pulling away again. Now, fearing what Clinton might do next, she stepped back a few feet more, all the time trying to distract him by talking about Hillary. This seemed to work for a moment, and Paula sat down at the end of the sofa nearest the door.

"Are you married?" Bill asked.

"I have a steady boyfriend."

Then the governor walked across the room toward her, and as he sat down on the sofa next to her, unzipped his pants, then lowered his trousers and underpants to expose his erect penis. "Kiss it," he ordered her.

Shocked, Jones leaped up from the couch and headed for the door. "I'm not that kind of girl," she yelled. "Look, I've got to go . . ."

"Well," said Clinton, who according to Jones remained on the couch, openly fondling himself, "I don't want to make you do anything you don't want to do."

He then stood, pulled up his pants, and said, "If you get in trouble for leaving work, have Danny [Ferguson] call me immediately and I'll take care of it."

As Paula walked toward the door, the tone of Clinton's voice changed dramatically. "You are smart," he said sternly. "Let's keep this between ourselves."

When she got back downstairs, Blackard said, Paula was "walking fast and shaking." Jones, distraught and crying, then drove to the office of another friend, Debra Ballentine, and told Ballentine what had happened. "I can't believe I was stupid enough to go upstairs," Paula said. "I can't believe I was so stupid . . ."

Even as her husband continued pursuing other women, Hillary was actively searching for ways to counter the allegations of infidelity Bill would surely face. At closed-door meetings with their inner circle of advisors—among them media consultant Frank Greer, Little Rock lawyer Bruce Lindsey, and pollster Stanley Greenberg—Bill again asked if it wasn't enough just to admit that he had "caused pain" in the marriage. Everyone agreed that it was—especially Hillary, who somehow managed to remain dispassionate as she coolly dismissed "all these lies being told about Bill."

Just as he had done during his 1983 reelection bid, Bill would seek to immunize himself against criticism by issuing a preemptive apology. The first test came at the Sperling Breakfast, a Washington ritual founded by veteran *Christian Science Monitor* columnist Godfrey Sperling Jr. At these informal biweekly gatherings, a candidate or office holder was given the chance to win over some of the nation's top political reporters.

To underscore the strength of his marriage, Bill brought Hillary along. When someone finally summoned the courage to bring up the subject of Clinton's rumored womanizing toward the end of the breakfast, Bill sniped, "This is the sort of thing they were interested in in Rome when they were in decline, too." He conceded his marriage had "not been perfect or free of difficulties. But," he went on, "we feel good about where we are and we believe in our obligation to each other, and we intend to be together thirty or forty years from now, whether I run for President or not . . . And I think that ought," he concluded, "to be enough."

Satisfied that they had disposed of the infidelity issue, Hillary turned her attention to another niggling problem: Bill's promise to Arkansas voters that he would serve out the remainder of his term as governor. At her suggestion, Bill took to the road for a full week that summer, traveling from town to town with the message that he was heartsick over breaking his promise. When he returned to Little Rock, he announced that the people of Arkansas were begging him to run, and as a result he was setting up an exploratory committee to look into the "possibility" of a presidential candidacy.

By summer's end, the tension at the Governor's Mansion was palpable. On the morning of Labor Day, 1991, Hillary left the Governor's Mansion in her blue Cutlass, only to come screeching back moments later. The state guards ran out thinking, in Larry Patterson's words, "that something was terribly wrong."

"Where's the goddamn fucking flag?" she demanded. "I want the goddamn fucking flag up every fucking morning at fucking sunrise!"

Unbeknownst to Hillary, Bill had also set out in late September to tie up yet another loose end. Juanita Broaddrick, the woman Bill allegedly raped in 1978, was attending a conference on state nursing home standards when she was called away. She stepped outside and was stunned to see Bill Clinton standing by a stairway, waiting for her.

"Juanita," he said, taking both her hands in his, "I am so sorry about what I did. I'm not the man I used to be. What can I do to make this up to you?"

Juanita Broaddrick, badly shaken, pulled away. "Go to hell!" she answered, and stormed off. That night, she told her husband and a few close friends about the bizarre encounter and wondered aloud about his motives.

A few days later, they had their answer. On October 3, 1991, before a crowd of several thousand gathered in front of the antebellum Old State House, Bill Clinton delivered the speech he had been preparing to make his entire life.

"Today we stand on the threshold of a new era," he proclaimed.

"This is not a campaign for the presidency. This is a campaign for the future, for the forgotten, hard-working middle-class people of America who deserve a government that fights for them."

When it was over, Fleetwood Mac's "Don't Stop Thinking About Tomorrow" boomed over the loudspeakers as Bill, Hillary, and Chelsea embraced and waved at the cheering throng. Father, mother, and daughter all had tear-filled eyes. So did Virginia, who had not told her son that, one year after she had undergone a modified radical mastectomy, her breast cancer had returned. The prognosis was grim, but she would not tell him until he was safely ensconced in the White House. In the meantime, Virginia would use the same technique for compartmentalizing she had taught her son and simply "box off" the fact that she was dying.

Later, at a small reception inside the Old State House, Bill stood at the head of the receiving line greeting well-wishers until a familiar face came into view. "Congratulations," Chelsea said, shaking her father's hand. "That was a fine speech, Governor." Before long, the sheer enormity of what her family was undertaking finally hit the personable eleven-year-old. "I hope it won't change things," she told a reporter wistfully.

From the moment he first met her in the Clintons' bedroom, George Stephanopoulos harbored no doubts about Hillary's all-important role in her husband's political future. While Bill stood by unselfconsciously in his underwear, Hillary warmly greeted their brash young deputy campaign director and then proceeded to pepper him with questions concerning the upcoming primaries.

But long before the primaries, in November 1991, they confronted their first sex scandal when supergroupie "Sweet, Sweet Connie" Hamzy talked about the day Clinton had propositioned her seven years earlier. Not surprisingly, Clinton's version of events differed from Hamzy's. He claimed that she had come up to him in a hotel lobby, pulled down her bikini top, and said, "What do you think of these?"

Clinton lit up as he told the story aboard his campaign plane, *Longhorn One*. But Hillary, sitting next to him, failed to see the humor. "We have to destroy her story," she said coldly.

By convincing a night editor at CNN to drop the story, Stephanopoulos would later boast, he had nipped the first "bimbo eruption" in the bud. That night, Hillary and Bill called to thank him from their hotel in San Antonio. No one mentioned the disturbing fact that Hamzy had taken a lie detector test—and passed.

For the next month, Bill took every opportunity to tout Hillary as his secret weapon in the campaign. "Buy one, get one free!" he would tell gatherings of supporters. "Two for the price of one!" As they crisscrossed the country addressing every issue from health care to education, he made it clear that Mrs. Clinton would be unlike any First Lady who had gone before. If I get elected, he said, it will be an unprecedented partnership, far more than Franklin Roosevelt and Eleanor. They were two great people, but on different tracks. "If I get elected, we'll do things together like we always have," Hillary agreed. "If you vote for my husband," she cracked, "you get me. It's a two-for-one blue plate special."

That shared sense of confidence was dealt a severe blow on January 16, 1992, when the *Star* ran a story accusing Clinton of carrying on affairs with five Arkansas women, including Flowers, former Miss America Elizabeth Ward Gracen, and former Miss Arkansas Lencola Sullivan.

The story had first surfaced during the 1990 gubernatorial campaign, when former state official Larry Nichols filed a libel suit against Clinton. Clinton claimed Nichols, who had been marketing director of the Arkansas Development Finance Corporation, had been fired for making 642 unauthorized phone calls to raise money for the Nicaraguan Contras. But Nichols's suit alleged he was forced out of his job because he "knew too much" about Clinton's use of state funds to pay for his various sexual liaisons. When all five women mentioned in the Nichols lawsuit denied they had had affairs with Clinton, the story disappeared and Bill was reelected.

Once again, Bill reacted blithely to the allegations resurrected in the *Star*. But one week later, at 6:30 A.M. on January 23, Stephanopoulos called campaign consultant James Carville from Washington's National (now Reagan) Airport and told him that Flowers had changed her story. In the new issue of the *Star*, Gennifer was admitting to her twelve-year affair with Bill, and she had tapes of their phone conversations to back it up.

Again, Bill seemed oddly detached, quietly reading *Lincoln on Leadership* as his campaign plane winged its way toward New Hampshire. While Stephanopoulos and Carville speculated about what had actually happened between their candidate and Flowers ("A blow job in a car ten years ago? A one-night stand or two?"), they were unaware that Bill had actually phoned Flowers the day the first *Star* story broke. He placed the call from a pay phone in the crowded lobby of a Boston hotel, just yards from an AP reporter and a Fox TV crew. "How could he have been so stupid?" Stephanopoulos later wrote. "So arrogant? Did he want to get caught?"

Cornered by a TV reporter, Bill was asked point-blank if he had ever had an affair. "If I had," Bill said, "I wouldn't tell you." As for Flowers: "The allegations in the *Star* are not true," he lied. "She's obviously taken money to change her story." Only a few months earlier, he was bragging to his security detail in Little Rock that Gennifer could "suck a tennis ball through a garden hose."

It soon became clear to Clinton's campaign staff that it was Hillary—not their candidate—who was in control of the situation. On several occasions, whether he was at a fund-raiser in Atlanta or shaking hands in St. Louis, Bill would stop at a pay phone to call her for advice. In each case, Hillary not only pledged to stand by him, but devised the strategy to destroy his accusers' credibility.

By way of distracting attention from the Gennifer Flowers scandal, Bill rushed back to Arkansas for the execution of Ricky Ray Rector, who had been convicted of killing a police officer. There was little doubt that the lobotomized Ricky Ray did not comprehend that he was to die by lethal injection. After his last meal of fried steak, baked chicken, beans, pecan pie, and cherry Kool-Aid, he said he was putting aside half the pie "for later." Then he spent ninety minutes trying to help his executioners find a vein.

Just as he had cited Scripture to explain why he believed oral sex did not constitute adultery, Bill told Stephanopoulos that capital punishment was not a violation of Christian teaching. Clinton had consulted with his pastor and determined that "Thou shalt not kill" really meant "Thou shalt not murder." Bill also realized that, by refusing to grant a stay of execution to the mentally deficient Ricky

Ray, he was showing himself to be as tough on law-and-order issues as any Republican.

Nightline had been pressuring the Clintons to do an interview, but Hillary wisely nixed the idea. The show's host, Ted Koppel, was a relentless interrogator who would not cut them any slack on the Flowers issue. Instead, they went with the top-rated CBS program *60 Minutes* and its huge post–Super Bowl audience.

The Clintons' political future hinged on their *60 Minutes* performance, and they knew it. The interview was to be taped that Sunday morning in a suite at Boston's Ritz-Carlton Hotel. The night before, in a tense meeting with their advisors, both Bill and Hillary were adamant about one thing: Bill would not admit to committing adultery, period.

The next morning, only minutes before the interview, a bar of lights overhead crashed to the floor, almost striking Hillary. She reeled back and into Bill's arms, where she stayed for a minute or so until they took their places for the interview. "It was very dramatic," said a CBS crew member, "and kind of touching."

60 Minutes correspondent Steve Kroft was more impressed by Hillary than by Bill. "She was in control," he said. "Hillary is tougher and more disciplined than Bill is. And she's more analytical. Among his faults, he has a tendency not to think of the consequences of the things he says. I think she knows. She's got a ten-second delay. If something comes to her mind she doesn't think will play right, she cuts it off before anyone knows she's thinking it."

Fortunately for the Clintons, Kroft's style allowed Bill to deny a relationship with Flowers without *technically* lying. Kroft said that Gennifer claimed a twelve-year affair with Bill. "That allegation is false," Bill replied, admitting only that the affair was not precisely twelve years long.

When Kroft asked if Bill was "categorically denying an affair with Gennifer Flowers," Bill replied: "I've said that before, and so has she." Again, all Bill was admitting was that he had denied it in the past.

But Kroft pressed on. "You've said that your marriage has had problems . . . What does that mean . . . Does it mean adultery?"

Hillary, sitting poker-faced at Bill's side, finally spoke up. "There isn't a person watching this who would feel comfortable sitting on this couch detailing everything that ever went on in their life or their marriage," she said. "And I think it's real dangerous in this country if we don't have a zone of privacy for everybody . . . that's all we're going to say."

Righteous indignation aside, Hillary offended one country music legend by saying, "I'm not sitting here because I'm some little woman standing by my man like Tammy Wynette. I'm sitting here because I love him and I respect him and I honor what he's been through and what we've been through together, and you know, if that's not enough for the people, then heck, don't vote for him."

Bill seized the opportunity to wax poetic about his family and what it meant to him. "If we had given up on our marriage—three years ago, four years ago, you know—if we were divorced," he said, "I wouldn't be half the man I am today, without her and Chelsea."

Bill would later say that he, Hillary, and Chelsea all watched *60 Minutes* together. When it was over, eleven-year-old Chelsea turned to them and said, "I'm glad that you're my parents."

In Nashville, Tammy Wynette sat down as soon as the interview was over and dashed off an angry letter to Hillary. "Mrs. Clinton," she wrote, "you have offended every woman and man who love that song—several million in number. I believe you have offended every true country music fan and every person who has 'made it on their own' with no one to take them to a White House."

Aware that it would be a major mistake to offend Wynette's legion of fans, Hillary quickly apologized. "I didn't mean to hurt Tammy Wynette as a person," she said. "I happen to be a country-western fan. If she feels I've hurt her feelings, I'm sorry for that."

Bill and Hillary emerged from the *60 Minutes* interview looking like a devoted couple who had stuck together to overcome some tough, if rather mysterious, obstacles in their marriage. But it was by no means the end, and throughout the campaign Hillary would have to field questions about her marriage and why she at times was evasive.

"We've been willing to work through all kinds of problems," Hillary conceded. "We have hard times because people overwork and they get short-tempered. Marriages go through rough times because you have problems with family members like we've had. It's very stressful. There are all kinds of things that happen. And I think it's inappropriate to talk about that. I don't believe in all that confessional stuff, because from my perspective you begin to undermine the relationship when you open it up to strangers. We don't talk about this kind of stuff in our marriage with family and friends. It's the way we are and the way we live. And I think it's the way most people live."

When British television interviewer David Frost asked if Bill and Hillary had ever actually discussed divorce, she stumbled.

"Not seriously," she said, then, catching herself, "No, no . . . I mean . . ."

Even the *60 Minutes* triumph was, as it turned out, rather short-lived. The very next day, Gennifer Flowers played tapes of her conversations with Bill at a nationally televised press conference.

On one tape, Bill talks about getting revenge on a political rival who was leaking stories about his affairs. "We stuck it up their ass," Bill said. "I know he lied. I just wanted to make his asshole pucker!"

On another tape, Gennifer asked Bill if he planned to run for President. "You can tell me that," she said.

"I want to, but I don't want to be blown out of the water with this," Bill replied in his unmistakably husky voice. "I don't see how they can hurt me so far. If they don't have pictures of me and . . . if no one says anything, they don't have anything. Or even if someone says something, they don't have much."

On September 23, 1991, Flowers asked him how to handle "snooping" reporters. "If they ever hit you with it, just say no and go on. There's nothing they can do . . . They're gonna try and turn this. If everybody kinda hangs tough, they're just not gonna do anything. They can't. They can't run a story like that unless somebody says, 'Yeah, I did it.' "

Bill sounded particularly adamant that Flowers not reveal that she had talked to him about obtaining a state job. Larry Patterson would testify that he was in the governor's car when Bill placed a call to state official William Gaddy and asked Gaddy to help Flowers with a recommendation. (A government grievance panel would later rule that Flowers was improperly given preferential treatment when she was then hired by the state Employment Security Department.) "If they ever ask you if you've talked to me about it," Bill told Gennifer, "you can say no."

There was no question that this was the voice of Bill Clinton. He never denied the tapes' authenticity. In fact, he picked up the phone immediately to apologize to Mario Cuomo for comments he made on the tapes implying that the Italian-American governor of New York had ties to organized crime. (Incredibly indiscreet, Clinton also told several people that Senator Edward Kennedy was so stupid "he couldn't get a whore across a bridge.")

Hillary was in her hotel room in Pierre, South Dakota, soaking in the spectacle as it unfolded on CNN. She reacted only once, flinching as if she had been struck in the face when he ended the conversation with Flowers by saying, "Goodbye, baby." Hillary called Bill and calmly waited for an explanation.

"Hillary, who's going to believe this woman," Bill said confidently. "Everybody knows you can be paid to do anything." Flowers had, in fact, reportedly been paid more than $100,000 by the *Star*.

"Everybody *doesn't* know that," she said, remaining remarkably calm. "Bill, people who don't know you are going to say, 'Why were you even talking to this person?'"

No matter. Now was the time for strategy. Everyone in the campaign was counting on Hillary, and she knew it. Rather than viewing this as yet another in a long line of betrayals by her husband, Hillary pointed her anger in the usual direction—at their enemies on the right.

"If we'd been in front of a jury," she mused on the flight to her next stop, "I'd say, 'Miss Flowers, isn't it true you were asked this by the AP in June of 1990 and you said no?' I'd crucify her." As soon as she got to Rapid City, she placed a conference call back to Bill and his staff in Boston. They would go on the offensive, she told them, attacking the Republicans and, of course, the press. This was the Hillary, her Rose colleague Thomas Mars said, who "could cut your heart out with her tongue."

"It was inspirational," Stephanopoulos later said of the call from Hillary. "If she was standing by her man, then so were we."

But for Hillary, the mounting humiliation was taking an unseen toll. At one point, she confided to her longtime friend Carolyn Huber, the office manager at the Rose Law Firm, "It's hurting so bad, Carolyn. The press doesn't believe you have any feelings. They sure don't believe in the Bible."

Late that January 1992, she sat on the dais at a Democratic National Committee roast of DNC Chairman (and future Clinton commerce secretary) Ron Brown in Washington. CNN's Larry King began his monologue with, "It's ten o'clock, Hillary. Do you know where Bill Clinton is?"

"He's with the other woman in his life," she said gamely. "His daughter, Chelsea." Bill was, in fact, with Chelsea at a father-daughter dinner-dance at the YWCA in Little Rock.

Brown, for one, was not amused. Gossip was swirling around Washington that Bill Clinton had made a pass at Brown's twenty-five-year-old daughter Tracey, an attorney in Los Angeles.

Bill did attend the YWCA father-daughter dinner in Little Rock. But on January 30 he left Chelsea behind at the Governor's Mansion to rendezvous with "Pretty Girl," his old paramour Dolly Kyle Browning, at a San Antonio hotel. Just as he had repeatedly assured Gennifer that she was the only "other woman" in his life, he had convinced Dolly that the stories in the *Star* and Flowers's claims had all been cooked up by his enemies.

"No truth to the stories?"

"Pretty Girl, of course not. You know you're the only one I ever loved, or ever will love." The woman he still referred to only as "The Warden" was, Dolly believed, not even in the running.

The next morning when Bill returned to New Hampshire, Dolly received a call from an editor at the *Star*. Panicked, she tried to get in touch with Bill, but was told curtly that he would not speak to her. "Bill can't talk to you," she was told. "But he wants you to deny the story. If you don't, we'll destroy you."

Dolly was stunned. "Are you telling me that Billy wants to destroy *me*?"

"If you don't deny the story," Dolly was told flatly, "we will destroy you."

Dolly did manage to kill the *Star* story simply by stonewalling. But she was furious at what she saw as an outright betrayal by her Billy. Several days later, Roger Clinton called at 1 A.M. from Los Angeles and began asking Dolly leading questions. It soon became evident to her that Roger, who had known about Bill's affair with Dolly for over twenty years, was taping their conversation. The tip-off: Roger repeatedly referred to the elder Clinton as "my brother Bill." Everyone who knew Roger was well aware that, whether he was talking to one of his drug contacts or directly to the governor himself, he referred to Bill Clinton one way and one way only: To Roger, he was always "Big Brother."

Not all of the presidential hopeful's liaisons took place on terra firma. According to witnesses aboard *Longhorn One*, the chartered Boeing 727 that served as the Clintons' campaign plane, Bill routinely groped, fondled, and otherwise sexually harassed flight attendants throughout the entire presidential campaign.

Clinton made his preferences known even before embarking on his first campaign trip aboard *Longhorn One*. The charter company that owned the aircraft, Express One, was told to staff the plane only with the company's most attractive blondes. Three women— Debra Schiff, Angela Fields, and Cristy Zercher—were chosen to serve the one hundred or so staffers, Secret Service agents, and journalists who generally accompanied the Clintons on the plane.

On his first trip aboard the plane, shortly before Christmas 1991, Bill climbed up the gangway and introduced himself to the three women. "Wow, this is great!" he exclaimed. "What did they do, go out and hire models?"

The very first night, Bill cornered Zercher in the small galley. "I could really get lost in those blue eyes," he said.

"Well, thank you," she responded. From that point, she said, she noticed that whenever he spoke with one of the attendants he usually "stood so close that our shoulders touched." Apparently close contact with the stewardess could also occur en masse. According to another Clinton campaign flight attendant, Sheila Swatzyna, Bill liked to engage in "cramming"—trying to see how many people could squeeze into the galley or a lavatory.

Zercher, who gave her account of what transpired aboard the *Longhorn One* in a sworn affidavit, also claimed that Bill repeatedly said, "Oh, we should run off to Bermuda," and complained that Zercher, Fields, and Schiff never stayed at the same hotel where he was registered. This was no accident: It was at Hillary's specific instructions that her husband's handlers made sure to book separate hotels for Clinton and the cabin crew.

Hillary also made it clear that the flight attendants were never to be photographed getting off the plane with Bill, or even on the tarmac at the same time. "We had to wait on the plane," said another member of the flight crew, "until Clinton got into his limo and was actually driven away. *Then* we could leave."

When she and the other women were with him, said Zercher, "there was almost never any conversation, about politics or even the weather. It was all sex, sex, sex."

To Zercher's amazement, Clinton made a habit of never locking the bathroom door. One night, she accidentally opened the lavatory door and saw him standing there with his pants unzipped.

"Well, why don't you come in and shut the door?" he said matter-of-factly.

Zercher apologized, but it quickly became clear that he was not joking. "Oh, no, don't worry about it, any time, come on in and shut the door."

Bill seemed intent on shocking the three women on board, and joked about the Gennifer Flowers scandal as it threatened to short-circuit his campaign. When the attendants were passing around a copy of Flowers's steamy interview in *Penthouse,* Clinton "seemed delighted," Zercher said. He asked each to pick out her favorite passage in the *Penthouse* piece, and beamed when Schiff selected Flowers's statement that Bill was "good" at performing oral sex. "That's pretty accurate," he nodded with a broad grin. "It's one of my favorite things."

But Zercher would claim Bill's inappropriate behavior on *Longhorn One* went far beyond the verbal. Once, while Angela Fields was taking snapshots in the galley, Bill came up behind Zercher, grabbed her from behind, pressed his body up against hers, and then squeezed one of her breasts.

"How's that?" he asked. Fields was so stunned that she did not take the picture.

The most egregious incident, according to Zercher, took place within feet of Hillary. The candidate's wife had her own schedule and her own plane, so she rarely traveled with Bill aboard *Longhorn One*. But on an overnight flight from New York to California, Hillary and Bill were stretched out asleep when Zercher walked to the front of the plane and sat on a jump seat not more than six feet away from the Clintons.

It was then that Bill, leaving Hillary behind, walked up and sat down next to the comely flight attendant. "Tell me all about yourself," he said.

"My life's boring," Zercher replied. "Aren't you tired? We had a really long day. Why don't you lie down?"

"No, I just want to sit here . . ." Then he rested his head on her right shoulder. Hillary, Zercher observed, was not only asleep but snoring—loudly.

At first his arms were crossed. "I just want to lay here and relax," he said as he snuggled more into Zercher's side, "and you do all the talking. Just tell me about yourself."

So she did. As Zercher talked, Bill began rubbing her left breast with his left hand. It was then, she said, "I just totally stopped talking. It was like I couldn't even swallow." She was afraid, she later said, that Hillary would awaken and discover what her husband was doing.

Bill asked Zercher to resume telling her life's story, so she began to talk about her two failed marriages.

"Was the sex at least good?" he asked. When she hesitated to answer, he kept demanding to know the answer. "Was the sex good? Was the sex good?"

Over a period of forty minutes, Bill continued to rub Zercher's breast intermittently. Finally, Debra Schiff walked up and saw Zercher's eyes wide open in a state of panic. "I really think," Schiff told Clinton, "you'd be more comfortable in your chair."

Schiff, unlike Zercher, apparently saw nothing wrong with Clinton's behavior. "You won't believe what he just said," she would often report to the others with a giggle. "He's *so* bad."

After an impromptu airborne dance party, Bill and Debra took a break and were seated next to each other when a photographer sneaked up to take some candid photos. At first Bill, unaware of the photographer's presence, stroked her bare knee and the inside of her thigh while she talked into the public address system. When he realized pictures were being taken, he withdrew his hand and smiled sheepishly.

"There isn't anything I wouldn't do for him," Schiff often told the others. Her loyalty would be rewarded with a job as a receptionist in the West Wing, where their special friendship would continue.

Judging by her brusque demeanor the few times she traveled aboard *Longhorn One*, it seems likely that Hillary had her suspicions about what some reporters called "Bill's flying harem." Hillary did not wish to be introduced to the flight attendants, and rarely spoke to them.

From Zercher's perspective, things weren't much better between the Clintons themselves. There were no tender, shared moments—no hugs or furtive kisses, no laughter. Only coldly analytical discussions of campaign strategy.

Years later, when rumors about what really went on aboard the campaign plane began circulating following Paula Jones's sexual harassment suit against the then-President, people began asking questions. Clinton troubleshooter Bruce Lindsey called Zercher. "What did they want to know?" she recalled Lindsey asking nervously. "Did they want to know if Clinton was flirting on the plane? Did you say anything to anybody?"

At that point Zercher told Lindsey, who would later admit making the call, that she had not yet told any reporters about what transpired aboard *Longhorn One*. If she did talk to a reporter, Lindsey instructed her, "say only positive things."

At about the same time, the police were called by an upstairs neighbor of Zercher who reported hearing someone break into her apartment. When she checked, Zercher found her cash, jewelry, and car keys, all untouched. But on closer inspection, she saw that the closet door had been opened and one item taken: a box containing her diary and most of the photographs she had taken aboard the Clinton campaign plane.

After a falling-out with Bill in 1991, Betsey Wright had been lured back into the Clinton camp just in time to set up what she called a "Truth Squad" aimed at stamping out "bimbo eruptions." The squad would first determine which women might present a problem for Bill, then assemble dossiers on them. Confronted with the details of messy divorces, illegitimate children, financial irregularities, abortions, substance abuse problems, and other embarrassing tidbits from their own pasts, many of these women were easily persuaded to remain silent.

Toward that end, the White House hired noted San Francisco–based private investigators Jack Palladino and Sandra Sutherland to delve into the pasts of Bill's potential accusers. They sought out people close to the women in question to undermine their credibility or cast doubt on their characters. Typical was the case of Sally Perdue, the former Miss Arkansas with whom Clinton had a fling in 1983. Palladino tracked down an estranged relative who was willing to make negative statements about Perdue and then, with the relative's permission, gave his name and phone number to the press. As a result of this and other hardball tactics aimed at silencing Bill's critics, the mainstream press ignored the stories of several women who came forward. "The approach," observed one *Washington Post* reporter, "appears to have worked."

However reluctant she may have been to display her affection toward Bill aboard *Longhorn One*, Hillary was genuinely upset about the physical toll the grueling campaign schedule was taking on him. She complained loudly and often to James Carville that he was not taking good enough care of her husband, who often seemed to be fighting a cold or a sore throat. "Bill is tired," she told Carville. "He needs his rest, and I have called you on that, and I'm not going to call you anymore, James. I want this done. Now."

Although it did trigger a brief dip in the polls, the Gennifer Flowers scandal did not derail the campaign. But the release of Bill's 1969 letter to Colonel Holmes in which he thanked the colonel for "saving me from the draft" came very close to doing just that.

After the *Wall Street Journal* ran a story about Bill's alleged draft evasion, he was back home in Little Rock with a bad cough and a fever, fighting off the effects of the flu. Hillary called an emergency meeting in the East Conference Room of the Governor's Mansion to talk about Bill's alarming twenty-point drop in the polls.

Pounding his fist against his knee and shouting ("The goddamn fucking middle-class tax cut is killing me!"), Bill had managed to convince himself that the Republicans were at the root of his problem, and not his own past come back to haunt him.

In what would be a scene replayed numberless times over the next several years, Hillary rallied the troops. "We're going to fight like hell!" she said of the primary contest in New Hampshire, only nine days away. "We're going to fight like we do in Arkansas. If this was Arkansas, Bill, you would be on every radio station, you would be out in every county fighting. In New Hampshire, they don't know you. But they're no different from the people in Arkansas. We have to fight. That is the problem."

Flowers and the draft issue would not sink the Clinton campaign. But for a time it looked as if Hillary might.

While Bill was literally flirting with disaster on his campaign plane, Hillary fended off attacks from every angle. Questions concerning Hillary's work at Rose resurrected the long-dormant conflict of interest issue. Then there was Whitewater—a catchall phrase that encompassed the Whitewater land development and the failure of Madison Guaranty Savings and Loan. Hillary and Bill were quick to point out that they actually lost $68,900 on the Whitewater deal—clear evidence, they maintained, that they had not sought to profit from any illegal or improper transaction.

More significantly, Hillary took the brunt of the criticism for the Clintons' espoused cocandidacy, and was even likened to Evita Perón. "The last thing we want," sniped one Republican, "is a First Lady Macbeth." Said her old nemesis Richard Nixon: "Hillary pounds on the piano so hard that Bill can't be heard. You want a wife who's intelligent, but not *too* intelligent."

At times, it did appear that Hillary was the dominant half of their highly touted partnership. When Clinton swept the Super Tuesday primaries and again when he won in Illinois, Hillary almost appeared to shove her husband aside to make a long, impassioned victory speech in the guise of an introduction. The actual candidate, meanwhile, waited impatiently in the wings.

In an awkward attempt to answer her critics, Hillary made an offhand remark during a stop at Chicago's Busy Bee coffee shop that would haunt her for years. "I suppose I could have stayed home and baked cookies and had teas," she said. "But what I decided to do was pursue my profession, which I entered before my husband was in public life."

Hillary's gaffe was interpreted as an indictment of stay-at-home mothers everywhere. Clinton's subsequent plunge in the polls was so drastic that Carville and pollster Stanley Greenberg put together a memo in April 1992 making the argument that Hillary should undergo an image makeover.

Focus groups and polls showed, said Carville and Greenberg, that most people thought Hillary was "going for the power. More than Nancy Reagan, she is seen as 'running the show.' The absence of affection, children and family and the preoccupation with career and power only reinforces the political problem evident from the beginning." The detailed memo concluded that Hillary should appear "affectionate and maternal," and suggested a wide range of staged events including "joint appearances with her friends where Hillary can laugh, do her mimicry," and "Bill and Chelsea surprise Hillary on Mother's Day." It was also suggested that the Clintons take a family vacation—preferably to either Disneyland or Disney World.

Heeding the memo's advice, Hillary pulled back immediately. She emerged two months later wearing pale pinks, blues, and yellows and looking every inch the prim, traditional, nonthreatening candidate's wife. Now she stuck to ribbon-cuttings, hospital visits, and photo ops with children. Chelsea, whose privacy they had so jealously guarded, was trotted out to underscore Hillary's role as a caring mom.

Whenever she got the chance, Hillary dismissed the idea that she would have any formal role in her husband's administration. He had promised he would not appoint her to a cabinet post, and she stressed that if he did she wouldn't accept. Neither of them was aware that, in accordance with a law passed after JFK appointed his brother Bobby attorney general, such nepotism was prohibited.

At the International Ladies Garment Workers Union convention, she demonstrated her prowess with a sewing machine. At a high school appearance in Conway, Arkansas, a student asked what her role would be. "I want," Hillary replied, "to be the voice for children in the White House." She told students at LaSalle University in Pennsylvania that "the most important thing in my life right now is my daughter, Chelsea."

"I'll do anything you want," Barbara Bush once told her husband's media advisor Roger Ailes. "But I won't dye my hair, change my wardrobe, or lose weight." Hillary, widely touted as the more independent of the two, was willing to do all those things—"whatever it takes," she told Bill, "to get us elected."

When she arrived in Los Angeles that June for the California primary, Hillary put the finishing touches on her transformation with the help of FOBs (Friends of Bill) Linda Bloodworth-Thomason and Academy Award–winning actress Mary Steenburgen, another Arkansan in Hollywood. Christophe, one of the industry's top hairstylists, chopped five inches off Hillary's hair and colored it yet again—this time to deeper, richer "honey-blond." Cliff Chally, who did the clothes for the Thomasons' hit television series *Designing Women*, helped her pick a new wardrobe of more tailored, sleek designer suits and dresses. Hillary joked that she had only one rule: "No Nancy Reagan red." Wrapped in a hotel bathrobe between fittings, she emerged with a wardrobe that was not only feminine but chic, classic, polished.

With the national spotlight trained on New York during the Democratic National Convention, Hillary seized the opportunity to undo all the damage done by her careless (if heartfelt) "tea and cookies" remark. She accepted a challenge from *Family Circle* magazine to compete with then–First Lady Barbara Bush in a cookie bake-off. "My friends say my recipe is more Democratic because I use vegetable shortening instead of butter," gushed Hillary, now resembling a blond Junior Leaguer in pearls and velvet headband.

In the same piece she described herself "as an old-fashioned patriot. I cry on the Fourth of July when kids put crepe paper on their bicycle wheels, so this is, like, just incredible—it's so extraordinary to me."

Although her cookies were actually baked by a friend's cook, Hillary won the contest. A *New York Times* article about the bake-off showed Tipper Gore and the new, nonthreatening Hillary enjoying tea at the Waldorf-Astoria Hotel.

On July 16, 1992, Hillary, clad in a pastel yellow silk suit, gazed adoringly at her husband as he accepted the Democratic presidential nomination at Madison Square Garden "in the name of the hard-working Americans who make up our forgotten middle class." Hillary grabbed Tipper Gore, wife of Clinton's running mate Al Gore, and did a little dance that, Bill would later say, reminded him of two "1960s teenyboppers recovering their lost youth."

It had been a banner day for the Clintons. Just hours earlier, H. Ross Perot, the Texas billionaire who had mounted a serious third-party candidacy, announced that he was dropping out of the race. For the time being, at least, it was a major shot in the arm for the Democrats.

The Hillary who chattered on about cookie recipes and claimed with a straight face to be "just a homebody at heart" was strictly for public consumption. Behind the scenes, she "basically ran the show," said one top aide. "Whenever she saw that he was flagging, she came up with a plan, a pep talk, whatever it took to get everybody back on track." As for her approach to the opposition: "Hillary is a lioness, protecting her lair and her mate. She has a real killer instinct—survival of the fittest. It was implicit in everything she said that it was a fight-to-the-death, us-or-them kind of thing." Accordingly, it was Hillary who dubbed Clinton's campaign nerve center "The War Room."

In her role as commanding general, Hillary spared no one—not even her husband, whom she continually berated for not being tough enough on his staff. During the New York primary, Stephanopoulos walked into their hotel suite one morning and saw Hillary "standing over him at the dining room table, finger in his face as he shoveled cereal into his mouth, his head bent close to the bowl." When Bill and Hillary fought, he noted, "it wasn't fun to watch."

Mary Matalin, James Carville's future wife and at the time President Bush's blunt-speaking campaign spokesperson, was brutal in her criticism of Bill. But she also knew what role Hillary played out of camera range. On Matalin's wall was a cartoon of Hillary as the Wicked Witch in *The Wizard of Oz*. The caption read: "I will get you, my pretty, and your little dog too."

Given her husband's erratic behavior, Hillary's desire to stay focused was only understandable. "After all," observed historian Gary Wills, "she does not know, from day to day, what she may have to cope with."

Yet she grew increasingly concerned about the state of his health, both mental and physical. At one point during the campaign when he was being pulled in several different directions by his advisors, Hillary demanded that he return to Little Rock to reflect on the issues and "recharge his batteries." When they continued to insist that he hit the road and appear on every television outlet from MTV to *Arsenio Hall*, she put her foot down. "Look," she told Stephanopoulos, Carville, Paul Begala, and the others, "he may agree with you. But he has to come to it in his own way." Hillary would employ this phrase—"He has to come to it in his own way"—whenever she felt Bill was in danger of being unfairly pressured to take a stand.

She was no less concerned about Bill's ballooning weight. The governor's eating habits were the stuff of Arkansas myth. When he ate an apple, he devoured the entire thing—core, stem, and seeds. "He would pick up a baked potato with his hands," recalled State Trooper Roger Perry, "and eat it in two bites. I've never seen anything like it."

In the course of the campaign, when a candidate would generally be expected to lose weight, Bill had gained twenty-six pounds, blimping from 200 to 226. "Christ, Bill," she would say, yanking a half-eaten cheeseburger from his hand, "you know you're not supposed to be eating that crap." Hillary made an exception for room service meals, which since childhood she had regarded as "the ultimate luxury." The couple would, an aide recalls, sit side by side on the sofa, "eating sundaes and giggling."

Dolly Kyle Browning, who had charted Bill's wildly fluctuating weight since they were childhood sweethearts, had a different explanation. "Billy is an addictive personality," she said. "He is addicted to sex, and when he doesn't have access to that, he replaces the sex addiction with a food addiction. You can tell the state of his sex life by his weight. When Billy's weight goes up, that means he isn't active sexually. When he slims down, then you know he's out there doing his usual thing."

Notwithstanding Dolly's weight-gain-as-sexual-barometer theory, the Clintons took advantage of every available photo op to portray themselves as a devoted couple. The public was soon awash in pictures of Bill and Hillary embracing, holding hands, sharing a private joke. "Oh, they're in love all right," said one close friend, "but let's just say they're a lot more in love when a camera's around." Another campaign worker, who went on to take a top staff position in the White House, added, "When you see his mouth wide open and they're grinning from ear-to-ear, they just realized the press was around. Chances are that under their breath they're talking about poll results or she's nagging him to lose weight."

Even those friends who saw obvious strains in the marriage insisted that the affection between them was real. "You couldn't sustain that level of irritation," one said, "if it were an arrangement." Concurred another lawyer friend of Hillary's: "I don't doubt that she's probably wanted to kill him sometimes—and with good reason. But this relationship is more than a cold, practical bargain. They like each other immensely."

In the closing days of the campaign, there were tender private moments between them. Often he could be seen reworking a speech while she stood behind him, massaging his shoulders. After a particularly hectic day that had taken a toll on the candidate's voice, Stephanopoulos walked into the Clintons' hotel suite and found Hillary on the couch with Bill, her legs slung over his lap, dipping slices of lemon in a jar of honey and feeding them to him.

"There were times," he said, "when they were affectionate—like little kids."

On election night, Hillary paced the floor of the Governor's Mansion in Little Rock. It had been her ritual since 1980, when exit polls showed her husband winning reelection as governor even as he was going down to defeat. Now she waited until Ohio put her husband over the top in the electoral college. Bill had received 43 percent of the popular vote, Bush 38 percent, and Perot 19 percent.

Bill now faced the task of winning over the 57 percent who voted against him. Hillary was confident that he could. She wrapped her arms around him, kissed him, and told him how much she loved him. She was proud, she said, that he had stood up to everything that had been thrown at him and never stopped believing in himself.

"You will be a great president," she said to him.

"You really think so?" Bill asked, as if suddenly struck by the enormity of the task ahead.

"Yeah," Hillary replied with a smile, "I really think so."

On election night the Clintons' car pulled up at the Old State House, where they were to make their first appearance before the nation as First Family–elect. Bill jumped out of the limousine and plunged into the crowd, leaving papers on the seat behind him. Hillary scooped them up and emerged clutching the papers in her hand. "Bill's speech," she said, hurrying with Chelsea to catch up to him.

After a night of celebrating, Hillary went to bed around 1 A.M. and was joined by Bill three hours later. At around 9 A.M., the phone rang in the mansion.

"Will you please hold," the operator told a hapless aide, "for President Boris Yeltsin?"

"No," Bruce Lindsey told the aide. "Let him sleep. Tell him to call back tomorrow." West German Chancellor Helmut Kohl and British Prime Minister John Major also called to congratulate the American President-elect, and were similarly rebuffed.

It would be hours before the next president and his First Lady finally stirred awake. Three days earlier, NBC's Tom Brokaw had asked Hillary what she thought she would do when they woke up that first morning and looked at each other. "Pull the covers over our heads," she had replied.

When they actually did awaken that morning, Bill and Hillary pulled the covers up to their necks, took one long look at each other—and burst out laughing.

I'm having to become quite an expert in this business of asking for forgiveness. It gets a little easier the more you do it.

—Bill

I could see in her eyes a real hurt, and a loss of bearings.

—*Henry Cisneros*

7

"WHO DO YOU want in the room," the reporter asked the President-elect, "when you make the big decisions?"

"Hillary." With a single word, Bill had erased any doubt that his wife would be unlike any First Lady before, occupying an important role in shaping administration policy. During the delicate transition period, Hillary dropped much of the pretense concerning her devotion to hearth and home. Now her staff referred to her as HRC—the name scrawled on the boxes containing her White House–bound files—and she made a point of always signing her name Hillary *Rodham* Clinton.

"It's rare that I think he's wrong," Hillary said. "We think so much alike and our values are so much alike." Accordingly, she sat in on his *Time* magazine "Man of the Year" interview, explaining their position on a variety of domestic and international policy issues.

Indeed, it quickly became clear that the White House staff had not one but two masters. Shortly after Stephanopoulus had worked out the ground rules for the way a small pool of reporters would cover the President-elect, the Clintons took their first postelection vacation to Hilton Head, South Carolina. Bill, Hillary, and Chelsea left their house to take a bike ride on the beach when Hillary noticed two pickup trucks carrying the pool reporters. She turned to one of the Secret Service agents and barked, "No trucks!" The reporters were instructed to leave, and the happy family trio went on their way, trailed by a dozen agents.

Later, as they headed back, Bill obliged the band of hungry photographers by joining in a game of touch football with Chelsea and thirty or so vacationers. Hillary, meanwhile, just glided by on her bike, never bothering to look back.

"If we disagree and I think I'm right," Bill said of their partnership, "I just go on and do what I think is right. And then she tells me, 'I told you so.'" But Bill actively sought out Hillary's advice, and seldom if ever declined to take it. For that—and the fact that he made no apologies for her activist role in his embryonic administration—Hillary was grateful. "I am," she would say periodically as they prepared for their greatest challenge, "so very proud of you."

They both had reason to be proud of Chelsea, who on Friday, January 15, said goodbye to the friends and schoolmates she had known her entire life growing up in Little Rock. When her school held a special assembly to say goodbye, Chelsea "told us to stay home," her father said. "She didn't want any press coverage for it. She just wanted it to be between her and her friends. So we did."

On Saturday, the Clintons prepared to leave Little Rock for Charlottesville, Virginia. The next morning, they were scheduled to attend a church service and then roll into Washington at the head of a bus caravan, following the route Thomas Jefferson took from Monticello 192 years before.

"Chelsea had a tough day Saturday when we left," Bill later recalled. "She cried . . . But I think she's really now looking forward to it. She seems to have sort of passed that watershed and I think she's kind of into it."

Saturday was a tough day for Chelsea's mother, too. Just before they left Little Rock airport, Hillary spotted trooper Larry Patterson escorting one of Bill's paramours—the wife of a Little Rock judge—to the farewell ceremony. "What the fuck do you think you're doing?" she asked Patterson. "I know who that whore is. I know what she's doing here. Get her out of here!"

Bill, standing only steps away, merely shrugged. So Patterson dutifully led "that whore" away, dropping her off at the Holiday Inn Center City.

Hillary apparently had cause to be upset. Even after winning the election, Bill continued to flirt with disaster by arranging trysts under the noses of the Secret Service agents. Women brought to the door of the mansion when Hillary was not home were told to identify themselves as either staff or cousins of the state troopers.

An attractive Arkansas Power and Light official who had been linked to Bill for years was ushered into the mansion one morning at 5:15. A trooper brought her into the mansion through a basement door that led into a game room where the President-elect was waiting. Once again, the troopers were told to stand guard and alert Bill if Hillary woke up.

The public was unaware of the tensions simmering beneath the surface during inauguration week, a five-day-long blur of staged events designed to play to the television cameras. "Clinton grew up in the age of television," NBC's Tom Brokaw observed, "and this is the first clear demonstration of it."

As soon as they arrived in Washington, the President-elect's family and his staff moved into Blair House, and then dove headlong into the festivities. There was a parade across the Potomac to Virginia, where Bill rang a replica of the Liberty Bell. The glittering lineup for Monday night's inaugural gala included Barbra Streisand, Aretha Franklin, Bob Dylan, Elizabeth Taylor, Michael Bolton, Stevie Wonder, Kenny Rogers, and Diana Ross. Judy Collins sang "Amazing Grace," and Fleetwood Mac reunited to belt out Clinton's campaign song, "Don't Stop (Thinking About Tomorrow)." For the grand finale, Bill, Hillary, Chelsea, and the Gores took to the stage and joined in a rendition of "We Are the World" led by Michael Jackson.

They returned to Blair House, where Bill, Hillary, and several key staff members worked on the President's inaugural address until dawn. As usual, as the time for the noon swearing-in ceremony approached, the Clintons were running late. While George and Barbara Bush were kept waiting at the White House for nearly a half hour, television cameras captured Bill emerging from Blair House, his jaw muscles rippling as he waited impatiently for Hillary.

Then he turned toward the door, and as a *USA Today* reporter would put it, "said some word the microphones didn't catch."

The Secret Service agents assigned to cover the new First Family and a park police officer heard precisely what he yelled—"That fucking bitch!"—and what Hillary replied as she dashed past him and into the waiting limousine: "You stupid motherfucker!"

George Bush was standing at the top step of the North Portico when the Clintons finally arrived at the White House. "Chelsea," he said, hand outstretched, "welcome to your new house."

At noon, Hillary stood gazing at Bill in practiced wonder as he placed his hand on the Clinton family Bible and took the oath of office from Chief Justice William Rehnquist. Then, in his first gesture as the forty-second President of the United States, Bill kissed his First Lady. Then he wrapped Hillary and twelve-year-old Chelsea in a bear hug.

After the swearing in, the new First Couple were escorted to a holding room in the Capitol before the traditional lunch with congressional leaders. After several minutes passed, a Capitol police officer was told to inform the Clintons that it was time to proceed to lunch. The officer opened the door, but withdrew as soon as he saw Hillary shrieking at her husband. "Goddammit, Bill," she screamed, "you promised me that office!"

The argument that had raged intermittently since Blair House, it turned out, was over whether Bill was willing to give Hillary the White House office traditionally assigned to the Vice-President. Ultimately, Al Gore got to keep his space. But Hillary got her way, as well. Although the residential and ceremonial East Wing had always been considered the First Lady's territory, Hillary demanded and got an office next door to the office of the White House Counsel.

After the congressional lunch, they piled into their bulletproof limousine and led the inaugural parade down Pennsylvania Avenue with an exhausted Chelsea squeezed in between them. The Clintons hopped out to walk the last three blocks to their new home, but after a few steps Chelsea, cold and windblown, got back into the car and rode the rest of the way.

That evening, Bill and Hillary, now sparkling in a blue lace gown by New York designer Sarah Phillips, swirled across the dance floor at no fewer than eleven inaugural balls scattered across town. Chelsea, wearing a green velvet dress with matching green necklace and earrings, joined them onstage at several before returning home that night.

"Home" was now 1600 Pennsylvania Avenue, and the Clintons spent their first night there wandering from room to room in a state of exhaustion and wonder. "It's simply overwhelming," recalled Hillary, who years later would claim that she had still not yet visited every room in the White House. "Overwhelming—and more than a little terrifying at first."

Even the family cat, Socks, was apprehensive. He had boarded for three days at Little Rock's Hillcrest Animal Hospital, getting his shots and being groomed for the move to Washington. Socks was also fitted with a new red harness for introductory walks around the White House grounds. Indoors, he wore a red jeweled collar. For his first act as the official White House pet, Socks threw up on the West Hall carpet—an act, according to one White House maid, he was prone to do with surprising frequency.

Hillary had gone to considerable lengths to make the transition less traumatic for Chelsea. So that the new First Daughter would not be alone during those first few strange nights in the White House, Hillary invited five of Chelsea's friends from Little Rock for a sleepover. To keep them entertained, the First Lady organized a scavenger hunt. The girls scampered all over the house looking for one particularly elusive object—a red bird. It was, Chelsea eventually discovered, a detail of a painting hanging in the Red Room.

A few months earlier, Hillary had been invited to lunch with Jackie Onassis at her sprawling Fifth Avenue apartment opposite New York's Metropolitan Museum. Much of their conversation centered on raising children in the fishbowl of the White House. During her time in the White House, Jackie had told Secret Service agents that it was not the job of "grown men to go around waiting on Caroline and John like servants."

"One of the things we talked a lot about," Hillary remembered, "was the effect of the press on children in ways that aren't always obvious, and adults around children in these roles who cater, or play up, protect, or give them all sorts of benefits, whether they earned them or not. She told me about how once the Secret Service intervened when her son encountered some bullies in the park. Obviously, she didn't want her children endangered, but when it came to ordinary give-and-take with kids she wanted them to handle their own problems."

Heeding Jackie's warning, Hillary tried to treat Chelsea the way any mother would treat her adolescent daughter. "I can't tell you," said a former aide, "how many times she used to ask, 'Chelsea, is your homework done? Is your room clean? It doesn't look clean.' (In reality, Hillary had been concerned about the effects of privilege on her daughter ever since she overheard a six-year-old Chelsea tell a friend that if the little girl didn't play the game Chelsea wanted to play, "I'll tell my daddy to call out the National Guard.")

To maintain some sense of normalcy for Chelsea over the course of the next four years, Hillary would often go shopping with her at Banana Republic and The Gap. In one instance, the First Lady hopped on a bicycle and, trailed by a small army of Secret Service agents on bikes and in cars, pedaled three miles to the National Zoo. There she joined Chelsea's class on a field trip.

After they had been in the Executive Mansion three weeks, Hillary decided she wanted to stock the second-floor kitchen so the staff would know what they liked to eat. "I picked up Chelsea at school," she recalled, "and we stopped at the first supermarket we saw. I opened my wallet and discovered that I had only eleven dollars."

She asked to speak to the manager. "Do you take credit cards?"

He just stood, stunned to see Hillary and Chelsea Clinton standing in line at his supermarket.

"Do you take credit cards here?" she asked again.

"We . . . we don't yet. But we're going to—soon. Like March."

"This is, like February," she said. "So I guess I can't buy anything today."

For the most part, Chelsea at least gave the impression of being a clear-eyed and confident eighth grader. Hillary occasionally escorted her to school, and on the second day of school she had to hit up Dad for lunch money (still in the habit of never carrying money, he borrowed it from his secretary). Chelsea signed on as goalie for the school soccer team, and would join her friends at the nearby Roy Rogers for an after-school snack—unperturbed by the ever-present Secret Service contingent tagging along.

Unlike Mom, Bill preferred to indulge his daughter any way he could. One Sunday night, George Stephanopoulos was dining in a Washington restaurant when his beeper went off. He dialed the White House from a pay phone, and was immediately put through to the Oval Office. Chelsea, who did her homework in the presidential study next door to the Oval Office, was having trouble with her school project on immigration. Contact the Immigration and Naturalization Service, the President told his top advisor, and get Chelsea the information she needed on border guards.

Within a matter of minutes, Stephanopoulos was able to contact the INS and get back to his boss with the information he requested. The President then passed it along to Chelsea.

At home, Chelsea rode her bike, ordered take-out pizza, and played card games (usually hearts or pinochle) with her parents. Once or twice a week they watched a first-run film in the White House movie theater. But after each screening, Hillary insisted that Chelsea sweep the popcorn off the floor.

For all the Clintons' efforts to maintain a zone of privacy around their daughter, she could not escape public scrutiny entirely. Even before they arrived in the White House, she had had to endure the humiliation of being cruelly parodied on NBC's *Saturday Night Live*. And when the populist President and outspokenly progressive First Wife chose to send their only daughter to the private Sidwell Friends School instead of a public school, there were cries of hypocrisy.

Yet, at least during her father's first term, Chelsea would suffer remarkably little—particularly in light of the scandals and controversies that buffeted her parents on a more or less continual basis. First came "Nannygate," the revelation even before Clinton took office that his nominee for attorney general, Zoë Baird, had failed to pay Social Security taxes for her household staff and that they were illegal aliens. After she withdrew, Kimba Wood was the appointee-designate—until it was discovered that she, too, had employed an illegal immigrant, although at the time, it was not illegal to do so. After one day, she withdrew her name from consideration.

(Judge Wood, a former *Playboy* bunny, would later make headlines with her own extramarital affair, the steamy details of which were recorded in the diary of her then-lover, New York financier Frank Richardson.)

The President's shifting position on gays in the military was another problem, soon to be followed by the furor caused when Air Force One held up air traffic at Los Angeles Airport so Bill could get a $200 haircut from Christophe. Then came Travelgate—the Hillary-engineered firing of longtime White House travel staffers and their replacement with cronies from Arkansas, specifically Clinton's distant "cousin" Catherine Cornelius and a firm run by Harry Thomason. "So much for opening like FDR or JFK," Stephanopoulos later recalled. "Our first Hundred Days were no honeymoon."

FOBs like the Thomasons, Bill's childhood friend and White House Chief of Staff Mack McLarty, Webb Hubbell, and actresses Mary Steenburgen and Markie Post wasted no time making themselves right at home in the White House. Their second night there, in fact, the Clintons invited the Thomasons and Post, the stunningly attractive blonde who starred in the hit television series *Night Court*, for dinner. Afterward, they all went upstairs to the family quarters. While Bill and Hillary changed, Post climbed up on the Lincoln bed and began jumping up and down. "We made it!" she yelled, bouncing violently and waving her arms as Bloodworth-Thomason joined her. "We're in the White House now!"

Away from the cameras, the Clinton style inside the White House could be charitably described as casual. The President and First Lady both padded around in sweat clothes, T-shirts, and running shoes; it was common to see him slouching in sweats and a baseball cap, gobbling down a banana smeared with peanut butter as he signed an executive order. But the laid-back attitude belied mounting tensions. From the beginning, Bill had complained that the Secret Service detail and others on the White House staff seemed remote, even hostile. "Those guys," he said of the Secret Service agents, "just don't like me."

He was right—some of them didn't. Following in the footsteps of the warm yet dignified Bushes, the Clintons offended many longtime White House staffers with their come-as-you-are attire, their lack of punctuality, and their oddly imperious manner. Many were shocked by the frequency and the intensity with which both the President and the First Lady employed choice Anglo-Saxonisms. "Everything," said one ex–White House staffer, "was fuck this or fuck that. They talked like that in front of congressman, senators, even Chelsea—although I have to say I never heard Chelsea use language like that. One time an ambassador was waiting to pay his respects to Hillary, and you could hear her plainly on the other side of the door, swearing like a sailor at some poor assistant. She can be very, very loud."

At least in public, Hillary's rages still paled in comparison to the verbal thunderbolts routinely hurled by her husband. Now that he had achieved his lifelong goal, several of Bill's underlings thought that he might mellow—that the "petty tirades," as Dick Morris once called them, might begin to fade.

Not so. Along with his ritual morning cup of coffee, staffers could count on being screamed at by the boss at the start of virtually every day—an eruption as predictable as Old Faithful and twice as gaseous. So unrelenting were the tantrums that George Stephanopoulos came to see himself as the President's permanent crash test dummy, there to absorb Bill's anger so that he could get on with the job of governing.

Often, Stephanopoulos pointed out, it was as if the President was "yelling not at you, but *through* you." A typical rant concerning a staffer who mistakenly excluded some people from a meeting: "I want him dead, dead. I want him killed. I want him horse-whipped. I want him fired." To Senator Bob Kerrey over the phone when it looked like Kerrey might vote against Clinton's economic plan: "My presidency's going to go down! Fuck you!" About a moderately critical story in the *Washington Post*: "This is *bullshit!*" (Chelsea inherited her dad's distaste for the *Post*, telling Dick Morris's niece she would never read it because "they don't like my parents.")

The First Couple's lack of self-control was quickly mimicked by staff members. After one prickly White House news briefing, Press Secretary Dee Dee Myers wheeled around and shouted at reporters: "Eat shit and die!"

Not surprisingly, Bill was at his angriest when it occurred to him that Chelsea was now old enough to read the published reports of his womanizing. "How is my daughter going to feel when she reads these lies, this horseshit?"

Morris went on to describe the frightening way in which Clinton's anger spiraled out of control. "His face became raw, red, and angry as he railed against the injustice and the violation," Morris recalled. "He wouldn't stop. On and on he would talk, into the night, pounding his fist . . ." Morris found the display "deeply disturbing . . . I watched him as if I were a small child watching a father lose control—frightening in its intensity . . . no less disquieting when it is a president of the United States."

Upstairs at the White House, however, Hillary appeared to have the upper hand. The pitched battles that had raged at the Governor's Mansion in Little Rock were now taking place with equal ferocity among the Federal-period furnishings and burnished antiques in the White House family quarters.

They had been in the White House only a matter of weeks when Hillary, in yet another fit of rage, was shrieking at her husband as a Secret Service agent observed them from the hallway. The agent saw Hillary pick up the lamp and throw it at the President. He ducked, and the lamp went crashing to the floor. Undeterred, Hillary continued screaming into her husband's beet-red face.

When the Secret Service agents who witnessed the incident leaked it to the press, Hillary was furious. Publicly, she laughed it off. Asked about the report of the tossed lamp, she replied, "A lamp or a Bible or a Mercedes-Benz, or, you know, there were many variations on it . . ."

Was it true, Barbara Walters asked, that she had certain Secret Service members put on another detail? "No, no, I wanted the situation cleared up—both for the Secret Service's sake . . . but also for my sake. I mean, you know, I have a pretty good arm. If I'd thrown a lamp at somebody I think you would have known about it, and you know, when those things are said, I just don't want that to get a life of its own."

But the American public *did* know about it, and Hillary had ordered that Secret Service agents be barred from areas of the family residence. Testifying before a congressional panel, Hillary's chief of staff Maggie Williams conceded that an incident had taken place that left the First Lady "feeling compromised."

After she was unable to convince the Treasury Department to replace her Secret Service detail with the Secret Service agents who had protected her husband during the 1992 campaign, Hillary's resentment toward the men assigned to guard her safety grew. Several times, in public, she admonished the agents to keep their distance in language that was, to say the least, colorful. "Stay the fuck back, stay the fuck away from me!" she yelled. "Don't come within ten yards of me, or else!"

In April rumors flew once again when the President appeared at a news conference with a lurid two-inch-long gash running from his right earlobe down his jawline and a smaller cut on his neck. Did Socks scratch the President? Press Secretary Dee Dee Myers was asked. No, she replied, the President had cut himself shaving.

But later, the President offered a different explanation. "I got hit playing with my daughter, I'm ashamed to say," he claimed. "Rolling around, acting like a child again. I reaffirm that I'm not a kid anymore."

When reporters pressed the issue and asked which story was true, Communications Director George Stephanopoulos joked, "We'd better get to the bottom of this! Sounds like a real scandal!" Away from the microphones, however, speculation was rife that Hillary had in fact inflicted the wound. Staff members were also perplexed by the conflicting stories. Chelsea was thirteen and it seemed unlikely that she would be "rolling around" with her father, or that in some way she could inadvertently inflict such a deep cut. Moreover, word had filtered down earlier from the second-floor staff that the President and First Lady had had another of their window-rattling rows. Despite continued prodding from the press, no further explanations were forthcoming.

Hillary may not have been able to fire the Secret Service agents whom she suspected of leaking stories to the press, but she had no trouble jettisoning the resident White House physician. The widely esteemed Dr. Burton Lee had spent thirty years at Memorial Sloan-Kettering Hospital in New York before becoming President Bush's physician and head of the White House Medical Unit. Lee had agreed to stay on a few weeks, but was unceremoniously dumped after just a few days.

On Friday, January 22, Lee had been summoned to the office of Deputy Appointments Secretary Nancy Hernreich and told to inject the contents of a vial into the President's arm. Lee was told the vial, which had arrived in the mail, contained Bill's allergy medication.

But Lee refused to administer the shot without first seeing President Clinton's medical records. The following Monday, Lee called Clinton's Little Rock physician, Dr. Susan Santa Cruz, and asked for the President's medical records. He was told that first Dr. Santa Cruz would have to get permission from the First Lady.

One hour later, Dr. Lee was informed that he was being fired. He was given two hours to clear out. "There isn't any question in my mind," Dr. Lee said, "that the person who fired me was Hillary." Navy Captain Dr. E. Connie Mariano, satisfied that the vial did indeed contain allergy medication, gave the President the shot.

For Lee, the swift and brutal reaction to a simple request for medical records was a clear signal that something was amiss. "I've never had anything like this happen in my whole career," he said. "At first I gave them the benefit of the doubt . . . But now, I've got to ask, what's the story here?"

Clinton's handling of his medical history paralleled that of his idol John F. Kennedy. In 1940, JFK's urologist, Dr. William P. Herbst, diagnosed his patient with gonorrhea. Sulfide drugs would clear up the gonorrhea, but for the rest of his life Kennedy would suffer from acute postgonnocal urethritis, a persistent, drug-resistant disease that caused inflammation of the genitals and a burning sensation on urination. Needless to say, JFK's venereal disease, which would ultimately have marital repercussions, was kept under wraps—along with his myriad other medical problems. The medical records themselves would not be made public until 1995—thirty-two years after JFK's assassination.

Facing reelection in 1996, Bill would finally allow himself to be interviewed on the subject of his health in lieu of releasing medical records as other presidential candidates have done in the past. Given his sexual history, the answer to one question took on added significance. "He said," the *New York Times*'s Lawrence K. Altman wrote, "that his press secretary, Michael D. McCurry, had been correct in saying that Mr. Clinton had never had a sexually transmitted disease." Not an outright denial—only the oddly worded explanation that his spokesman was "correct" in repeating what he was told.

Bill was keenly aware that JFK, who also suffered from a wide range of allergies, went to considerable lengths to conceal his venereal disease and his Addison's disease from the American public. The President mentioned to George Stephanopoulos and others that he was astounded to learn that JFK's potent cortisone treatments had acted as an aphrodisiac, supercharging his sex drive.

This was no idle observation. As part of his treatment for persistent back pain and for a subsequent knee injury, Bill was given medication containing cortisone. As with JFK, this may have intensified his already formidable libido, and contributed to his continued sexual recklessness inside the White House.

As Bill Clinton well knew and Dr. Lee quickly discovered, Hillary Clinton was not one to be crossed. While her husband floundered during his first one hundred days in office, she carved a new and controversial role for herself unlike that of any previous First Lady. Not even Edith Wilson, who played a major role behind the scenes after her husband, Woodrow, suffered a stroke, would wield as much power as the woman known around the White House as HRC.

Although her role model when it came to handling problems in her marriage was undoubtedly Jackie Kennedy, Eleanor Roosevelt was her hero. "I'm a die-hard Eleanor Roosevelt fan," she said. "She was often attacked and criticized, but there was never any confusion in her own mind about what constituted a meaningful life. She refused to be categorized or stereotyped, which, of course, greatly frustrated her critics."

But Hillary would go further than Eleanor, whose only official post during FDR's thirteen years in office was an unsalaried position as deputy director of the Office of Civilian Defense. Bill had been in office less than a week when he named his wife to head up his

Health Care Task Force. Her assignment: to draft a bill that would completely revamp the country's unwieldy and inefficient $800 billion health care system.

Five days later, Hillary fussed over the menu for her first White House affair—a black-tie dinner for the nation's governors. In her role as First Lady, she added more fruits and vegetables to the White House mess menu and declared the entire White House complex smoke-free. She also took time off to watch her daughter play goalie at a Sidwell Friends School soccer match (Chelsea's team won 4–1).

"She is representative of what a majority of women are doing today," her press secretary, Lisa Caputo, explained at the time. "And that is balancing career with family and entertaining."

"Career" was the operative word, however, as it rapidly became apparent that the tea-and-cookies Hillary who had helped her husband win the election now felt free to be who she really was—her husband's partner in power. More senior aides were assigned to Hillary than were assigned to the Vice-President. "The administration is something entirely new in American life," marveled Howard Fineman and Mark Miller in *Newsweek*. "It's a Team Presidency whose own act has no script—and whose political consequences are unknown."

Nowhere was this more evident than in her handling of health care reform. Hillary worked with her aide Ira Magaziner to build her own empire inside the White House. Again, Hillary set up a war room to wage her very personal health care battle, only this time it was called the ICU—Hillary's "Intensive Care Unit."

Clad in designer armor—power suit, pearls, black stockings, high heels, and an ever-blonder coif—Hillary, backed by her own national FOH (Friends of Hillary) network, charged into battle. She presided at public hearings, met behind closed doors with key senators and congressmen, and crisscrossed the country with her messages of cost control, preventive medicine, and universal coverage.

At first, the Hillary health juggernaut sent her popularity skyrocketing. Not for long. Unwilling to compromise on even the smallest provisions of her plan, a defiant Hillary squared off against a multitude of special interest groups opposed to reform—and lost. Even her supporters inside the White House agreed that the bill

Hillary's task force crafted was destined for defeat. Like the woman who guided it, Stephanopoulos observed, the plan was "ambitious, idealistic, and highly logical; but it was also inflexible, overly complex, and highly susceptible to misinterpretation."

The Clinton health plan would not only prove to be an unmitigated disaster, it would focus the press's laserlike gaze on the woman behind it. By taking on an unprecedented policymaking role, Hillary opened herself up to increased scrutiny by the press—specifically, concerning her involvement in Whitewater, her work at the Rose Law Firm on behalf of the failed Madison Guaranty Savings and Loan, and those curious short-term commodities transactions that earned Hillary $100,000 on an initial investment of $1,000.

Of these, Hillary's representation of Madison Guaranty raised the frightening possibility that the First Lady of the United States might actually face a criminal indictment. During the freewheeling deregulation days of the 1980s, Bill's pals Susan and Jim McDougal took over Madison Guaranty. They then proceeded, through a series of fraudulent real estate loans, to divert an estimated $17 million to themselves, their relatives, and dozens of political cronies.

Madison Guaranty finally collapsed in 1989, but not before chalking up losses of $60 million—to be paid, of course, by taxpayers through the Federal Deposit Insurance Corporation. Seven years later, after investigations by independent prosecutors Robert Fiske and Kenneth Starr, the McDougals and their partner, Arkansas Governor Jim Guy Tucker, would be convicted on numerous counts of conspiracy and mail fraud.

Hillary was frantic that she might be made the scapegoat for her husband's less-than-aboveboard wheeling and dealing with the powers-that-be in Arkansas. At one staff meeting about Whitewater, she openly wept. "I know everybody's looking out for Bill," she sobbed, "but nobody's out there fighting for *me*." She also sobbed when a scheduling snafu resulted in her husband giving a press conference on health care the same night Hillary's chief of staff testified before the Whitewater grand jury.

While Hillary was generally perceived to be tougher than "The Big Guy," as staffers called him, there were those at the White

House who felt the reverse was true. "He has the soft exterior but there is this hard, cold core," Stephanopoulos said. "She has the tough exterior but inside she's much more real and vulnerable."

Her emotions surfaced in March 1993 when her father suffered a stroke in Little Rock. Hillary flew to her father's bedside. "When we got there," Hillary said, "for the first couple of days he knew we were there, and it was wonderful." Over the next two weeks, she shuttled to and from the hospital as Hugh Rodham hovered between life and death.

While Hillary was keeping a vigil at the bedside of her dying father in Little Rock, Bill was entertaining Barbra Streisand back at the White House. The President's mother had taken a special liking to Barbra, a longtime Clinton booster who had raised millions for Clinton's candidacy and performed at presidential galas.

Clinton often got together with Streisand when he visited California. According to Mike McGrath, who was then chief White House steward, Clinton and Streisand had become "pretty playful" when she accepted an invitation to join him at his hotel suite. McGrath was told by Secret Service agents on the scene that Bill "chased her around the piano."

Bill had arranged similar hotel rendezvous with the stunning blond star Sharon Stone when he was in California. According to Dick Morris, the President was "really, really hot for Sharon Stone. He has it bad for her." During one trip to the West Coast, Clinton changed his schedule so that he and Stone could both be in San Francisco at the same time. Clinton often gushed to friends about his favorite Sharon Stone scene—predictably, the graphic leg-crossing shot in *Basic Instinct*.

Now, with Hillary keeping a deathwatch in Arkansas, Barbra slept in the Lincoln Bedroom. It was only when she returned to Washington that Hillary learned Streisand had been an overnight guest. Whether out of jealousy, rage at Bill's apparent insensitivity, or just concern over the way things looked, Hillary was furious—and reportedly banned Streisand from the White House before returning to Little Rock.

"Barbra got her notch, he got his notch," said one frequent White House guest. "Hillary was livid, but Barbra was too important to the Clintons as a fund-raiser to alienate. So Hillary gave orders that Barbra was never to be at the White House when the First Lady is not there."

"When does life start?" Hillary asked a crowd of ten thousand at the University of Texas the day after her father died at age eighty-two. "When does it end? Who makes those decisions? How do we dare to impinge upon these areas of such delicate, difficult questions? And yet, every day in hospitals and homes and hospices across this country, people are struggling with those very profound issues . . ."

At her father's funeral, Hillary was flanked by the two men she loved most in the world: Bill and Vince Foster. "Bill was very tender and comforting toward Hillary," a friend of the family said. "But so was Vince. He cared deeply for her, and you could see it in his face at the funeral. Vince was devastated because she was in so much pain."

Understandably, the death of her adored father hit Hillary hard. For months she was in mourning, taking solace from her strong Methodist faith and Vince Foster's words of comfort. "It comes up on you at odd times," Hillary said of the waves of grief that would suddenly overtake her in the middle of a speech or during her travels as First Lady. "I was in Montana—something I'd promised to do for a long time. I did not feel like going. I was so tired, drained, but I'm really glad I went, because the people were wonderful and a lot of them engaged me in talking about my father and were generally sympathetic. Today I feel pretty good. I feel we're back to settling in and trying to get rooted again."

Not long after Hillary lost a beloved member of her family, Bill suddenly discovered a family member he never knew he had. On June 20, 1993—Father's Day—Henry Leon Ritzenthaler of Paradise, California, stepped forward to declare that he was the President's half brother. Ritzenthaler, who took his adoptive father's surname, was born Henry Leon Blythe in 1938, the son of William Jefferson Blythe and Blythe's first wife, Adele Gash.

"I don't want nothing from Mr. Clinton at all," Ritzenthaler, former owner of a janitorial service, told *CBS This Morning*. "I don't want no favors or nothing . . . I'd just like to meet him." Ritzenthaler suffered from heart disease, and wanted to find out if Clinton shared any of his medical problems. It turned out there were other things the two men had in common: They were chronically late, had hair-trigger tempers, and loved fast food.

The President, who had heard rumors over the years that he might have a half brother, called his mother as soon as he read Ritzenthaler's story in the *Washington Post*. It came as a complete shock to Virginia; she was not even aware that Bill's father had been married before—let alone twice (in truth, William Blythe had been married three times before and fathered at least three children before Bill).

Immediately, Bill phoned Ritzenthaler and left a message on his answering machine. When he discovered Ritzenthaler had flown to New York to tell his story on television, Bill left a message for him in New York. When they finally spoke, Bill graciously invited his newest sibling to the White House.

Ritzenthaler was only the latest in a series of embarrassments that often made Clinton's aides feel as if they were "back in Dogpatch." Six months earlier another closet relative, Bill's stepsister Diane Welch, attacked the President for shunning her. When she and Bill were both twenty-two years old, Welch's father, Jeff Dwire, had married Bill's mother, Virginia.

Welch, it turned out, was a convicted bank robber and drug dealer who had served six years of a forty-five-year sentence at Mountain View Maximum Security Prison in Gatesville, Texas. According to Welch, she was spirited away to a Holiday Inn by Clinton operatives the day before the 1992 elections and told to speak with no one.

"They didn't need to intimidate me like that," said Welch, who proudly watched her stepbrother's victory speech on television the next night. "I wasn't about to go public at that time and blow Bill's election chances." Later, in 1993, it would be revealed that Welch's son Jeff, a convicted drug dealer and forger, was a member of the Ku Klux Klan.

In August, Sharon Pettijohn—born Sharron Lee Blythe in 1941—surfaced in Tucson. Pettijohn, Bill was no less stunned to learn, turned out to be a half sister he was "completely unaware of," the daughter of William Jefferson Blythe and Wannetta Ellen Alexander.

Like the President's senior staff, Hillary hardly knew what to make of her husband's ever-expanding family tree. On one level, she knew that the sudden appearance of Henry Leon Ritzenthaler and Sharon Pettijohn had to be a source of some pain for Virginia. Hillary had agreed in July that Bill should invite Ritzenthaler to the White House, but she saw no need for a repeat performance with Pettijohn.

Hillary drew the line when Diane Welch publicly appealed for Bill to get in touch with her ("He can call me—collect," she said). Snapped the First Lady: "Don't even think of it." As for KKK member Jeff Welch: "Jesus, Bill. I know you've got all these red-neck relatives out there. But the *Klan*?"

That summer of 1993, heavier things were weighing on the President's mind. In retaliation for a planned attempt on the life of former President Bush sanctioned by Iraqi strongman Saddam Hussein, Bill ordered air strikes on Baghdad. Saddam would be only one of several foreign policy thorns in Clinton's side. With the exception of the historic mutual recognition agreement signed by Israeli Prime Minister Yitzhak Rabin and PLO leader Yasir Arafat at the White House on September 13, 1993, there were few bright spots as the administration faced one foreign policy nightmare after another: Somalia, Bosnia, Kosovo.

Just as he did on health care, welfare reform, and economic policy issues, Bill consulted Hillary every time he made an important foreign policy decision. But, realizing the political pitfalls for the President, she rarely ventured beyond health care and the rights of women and children.

On those occasions when she did offer an opinion on foreign policy—her advocacy of an independent Palestinian state, for example—she invariably regretted it. "You can be very involved and on the front lines like Mrs. Roosevelt and be criticized," she said. "Or you can be totally concerned with your family and not venture forth and be criticized. It is a no-win situation."

At times Hillary felt compelled to take a stand regardless of the international ramifications. In 1995, Hillary offended her Chinese hosts at the United Nations World Conference on Women when she bravely blasted human rights violations in that country. "It is a violation of human rights when babies are denied food, or drowned, or suffocated, or their spines broken, simply because they are born girls," she said. "It is a violation of human rights when women and girls are sold into the slavery of prostitution. It is a violation of human rights when women are doused with gasoline, set on fire, and burned to death because their marriage dowries are deemed too small . . . If there is one message that echoes forth from this conference, let it be that human rights are women's rights, and women's rights are human rights, once and for all. Let us not forget that among those rights are the right to speak freely. And the right to be heard."

Yet even when they were addressing the most compelling issues, it was impossible for the Clintons to be heard over the din of tabloid headlines. Hillary, Chelsea, and the First Lady's entourage had stopped off in Little Rock to visit Hillary's widowed mother when the phone rang at 9:25 P.M. on July 20, 1993.

On the other end was Mack McLarty, his voice cracking with emotion.

"Hillary, I have terrible news. Vince is dead."

"What?"

"Vince committed suicide. We just got the news. They found him . . ."

Hillary, in the words of a staff member, "just lost it—screaming, crying. She was clearly devastated by the news." Based on Hillary's reaction, her press secretary Lisa Caputo immediately assumed that the President had been assassinated.

Once he had told Hillary what little he knew about Vince's death, McLarty hung up the phone and walked across the hall to the West Wing library where President Clinton was winding up a live interview with CNN's Larry King. At the commercial break, McLarty signaled Bill to say his goodbyes to King and then, on the way to the elevator, told his boss the terrible news. The President's chin dropped to his chest, and for a brief moment it looked as if he might collapse.

Bill's first call was to Hillary. He had been well aware of the rumors that had been circulating for years about his wife and her law partner. But he had known Vince his entire life—as small children they had lived next door to each other in Hope—and he felt the loss almost as keenly.

Hillary was sobbing uncontrollably, blaming herself for Vince's suicide. Bill, struggling to control his own emotions, told her it was not anyone's fault. *He just snapped.* Immediately after hanging up, Bill left to console Vince's wife, Lisa.

Conversely, the First Lady did not call Vince's wife that night to express her condolences as might have been expected. Nor did she call Lisa Foster the next day. In fact, phone records indicate that Hillary never phoned Vince Foster's widow following his death.

Bill and Hillary were, in fact, both well aware that Vince Foster was depressed—perhaps even suicidally so—and they knew why. Back in Little Rock, Hillary was still consumed with guilt over Vince's death. "It's my fault, it's all my fault," she kept repeating after she hung up the phone with McLarty.

It had begun the previous November: When the Clintons had first asked Foster to join the new administration as deputy White House counsel, he hesitated. The White House job meant a 50 percent pay cut—he earned $298,000 a year at Rose—and it meant uprooting his family and leaving his beloved Arkansas. Hillary first urged, then begged him to come to Washington. He later recalled her exact words: "We need you, Vince. I need you . . ."

With their two eldest children away at college, Vince made the move to Washington while Lisa waited behind in Little Rock while their youngest son, Brugh, finished his junior year in high school. He stayed with his sister Sheila and brother-in-law Beryl Anthony in their northwest Washington home for three months before settling into a three-bedroom brown brick house in Georgetown.

Almost from the moment he set foot in the White House, Vince realized he had made a huge mistake. In April his old friend Judge Richard S. Arnold asked if he was having fun yet. "Not yet," Foster answered soberly. A month later one of his old law associates, Amy Stewart, asked how he liked his new work. "Interesting, yes," he answered. "Fun, no."

In a letter to a friend just weeks before his death, Foster wrote: "I have never worked so hard for so long in my life. The legal issues are mind-boggling, and time pressures are immense. The pressure, financial sacrifice and family disruption are the price of public service at this level. As they say, 'The wind blows the hardest at the top of the mountain.' "

Yet even by Washington standards, Foster found himself caught in a maelstrom of controversy. Nannygate, Travelgate, and the Whitewater imbroglio had all taken their toll on the man Hillary and Bill both repeatedly referred to as "our Rock of Gibraltar."

To be sure, the Clinton White House had been under continuous fire since Bill's first day in office. And like his friends Bill and Hillary, Vince took it personally. Unlike his friends, he directed his anger inward. The night Zoë Baird withdrew her name from consideration as attorney general, Foster experienced what his coworkers later described as an anxiety attack. When his face was etched alongside a *Wall Street Journal* editorial assailing the Clintons' Arkansas "cronies," Foster became frantic. "Vince was afraid," said a White House colleague, "that he had failed Hillary."

On July 2, when two other White House aides were officially reprimanded for their role in the Travelgate affair, Vince felt ashamed that he had not been punished. "This is *my* blame," he told Hillary's old Watergate friend Bernie Nussbaum, now ensconced as White House counsel. "Let *me* take it."

Foster was not allowed to officially take the blame at the time. But there were strong indications that he might eventually be called on to make a sacrifice and, as one observer put it, "fall on his sword to protect the First Lady."

Meanwhile, the President's wife made her displeasure known. Just as Bill vented his anger at George Stephanopoulos, Vince routinely absorbed Hillary's wrath during this period. Said one White House staffer: "If she was mad at anyone—it didn't matter who it was— Vince got it."

To make matters worse, Vince had been quietly battling depression. Foster's Georgetown housekeeper, Loretta Sears, watched him gradually grow more and more despondent. "When I first met him, he literally bounded down the steps when he left for work. When I'd ask how he was, he'd smile and reply, 'Wonderful.'

"But as the weeks went by, he became very unhappy. He looked like a man carrying the troubles of the world on his shoulders. In the final days," Sears said, "his eyes revealed he was hurting bad. His shoulders seemed to stoop, he looked exhausted, and he always appeared to be brooding about something. He'd come home and read the newspapers cover to cover—sadly shaking his head."

One day she walked into the living room as he was hunched over the newspapers. "Wrong, wrong, *wrong*," he said. "They don't understand how difficult it all is." The change in Foster's mood left Sears "worried sick" about his state of mind. "I wanted to ask him what was wrong," she said, "but it wasn't my place . . ."

Job pressures were taking their inevitable toll, but those closest to Foster did not feel they were proving too much for him. "You have to be in the office by 7 in the morning and you're dog tired at 9 or 10 at night when you leave," Vince told his friend Joe Purvis. "But then you look at the bright lights of the White House and see what a magnificent sight it is, and you're sort of overcome by the awe and the wonder." Amy Stewart felt her old friend was "really happy—to the extent you could be happy and exhausted and pressured."

Foster was not accustomed to being pilloried in the press. "His temperament was not such," said his brother-in-law Beryl Anthony, a former Arkansas congressman, "that he was ready to deal with a press that can get as ugly as it can get." Vince was stung by what he saw as vicious, unwarranted attacks on his character. "Before we came here," he told *Time* magazine's Margaret Carlson not long before his death, "we thought of ourselves as good people."

Yet those who knew him best did not think these alone were reasons enough to push Vince Foster over the edge. "I don't think Vince was at all green," said Carolyn Staley. "He was very sophisticated and led a fairly pressured life himself."

What had changed dramatically in that final month was Foster's relationship with Hillary. After sixteen years "joined at the hip," as one friend put it, Hillary, angered at what she felt was the mishandling of the Travelgate scandal, had abruptly cut Vince off. For the three weeks prior to his suicide, she refused to see Vince or even take his calls. "When Hillary is stung she reacts viscerally and closes up," Dick Morris observed. "There is no colder feeling on the planet."

Lisa Foster, who finally made the move to Washington in June, knew her husband was beginning to unravel. When a friend from Little Rock told her she was thinking of taking a job with the administration in Washington, Vince's wife replied without hesitation, "You are making the biggest mistake of your life."

Even before she left Little Rock, Lisa Foster was concerned about her husband's state of mind—so concerned that both she and their oldest son repeatedly asked White House aides about Vince's "mood." In a matter of weeks, he had lost twelve pounds—the result, he said, of anxiety.

There were added, unseen pressures known only to the Fosters and a few close friends. Lisa Foster confided to her friend Ileene Watkins, wife of White House aide David Watkins, that she had moved to Washington in a last-ditch effort to save their marriage—a marriage threatened by Foster's affair with Hillary.

On July 16, just four days before his death, Vince was having dinner with his wife when he broke down and began to cry. He talked of resigning, but then pulled back; he just couldn't face what he called the "humiliation" of quitting and returning to Arkansas. Two days later, Vince told his mother that he was unhappy because his work was "a grind."

Finally, Foster decided to seek professional help. He was going to see a psychiatrist. But in the meantime, he called Dr. Larry Watkins, his physician in Little Rock, and received a prescription for the antidepressant Desyrel. That night, July 19, Bill Clinton invited Vince to attend a screening at the White House of the film *In the Line of Fire*. Curiously, the film starred Clint Eastwood as a veteran Secret Service agent eager to sacrifice himself for his commander in chief. Vince declined the President's invitation.

The next day, Foster stood in the White House Rose Garden while his friend the President announced the appointment of Louis Freeh to head the FBI. Around noon he joined Nussbaum to watch the televised confirmation hearings for Supreme Court nominee Ruth Bader Ginsburg.

"Hey, Vince," Nussbaum said, "not a bad day . . . We hit two home runs . . . I think we're doing our job, and I think we're doing it well."

Foster "just sort of smiled," Nussbaum remembered. He returned to his office, had lunch at his desk, then left the White House around 1 P.M. "I'll be back," he told his secretary.

The inevitable flood of conspiracy theories notwithstanding, even Clinton nemesis Ken Starr would later conclude that this is what happened next: Foster drove his gray Honda Accord seven and a half miles across the Potomac to Fort Marcy Park in McLean, Virginia. Then he sat on a grassy hill in front of a Civil War cannon, grabbed the butt of a .38 caliber pistol with both hands, put the barrel deep in his mouth, and pulled the trigger with his right thumb.

The bullet exited the top of his head, and he toppled back, his legs straight out, his arms falling to his side. The gun stayed in his right hand, his thumb stuck in the trigger guard. He was forty-eight years old.

For all their shared sorrow ("It was personal grief—men were crying," recalled a senior White House official), White House staffers moved quickly, rifling through Foster's office in search of anything that might be incriminating to the President or the First Lady. Or both.

Even though she never did contact Lisa Foster to convey her sympathies directly, Hillary did place a series of calls immediately after learning of Vince's death. At 10:13, just forty-five minutes after first hearing the news, Hillary phoned her chief of staff Maggie Williams. As soon as she hung up, Williams rushed to Vince's White House office to look for a potentially embarrassing suicide note before police arrived—only to find another White House official, Patsy Thomasson, there on the same sensitive mission.

Then Hillary called Harry Thomason in Los Angeles. While she was visiting the Thomasons, Hillary had told her show business friends that she was aware Vince had been depressed. But she was still angry over the way Travelgate had been mishandled. Now she sobbed to Thomason over the phone, "He did it, Harry. He really did it."

The next call—at 11:19—was to her high-powered New York lawyer friend Susan Thomases, who would go on to play a pivotal role in advising Hillary on how to handle the thorny legal issues that might surface in the wake of Vince's death. Hillary and Thomases spoke for twenty minutes, after which she called Mack McLarty's office. At 12:56, she called Bill.

Vanishing files, convenient memory lapses, and White House Counsel Nussbaum's insistence on keeping Foster's papers to protect attorney-client privilege combined with sloppy police work at the scene to spawn countless conspiracy theories. The most extreme of these suggested Foster had been murdered to protect the Clintons.

More fuel was thrown on the fire when on July 26, six days after Foster's death, a White House assistant inexplicably discovered a note torn into twenty-eight pieces at the bottom of Vince's briefcase. The discovery was all the more strange given the fact that the police had thoroughly examined the briefcase five days earlier and found nothing.

The note gave some insight into Foster's tortured state of mind. "I made mistakes from ignorance, inexperience and overwork," Vince wrote. "I did not knowingly violate any law or standard of conduct, including any action in the travel office. There was no intent to benefit any individual or any specific group." He went on to accuse the FBI of lying in its report to the attorney general, and the press "for covering up the illegal benefits they received from the travel staff . . . The public will never believe the innocence of the Clintons and their loyal staff.

"The WSJ [Wall Street Journal] editors lie without consequence," Vince went on. "I was not meant for the job or the spotlight of public life in Washington. Here ruining people is considered sport."

To the inevitable charges of a White House cover-up, veteran Clinton fixer Betsey Wright said, "People were trying to protect him in death in a way that they felt that they were unable to in life. Embracing him in death made it look like a cover-up."

Cover-up aside, there is little question that both Bill and Hillary were crushed by Foster's death. "No one can know why things like this happen," said Clinton, his eyes red and swollen from crying. "He was usually the Rock of Gibraltar when other people were having trouble. It is very important that his life not be judged simply by how it ended, because Vince Foster was a wonderful man."

The President suggested there was a lesson to be drawn from his friend's tragic death. "We have to pay maybe a little more attention to our friends and our families and our coworkers and try to remember that work can never be the only thing in life, and a little humility in the face of this is very, very important."

Worried about the impact all this might have on his overworked and overstressed staff, the President called a meeting of White House personnel in the Old Executive Office Building and reassured them that "Vince's death was a mystery about something inside of him." Still, over the next several days several of those who worked closest with Foster sought professional help.

Bill dealt with his grief in his own way. "His family, his friends, his coworkers have been up real late two nights in a row now, remembering and crying and laughing and talking about him," he told a group of reporters. "I don't think there is anything else . . ."

With Hillary away, White House logs showed that Bill spent the night of Vince's death in the family quarters with his self-described "old hippie girlfriend" Marsha Scott. Another exuberant, attractive Arkansas blonde, Scott spent the 1970s bombing from town to town in a Volkswagen bus. Where she would live was decided by where the bus ran out of gas. Her first official act as $98,000-a-year director of correspondence at the White House was to fire twenty longtime staffers and watch more than one million letters pile up in a matter of weeks.

The morning of Vince's funeral, Scott told her friend Ileene Watkins that she had slept with the President the night before to comfort him. "I spent the night with Bill in his bed," she blurted out to Watkins. "I had my head in his lap and we reminisced all night long. I'm wearing the same clothes as yesterday and I'm going to have to wear them the whole day again." In June 1996, Scott would state in a sworn deposition to a House committee that she remembered going to the White House those nights but that the rest was "a blur."

At Vince's funeral, mourners took note of the curious way Foster's family was treating the First Couple. While Bill embraced the widow and Vince's children, a heartbroken Hillary was kept at arm's length, Watkins said, "because the Foster family knew all about Hillary's involvement with Vince."

In Austin, Texas, Dick Morris confirmed the romantic relationship between Hillary and Vince while watching television coverage of the service with Barbara Plafflin. "I mentioned how grief-stricken Hillary was," said Plafflin, Morris's longtime mistress.

"It doesn't surprise me," remarked Morris, one of those political advisors closest to Hillary. "They had an affair back in Arkansas."

Even as Foster's death rocked Washington, Bill was secretly maneuvering to avert yet another scandal. In mid-1993 the President acted swiftly when he learned that several of the Arkansas state troopers who were part of his security detail back in Little Rock were about to go public. That July he appointed their former captain, Buddy Young, to run the regional Federal Emergency Management Agency office in Texas at an annual salary of $92,000.

Troopers Larry Patterson and Roger Perry, however, were about to blow the lid off Bill's sex life in Arkansas—and the President was frantic to stop them. Young called Patterson, then sent him a note expressing concern for his "health."

When that didn't work, Bill intervened directly. He called Ferguson and told him to "tell Roger he can have whatever he wants." Later, Bill called Ferguson again. "If you tell me what stories Roger and Larry are telling," President Clinton said, "I can go in the back door and handle it and clean it up." In return for his help in cleaning up the mess, Bill reportedly offered Ferguson a federal job.

When the troopers went public in *American Spectator* that December, Betsey Wright admitted to White House counselor David Gergen, "as far as I can tell, they're telling the truth." Stephanopoulos quickly learned, despite his boss's denials, that the President *had* talked to the troopers. "How could he be so reckless?" Stephanopoulos asked himself. "He's so sure he can talk his way out of anything that he doesn't even think about the consequences." But none of this kept Wright, Stephanopoulos, or the other "Masters of Disaster," as they were now called, from going on the attack.

Hillary, meantime, also came out swinging. Although in December 1993 she was under heavy fire herself for withholding Vince Foster's papers and for not cooperating in the Whitewater investigation, the First Lady took time to blast her husband's accusers for their "outrageous, terrible stories. For me, it's pretty sad that we're still subjected to these kind of attacks for political and financial gain from people, and it is sad that—especially here in the Christmas season—people for their own purposes would be attacking my family."

She conceded that a scandal like this "hurts. Even though you're a public figure, which means apparently in America they can say anything about you, even public figures have feelings and families and reputations.

"I think my husband has proven that he's a man who really cares about this country deeply and respects the presidency and believes strongly that he's doing the right thing, and when it's all said and done, that's how most fair-minded Americans will judge my husband. And," she added, "all the rest of this stuff will end up in the garbage can where it deserves to be."

Hillary was indeed hurt, and angry that Bill's sordid past was back to haunt them yet again. The Clintons had a social agenda—hers as much as his—that was far too important to be derailed by her husband's priapic excesses. But as long as these were sins of the past—as long as he was no longer jeopardizing all they had worked for by cheating on her—the First Lady was willing to, as one aide put it, "stick her neck out—way, way out—for the guy."

But even as his wife, caught up in her own battle for survival, prepared to do battle for him, Bill was risking it all. Kathleen Willey was married to Virginia real estate lawyer Ed Willey when she first met Bill Clinton at a political fund-raiser in 1989, and they quickly struck up a friendship. That Bill had something more in mind became obvious in 1992, when he called her after the first presidential debate in Williamsburg and told her he would "make the Secret Service guys scarce" so she could bring him chicken soup for his sore throat.

Willey, realizing that Bill had "something more than my bringing him chicken soup" in mind, declined the invitation. After the election, however, the striking redhead went to work as a part-time volunteer in the White House.

By the fall of 1993, Kathleen's twenty-two-year marriage to Ed Willey began to fall apart amid charges that he had embezzled $274,500 from a law client. At first she resisted, but eventually Kathleen Willey agreed to cosign a repayment note that meant she shared financial responsibility for restoring the funds her husband had stolen. The note, she later testified, "put the fear of God into me." To make matters worse, the Willeys also owed more than $500,000 in back taxes.

On November 28 the couple had what a neighbor described as "another huge fight." Kathleen later said that she told her husband, "If it takes my going to Washington and getting a paying job . . . and our selling everything we own, then we all need to change course." When she declared she was going to seek help from "Bill," Ed Willey angrily stormed out of the house.

The next day Kathleen Willey went to the Oval Office to ask the President for a paying job. "I have a serious problem," she said. "I need your help."

But first Clinton offered her a cup of coffee. When she said yes, he walked out a door on the other side of the Oval Office into a small kitchen. A steward was standing there, but rather than ask him to do it, Bill retrieved a Starbucks coffee cup from the pantry and poured Willey a cup of coffee himself. Then he poured a cup of coffee for himself, and the two began to walk down the hall back toward the Oval Office.

"Why don't you come in here, into my study?" he said. "We can talk better in here . . ."

According to Willey, just as they got to the door, he turned and gave her a hug. "I'm sorry this is happening to you," he said, referring to her financial and marital woes. Then he kissed her on the mouth, pulling her closer to him.

"What in the world is he doing?" she thought, trying to push him away. Instead, he tightened his arms around her and, in a motion similar to the one recalled by flight attendant Cristy Zercher, grabbed her breasts.

Leaning down, he whispered in her ear, "I——I've wanted to do this ever since I laid eyes on you."

"Aren't you afraid somebody's going to walk in here?" she asked.

"No, no. I'm not," he replied matter-of-factly. Then he took her hand and placed it on his aroused genitals. It was as if, Willey recalled, it was all happening in slow motion.

"This is not happening," she thought. "Maybe I should just give him a good slap across the face . . ." But then she thought, "Well, I don't think you slap the President of the United States like that."

Willey pushed him away. "I think . . . I think I'd better go," she said. But Clinton just kept looking at his watch. He had a meeting, he told her, but then he added, "They can wait."

Willey fled. She would later tell *60 Minutes'* Ed Bradley that she was in a state of shock. "I just could not believe . . . the recklessness of that act . . . Of that . . . of him . . . doing that right outside the Oval Office. I mean, there are Secret Service people around, there are stewards around. His staff is around. I just thought it was extremely reckless."

As she left, Willey passed Lloyd Bentsen. During the entire groping episode, the distinguished secretary of defense, former Texas senator, and vice-presidential candidate, was standing only a few yards away waiting for the President to keep his 3 P.M. appointment.

At about the same time, Ed Willey drove his Isuzu Trooper into the woods as far as he could. Then he walked two hundred feet into the trees, placed a gun to his head, and pulled the trigger. His body lay where it fell for twenty-four hours before hunters stumbled upon his truck.

A month later the President arranged for Willey to be hired by the White House counsel's office. After that, he appointed her to serve on U.S. delegations to conferences in Denmark and Jakarta, as well as an unpaid post at the USO.

Willey would later say she often thought about the President's pass at her, and that it made her "angry—that I had been taken advantage of." But she would not go public with her accusations for another four years—after Paula Jones and Monica Lewinsky had become household names.

The President would claim that she was distraught when she came to see him, and that he may have hugged her and kissed her "to calm her down." Her charges, he said, had left him "mystified and disappointed."

But while he portrayed himself as a hapless victim, behind the scenes he and Hillary would launch an all-out counteroffensive to discredit Willey. Within days, the White House would seek to undermine her story by releasing fifteen letters Willey had written to Bill before and after the Oval Office incident. In one, Willey gushed, "Take heart in knowing your number one fan thanks you." Most of the letters were signed, "Fondly, Kathleen."

Experts in the field would later point out that Willey's attempt to stay on good terms with the President was a common reaction among victims of sexual harassment in the workplace. "We're talking about somebody you think has harassed you but who also holds the key to your future employment," said attorney and author Barbara Kate Repa. "It's not unusual, especially for women, to want to smooth over the waters."

Hillary Clinton, however, was no "usual woman." She had to swallow hard every time there was a new revelation, and convince herself—for the sake of Chelsea and, she felt, for the sake of the country—that their right-wing enemies lurked behind every sordid tale. By now she was, like her husband, expert at "boxing off" unpleasant things so she could get on with helping her husband run the country.

In the early morning hours of January 7, 1994, the President was awakened by a call from his stepfather, Dick Kelley. Bill's mother had died in her sleep, at age seventy the victim of breast cancer. Only ten days earlier Bill had given Virginia a goodbye hug on the porch of her lakeside home in Hot Springs before joining Hillary and Chelsea in Hilton Head. Stricken, he wandered into Hillary's room and woke her up. According to friends, they both broke down and wept.

Coming on the heels of Hugh Rodham's death, Vince Foster's suicide, and the torrent of scandals from Whitewater to Troopergate, Virginia's death brought Bill and Hillary closer together than they had been in months. "You could see it when she hugged him as he left for Little Rock," said a woman lawyer friend, "and later when she joined him at the funeral. Virginia's death brought up all those feelings she had been suppressing since her own father's death. And Hillary knew how big a part of Bill's life Virginia had always been—she was the one who pushed him from the beginning. Deep down Hillary knew that she never would have been in the White House if it hadn't been for Bill's mom."

At the funeral, Roger Clinton sobbed openly. But Bill, supporting his brother by the arm, clenched his jaw and fought off the tears. "Roger did all the bawling," said one of the one thousand people who attended the funeral service that day. "But you could see in their faces that nobody was hurting more than Bill, Hillary, and poor Chelsea."

Virginia's friend Barbra Streisand was also at the funeral, but Hillary was apparently still holding her grudge over Barbra's earlier White House visit. According to a White House insider, Hillary made it clear that, among other things, she did not want Streisand riding in the family car to the cemetery. "Just tell her," Hillary instructed an aide as she leaned back in the spacious limousine, "that there isn't enough room."

It quickly became clear that they would have to hang tough if they were to survive. As the Whitewater scandal continued to dominate the news, other shoes began to drop. Hillary's questionable commodities trades were revealed, there were new questions about Vince Foster's death, and—far and away most significantly—a heretofore unknown young woman named Paula Jones came forward to accuse the President of sexual harassment.

Ironically, the trigger for Paula's outrage was the *American Spectator* Troopergate story. The piece had mentioned a woman named Paula who supposedly offered to be Governor Clinton's girlfriend. On February 11, 1994, an outraged Paula Jones announced that she was filing a $700,000 sexual harassment suit against the President. Was it true that he used the Arkansas state troopers to bring him women like Paula? "I may be a fat old man now," he told Stephanopoulos, "but in my younger days I never needed any help getting women."

Nor, in fact, did he now. Even as the Paula Jones case grew exponentially, Bill continued ongoing extramarital relationships with several women inside and outside the White House, and was actively on the hunt for more.

Hillary, meanwhile, was coping with the likely collapse of her unwieldy health care initiative and the ever-present specter of indictments stemming from Whitewater. At a White House meeting that January, she had raged at top aides for abandoning her in her hour of need. "We were out there alone," she began to sob, "and I'm feeling very lonely right now.

She knew full well that, to a large extent, she was taking the rap for her husband. It was Bill who hooked them up with the Mc-Dougals and got her involved in what was later revealed to be a crooked land deal in the first place. She was in far too fragile a state even to consider the possibility that this Paula Jones, like the others, might be telling the truth.

Once again, Hillary would urge her husband and his lawyers to go on the offensive. Bill did not need any prodding. When Jones's lawyers said that she was prepared to describe "distinguishing characteristics" of the presidential genitalia, he told his aides he would have a urologist visit the Oval Office and "examine me right here" to prove she was lying.

Jones's legal team was eager to take him up on that offer. "If he can show them to a woman he met for three minutes in the Excelsior Hotel in Arkansas," said her advisor Susan Carpenter-McMillan, "that woman has a right to go before a jury and say 'Here's my evidence of exactly what was shown to me.' This is prime evidence in this case."

Regardless of his statements to his staff proclaiming his innocence, Bill's lawyers would spend the next several years furiously battling all attempts to enter photographs of the President's sexual organs into evidence.

Paula was instantly branded "trailer trash" and worse by Clinton's defenders. Bill's high-profile Washington attorney Bob Bennett likened her to a dog. He also threatened on national television to ruin Paula's reputation by delving into her past sexual history—a statement that rebounded so that he was forced to back down publicly.

But neither Bill nor Hillary wanted him to. After he made his harshest attacks against Paula, Hillary phoned Bennett to praise him for going after the Clintons' enemies.

As with past scandals, Bill and Hillary had several chances to put the genie back in the bottle. Initially Paula Jones insisted she would drop the suit if the President simply apologized for his boorish actions. In May 1994, Bennett did convince his client to offer to make an apology of sorts. It read: "I have no recollection of meeting Paula

Jones on May 8, 1991, in a room at the Excelsior Hotel. However, I do not challenge her claim that we met there and I may very well have met her in the past.

"She did not engage in any improper or sexual conduct," the statement continued. "I regret the untrue assertions which have been made about her conduct which may have adversely challenged her character and good name."

But Paula's lawyer, Joseph Cammarata, had a simpler statement in mind. Paula would drop the lawsuit immediately if Bill agreed to read the following statement to the press: "I do not deny meeting Paula Jones on May 8, 1991, in a room at the Excelsior Hotel. She did not engage in any improper or sexual conduct. I believe her to be a truthful and moral person."

Bill was on the verge of accepting the deal when Hillary intervened. "There is no way I am going to let you read that," she told him at a closed-door meeting with his legal team. "That's as good as admitting you're guilty." The next day, the First Couple was all smiles, joking and laughing for the cameras at a Mother's Day tribute in the Rose Garden.

In a last-ditch effort to save her health care package, Hillary went on a bus trip across the country. At every stop she was met by angry, jeering protesters waving placards that screamed HILLARY IS A COMMIE BITCH or GO BACK TO RUSSIA. She smiled and waved and pressed on, but in private Hillary was deeply shaken.

While she fought for her husband and his administration, Bill was up to his old tricks at the White House. According to Chief White House Steward Mike McGrath, on one particular Saturday he was manning the pantry just outside the Oval Office study, where the President was working, when Debra Schiff appeared in a short skirt and high heels—"a knockout," McGrath recalled.

Schiff went straight to the door that was always left open between the pantry and study, swung it closed, and then shoved a doorstop under it to keep it that way. "We don't want to be disturbed for twenty minutes," she told McGrath, who was now for all intents and purposes locked inside the pantry. "I couldn't believe it," McGrath said. "I just waited. I remember being really shocked and surprised."

Twenty minutes later, Schiff "came whipping out by me," McGrath said. "She opened the door, kind of smiled, and took off. She was in a real hurry—she didn't say a word and didn't look me in the eye. She seemed a little embarrassed." A few minutes later, he went to check on the President, but he had already gone up to the family residence. Later it would be revealed that after a sexual encounter with Monica Lewinsky, Bill sometimes went upstairs to shower.

It was rare that Schiff had to go to such lengths for her "twenty minutes" with the President. When the former flight attendant first arrived at the White House at the start of the administration, Deputy Chief of Staff Nancy Hernreich blocked her access to the President. After three months, she went to Bill directly.

"I have my twenty minutes with him every morning now," she told Linda Tripp, who was then working at the White House.

"For what?" Tripp asked.

"You figure it out," Schiff smiled.

Although Schiff would later deny having an affair with the President, Secret Service agent Gary Byrne later told a federal grand jury that he came upon Clinton and Schiff sharing an intimate moment in the Oval Office study. Byrne testified he "felt the rumors about them having some kind of physical relationship were true." (At the height of the Monica Lewinsky scandal, Schiff was transferred out of the White House to a higher-paying position in the State Department.)

Schiff, it turned out, had to stand in line for her twenty minutes alone with the President. After he took his morning run, Clinton usually stopped by the office of Catherine Cornelius, a blond Texan who was not yet twenty when she came aboard at the White House. As an advance person in the travel department, Cornelius would often accompany the President when he went abroad *sans* the First Lady. "He got together with her all the time on their overseas trips," Lewinsky would later complain to Linda Tripp.

Hillary was on her grueling "Health Security Express" bus trip when Bill flew down to Little Rock for his thirtieth high school reunion on July 23. He approached Dolly Kyle Browning several times, but she avoided him. Bill may have forgotten that his underlings had repeatedly threatened to "destroy" her if she talked to the press about their affair.

Once Bill finally did corner Dolly and ask her how she was, she shot back, "You are such an asshole. I can't believe you'd even bother to ask!" As the crowd gasped, a Secret Service agent moved toward her but was waved off by the President. "It's OK, it's OK," he said.

They sat down and, surrounded by hundreds of people and with Secret Service agents only a few feet way, had an emotional forty-five-minute-long conversation about Bill's promiscuous behavior. Marsha Scott, the former "hippie girlfriend" who had slept with Bill the night before Vince Foster's funeral, hovered nearby. But, according to other guests at the reunion, the blaring sixties music made eavesdropping virtually impossible.

Bill apologized for the earlier threats to "destroy" her, and asked her to move to Washington, where he would find her a job. She declined, telling him instead that she had finished writing a transparently thin account of their relationship, *Purposes of the Heart*. "People will figure out it's me you're writing about," he said.

Yes, she nodded.

Hillary was totally unprepared for the devastating losses incurred by the Democrats in the 1994 elections. Led by Newt Gingrich, Republicans took control of the House of Representatives for the first time in forty years. The GOP also regained control of the Senate, and for the first time since 1970 won a majority of the nation's governorships.

It was the First Lady, and not the President, who drew the harshest criticism and most of the blame. In pushing her ill-fated health care program, she had appeared arrogant and shrill. As much as anything, it had been a referendum on the Clintons' vaunted co-presidency.

"I just don't know what to do," she told Dick Morris. "I just don't know what works anymore. I don't trust my own judgment. Everything I do seems not to work." Depressed and withdrawn, Hillary no longer attended the White House strategy sessions that she once dominated. It was, Morris told writer Gail Sheehy, "almost an abdication."

Around that time, Paul Newman and his wife, Joanne Woodward, joined the First Family and friends for a screening of Newman's new film, *The Hudsucker Proxy*. To the delight of the President and his guests, Newman served them his Newman's Own popcorn. But Hillary, in the words of one guest, "was a total zombie—expressionless, dazed. She was *so* unhappy, it was just heartbreaking. I cried for her on the ride home."

Looking for some sort of guidance, she consulted her old Methodist mentor Don Jones and even invited New Age gurus Marianne Williams and Tony Robbins to Camp David. When all the self-help sessions and inspirational speeches were over, Hillary decided to return to the issue dearest to her heart: children. She began writing a syndicated newspaper column patterned after Eleanor Roosevelt's "My Day," and published her thoughts on child development in the best-seller *It Takes a Village*. Her next literary effort, a collection of letters written to the First Family pets, titled *Dear Socks, Dear Buddy*, was more than faintly reminiscent of Barbara Bush's *Millie's Book*.

To Hillary's surprise, the more traditional role of First Lady—albeit one that still allowed her to raise millions for the party and speak out on issues like human rights—suited her. It also gave her more time to spend with Chelsea.

By now the public was given only fleeting glimpses of Chelsea—practicing with the Washington Ballet for her role in *The Nutcracker*, greeting her father as he got off Marine One on the White House lawn—and then usually to take the heat off her parents. The general public had yet to hear her utter a single sentence. Her parents often refused flat-out to answer questions about her, and interviews with the First Daughter were strictly verboten. "There was a line in cement that you didn't cross," Hillary's former press secretary Neel Lattimore recalled. "We didn't discuss Chelsea."

"She would call me an overprotective mother," Hillary confessed. But the strategy seemed to work. "Chelsea is as unaffected by her parents' status as it is possible for a President's daughter to be," said Dick Morris, who has known her since she was a toddler. "She has a clear sense of herself, of who she is, and she marches to her own beat . . . There is no trace of conceit, arrogance, or class-consciousness about her."

The world got a glimpse of these qualities when Hillary took Chelsea along on a ten-day tour of South Asia in 1995. Often photographed holding hands, the affectionate mother-daughter team visited Mother Teresa's orphanage in Calcutta and mosques in Pakistan. "One could see how close they were," said Benazir Bhutto, Pakistan's former prime minister. As they moved through the narrow streets of Lahore, on the way to a state banquet, Hillary was careful that Chelsea "was right there with her, that she didn't get left behind in the crowd."

Back in Washington, Bill was also making his way through a crowd—shaking hands with supporters who lined his path to the presidential helicopter, Marine One. As he made his way down the line, an attractive young woman wearing a sage-green J. Crew suit caught his eye. He stared at her ("He gave me the full Bill Clinton," she would later say) and then took her hand. "The rest of the crowd disappeared," the young woman remembered, "and we shared an intense but brief sexual exchange. He undresses you with his eyes. And it is slow, from the bottom of your toes to the top of your head back down to your toes again. And it's an intense look. He loses his smile. His sexual energy kind of comes over his eyes, and it's very animalistic."

She went home, ironed her "lucky green dress," and returned the next day to attend a forty-ninth birthday party for the President on the South Lawn. This time, after she wished him Happy Birthday, he casually brushed up against her breast. A few weeks later, the young White House intern bumped into him again, this time while waiting for a friend in the basement lobby of the West Wing.

"Hello, Mr. President," she said nervously. "I'm Monica Lewinsky."

"I know," Bill said, looking deep into the eyes of the twenty-two-year-old. "I know."

They've all underestimated our capacity for pain.

—*Hillary*

■

I love you, Butthead.

—*Monica Lewinsky,*
to the President

At least we want to know that Hillary kicked his
butt.

—*Patricia Ireland*

■

8

"SHE BOUNCES BACK easily, she really does," said the man who first introduced Bill and Hillary, former Labor Secretary Robert Reich. "Except in the one domain of trust."

Hillary was, she would tell her friends, happier than she had ever been. She had survived testifying for four hours before a federal grand jury investigating the mysterious reappearance of her Rose Law Firm billing records, weathered a new controversy over her hand in collecting FBI files on Republicans, and stood fast by her man as he fended off sexual harassment charges from Paula Jones. She even managed to "box off" the possibility that she might be indicted, although the initial threat had, said one confidant, "stung her really hard, put her in shock."

But she had bounced back—albeit this time in a decidedly dignified, nonthreatening way. During Bill's 1996 campaign, she worked behind the scenes with Dick Morris to define the more centrist strategy that got her husband reelected. She hit the campaign trail, but—determined not to compete with Bill for attention— banned the national media from her plane.

"She was seared, and seared badly," a White House aide observed. "She's trying to carve her niche so she can be remembered." Even though four years of public battering had taken their toll, Hillary came out smiling for her husband—as he blew out the fifty candles on his American flag–shaped birthday cake, as he delivered his second inaugural address and each new State of the Union address, as he hobbled around on crutches for weeks following knee surgery.

Sometimes the resentment that lingered just below the cool exterior bubbled to the surface. She told a group of delegates at the 1996 Democratic Convention that a friend warned she would have everything but the kitchen sink thrown at her. "Well," she said, "I just saw it go by."

In the past, she would have caught the sink and thrown it back. Now Hillary merely ducked. "She was trying to figure out," said her old friend Diane Blair, "how she could be who she is—a thinker, a doer—without arousing hostility from those who felt she was overstepping her bounds. I think she's figured it out."

Both she and Bill had come to another realization: The most important person in their lives would soon be leaving them. In the meantime, they were intent on savoring every moment with Chelsea. For her seventeenth birthday, the President and First Lady commandeered two helicopters, Air Force One and a backup jet, a battalion of Secret Service agents, and a fleet of limousines to take in a Broadway show and a late supper at New York's exclusive "21" Club.

Six weeks later, mother and daughter embarked on a two-week tour of Africa. It was during a ceremony at Kilimanjaro International Airport in northern Tanzania that Hillary yielded the floor to her daughter. The sound of Chelsea's voice came as quite a shock; Americans realized that, after five years in the White House, this was the first time they had actually been permitted to hear the President's daughter speak.

"We have a big problem with violence in our country in all spectrums," Chelsea confidently told her African hosts. "We have a big problem with drugs, and we have a big problem with people not thinking they have a future. There's a lot of hopelessness."

Chelsea went on to say that the solution to violence "has to come from the young people themselves . . . We have to try to realize that we are the future and we make of our future what we make of it."

A month later at the Sidwell Friends annual mother-daughter banquet, Hillary donned a pink tutu, put her blond hair in a ponytail, and took to the stage to imitate the Clinton who starred in a school production of *The Nutcracker*. "Your mother embarrasses you in front of maybe a couple hundred people," Hillary whined in character to another mom playing a daughter. "*My* mother embarrasses me in front of *millions*."

When she was handed her high school diploma during graduation exercises at Sidwell Friends School in June 1997, Chelsea walked over to her father and threw her arms around him. "I love you, Dad," she whispered.

"I love you," Bill answered, fighting back tears, "and I'm very proud of you."

Understandably, Bill had been an emotional wreck as he delivered the commencement address. He recalled Chelsea's first day in school, her favorite books (*Good Night Moon*, *Curious George*, and *The Little Engine That Could*) and "all the triumphs and travails between then and now.

"Though we have raised you for this moment of departure and we are very proud of you, a part of us longs to hold you once more as we did when you could barely walk, to read to you just one more time," he said, his voice faltering. So, he asked Chelsea's class, "indulge your folks if we seem a little sad or we act a little weird."

Hillary conceded that her husband "was so nervous about making the speech. He was just overcome by the emotion of it." But what really got to him was the hug. "When she came back and put her arms around me," he said, "it was like I was reliving her whole life there in that few seconds."

Even more troubling for Mom and Dad was Chelsea's decision to attend Stanford University—inspired in part, perhaps, by her interest in a Stanford sophomore she had known for four years, former Congresswoman Marjorie Margolies-Mezvinsky's son Marc Mezvinsky.

"But," Hillary reacted, clutching her chest, "it's so far way." Bill was more philosophical. "Well," he said, "the planes run out there and the phones work out there. The e-mail works out there. So we'll be all right."

Still, Chelsea's departure that September hurt. Just so she could savor every remaining moment, Hillary rushed home following a twenty-hour trip to Mother Teresa's funeral in Calcutta to help Chelsea pack. "We have maintained a level of personal intimacy with Chelsea that I am very proud of, and pleased by, and very, very grateful for," Bill said. "I'm going to miss her when she's gone."

Indeed, the President would interrupt even the most important staff meetings to take a call from his daughter. And he could count on Chelsea, the other night owl in the family, to be up for a midnight game of hearts. "The phone doesn't ring as much—not nearly as much," Bill said, his voice tinged with sadness. "And every now and then, we ease into her room and look around." But, he conceded, "she was ready to go. We felt sad for ourselves but happy for her. It's a lot quieter here . . ."

"She was always Daddy's little girl," said an Arkansas friend. "They are close, but Hillary is almost more of a soul mate. They have a wonderful, kidding rapport with one another." One day Chelsea asked her mother, "What would you do if I came home with half my head shaved and the other half dyed purple?"

Answered Mom: "It's your head."

And when they threw a birthday party for Chelsea at the White House: "I would hasten to add," Hillary quipped, "that the best way to have a party for thirty-six teenagers is to have the Secret Service and the military there."

In her newspaper column, Hillary wrote, "I am dreading the moment Bill and I have to say goodbye to Chelsea . . . I'm wondering why I ever let her skip third grade." Later, she quipped, "I'm looking for ways to divert myself from my empty nest, and I'll take just about any dinner invitation I can get."

Even as she bade goodbye to her only child, Hillary faced yet another milestone. "It's my daughter going to college more than any birthday that's marked a turning point," Hillary said. Perhaps. But after one month away at college, Chelsea flew back in late October to surprise Mom on her fiftieth birthday.

"It's not exactly the kind of thing you want to have everybody make a big deal about," Hillary said of all the ballyhoo surrounding her birthday. But since the First Lady was one of the country's two most celebrated baby boomers, quite a lot was made of her reaching the half-century mark. *Time* magazine devoted a cover story to Hillary turning fifty, and there were rounds of parties in Washington and her hometown of Chicago, where, among other things, she appeared on *The Oprah Winfrey Show*.

"Don't you think you look better than ever?" Oprah asked.

"Well, some days I look OK."

"Really, I think you've found your place," Oprah said to the enthusiastic applause of her mostly female audience. "I think the hair, it's there. It's there."

"We've finally found a haircut for me?" Hillary joked.

But Hillary *did* look more attractive than ever before. And to those closest to them, it seemed that the President and the First Lady were closer than they had been in years. By the fall of 1997, servants in the White House residence were reporting that the shouting matches had ceased. More and more, friends and staff members were seeing moments of genuine affection between the two. On at least one occasion, when he was still using crutches after knee surgery, a playful President resorted to the cloying baby talk he had used when he had lost his voice during the 1992 campaign: "Oh, Hiddawee, pweeze get me a dwink." There was even talk of replenishing their empty nest: For a fleeting moment, they considered trying one last time for another child of their own, then went public with the news that they were thinking of adopting.

At one of Hillary's fiftieth birthday parties—this one held in the ballroom of Washington's Ritz-Carlton Hotel—Bill seemed to bask in Hillary's reflected glory. Hillary's glow might have had something to do with her standings in the polls—at 60 percent her highest approval rating in four years.

"She was absolutely radiant," said the spouse of a cabinet member, "as if she'd really come into her own. We were talking to the President when suddenly we realized he was watching her from across the room. He said, 'Would you look at Hillary? Isn't she just beautiful tonight?'" Stephanopoulos agreed. "As Hillary swirled around the dance floor in her husband's arms, surrounded by family and friends," he recalled, "she seemed as happy as I'd ever seen her."

Yet neither Hillary nor Chelsea could have suspected that the husband and father who agonized over his daughter's departure and gloried in his wife's phoenixlike rise was at the very same time betraying them.

Soon the world would be engulfed in an avalanche of bizarre and often sordid detail: blue thong underwear, displayed to the President by a flirtatious twenty-two-year-old intern; phone sex, oral sex, and masturbation into the sink of the Oval Office bathroom; a hatpin, sunglasses, a bag from the Black Dog restaurant on Martha's Vineyard; embroidered kneepads; ties worn to send a message; a cigar used by the President as a sex toy. *Leaves of Grass.* A Valentine's Day love poem from Monica to the President published in the *Washington Post.*

Monica called him "Handsome" or "The Creep" or "The Big Creep" or, playfully, "Butthead"—depending on her mood. She thought of him as her "sexual soul mate," and told him she loved him. "That means a lot to me," he answered, but never said he loved *her.* "I don't," the President said, "want to get addicted to you."

The timing of many of these episodes, though confirmed by the principals themselves under oath, simply defied belief. The first had occurred on November 15, 1995, at the height of the government shutdown and the budget crisis that triggered it. The third was on New Year's Eve. The President tried to break it off on February 19, 1996—Presidents' Day—only to violate her with a cigar a month later. Their next sexual encounter was right after church on Easter Sunday—just days after Commerce Secretary Ron Brown, a close friend, was killed in a plane crash.

During one phone conversation, Monica realized that he was becoming aroused as they talked about the situation in war-torn Bosnia and the call ended in phone sex. Another time, she performed oral sex on the President in his study off the Oval Office while Bill was talking to Republican Congressman H. L. "Sonny" Callahan of Alabama about the deployment of American troops in Bosnia. And later, she performed fellatio on Bill as he discussed politics over the phone with Dick Morris.

When Hillary went on a goodwill visit to Ireland, and when she and Chelsea grabbed headlines in Africa, the President was being visited by Monica Lewinsky. Bill was even able to deceive his family as he carried on right under their noses. The day after Chelsea's seventeenth birthday, for instance, Monica paid her fateful call on the President wearing her famous navy-blue dress from The Gap.

Bill's steamy meetings with Monica, as well as his similar closed-door encounters with a number of other young women, nearly all took place in the tiny, book-lined study with its small desk, leather-upholstered rocking chair, and large globe. Usually he sat in the rocker while his guest would take her place in the black swivel chair at his desk. A portrait of John F. Kennedy stared down from one wall—a silent witness to his successor's "inappropriate" actions with a young girl twenty-seven years his junior.

Throughout all of his sexual trysts with young women, Bill kept the Bible on his desk open to the Book of Galatians, chapter 6, verse 9:

Let us not be weary in well-doing, for in the season we shall reap if we faint not.

By his actions inside the walls of the White House—even as he battled a bad back and used crutches—Bill had mimicked his idol's life to an almost frightening extent. Paradoxically, he had also grown jealous of Kennedy, resenting the fact that he could romp in the White House while Jackie was away without consequence. "The press was always covering up for Kennedy," Bill now complained bitterly. "So why in the hell do they want to crucify me?"

At times it seemed that Bill was actually courting crucifixion. For example, he always left the door to the study ajar during these sexual encounters—risking discovery by the hovering Secret Service agents, stewards, secretaries, and advisors. On several occasions, Bill came dangerously close to being caught in flagrante.

On March 29, 1997, while Hillary and Chelsea were in Africa, Bill hobbled into his study on crutches, and this time he agreed to more than fondling and oral sex. It would, according to Monica, be their final sexual encounter. Two months later, on Saturday, May 24, 1997—Memorial Day weekend—Bill summoned Monica to the

Oval Office. She wore a straw hat instead of her trademark beret and, as usual, brought gifts: a Banana Republic shirt and a golf puzzle. Convinced that he loved her as much as she loved him, Monica was not prepared for what the President was about to tell her.

With Hillary and Chelsea splashing in the White House pool just outside, Bill took Monica into his study and told her their affair was over. He then confessed to Monica that his entire life had been a tissue of lies. Ever since he was a little boy he had led a secret existence that even his mother had never known about. Marriage to Hillary hadn't changed that; over the years, Bill said, he had had "hundreds" of extramarital affairs that left him filled with remorse. He told Monica that when he turned forty he was so desperately unhappy in his marriage that he considered divorce, but instead decided to "be good" and work on his marriage for Chelsea's sake. Then they both broke down.

Like countless other women who passed in and out of Bill's life, Monica thought little of Hillary. Monica actually met the First Lady, and the two women shook hands on several occasions. At public gatherings, Bill acknowledged Monica with a smile or wave even with Hillary standing next to him.

Consequently, it was easy for Monica to view the First Lady as a "marginal figure"—one of two "brilliant" people whose marriage existed on a lofty intellectual plane. "There were days when I thought that maybe they won't be together when his term ends and he will be free," Monica said. "Other times I just accepted that they would be married forever." Monica's nickname for Hillary: Baba, short for the Russian babushka.

Bill picked one more holiday—July 4, 1997—to drop yet another bombshell on Monica. This time he summoned Monica, who had been transferred to the Pentagon, into the Oval Office to chastise her for threatening to tell her parents about their affair. "It is illegal," he warned her, "to threaten the President of the United States."

With that, Monica burst into tears, and Bill went to comfort her. They caressed until Monica realized a gardener was working right outside the window, and they moved to the bathroom doorway.

"I wish I could spend more time with you," he said, holding her as he stroked her black hair. "I wish I had more time for you."

"Maybe you will in three years," she replied hopefully.

"I don't know. I might be alone in three years."

Monica was taken aback. Did this mean what she thought it meant—that after he was out of office he would divorce Hillary? Rather than press him, she said, "I think we'll make a good team."

"Yeah," he said, "but what are we gonna do when I'm seventy-five and have to pee thirty times a day?"

"We'll deal with it," she answered.

The President's offhand remark about being "alone in three years" was enough for Monica to subtly pursue the nature of his relationship with Hillary. "I know it's not my business," Monica said, "but I think you and your wife connect at a level that most people can't understand. I don't doubt that you have a deep bond, but to me I think she has cold eyes. You seem to need so much nurturing and the only person you seem to have worth for is your daughter. You are a very loving person and you need that, and I think you deserve it."

It did not take long for Monica to come to the realization, however, that Bill's comments had been self-serving. When she met with presidential fixer Vernon Jordan to discuss finding her a job, she asked him if he thought Bill would stay married to Hillary.

"Yes," Jordan said. "He will, as he should." He later claimed he found Monica's question concerning the possibility of a Clinton divorce "astonishing and disturbing."

Certainly, the well-connected Washington lawyer had no illusions about Bill's fidelity. "Well," he added blithely, "maybe you two will have an affair when he gets out of office." The comment was vintage Jordan. When asked away from the cameras just what it was he and the President were always chatting about, Jordan invariably replied with a single word: "Pussy."

Hillary, of course, was not Monica's only competition. Nor was Monica the first female acquaintance of Bill's—romantic or otherwise—to be blocked by the cadre of female gatekeepers Clinton's Arkansas woman friends called "the Barracudas." Recalled one platonic friend of more than twenty years: "If you were a woman and you wanted to talk to Bill, you just couldn't get through to him. It didn't matter who you were, the Barracudas saw every other woman as competition, and they made it their mission to keep every woman away from him."

There was Marsha Scott, Bill's old "hippie girlfriend" who had spent two nights with him at the time of Vince Foster's death. Monica blamed Scott for blocking her return to the White House. To one of the Clintons' most intimate confidants, this came as no surprise. After spending the night in the Lincoln Bedroom, the friend encountered Scott, whom she had known in Arkansas, and asked, "So what are you doing these days?"

"The President," Scott replied without missing a beat.

Then there was Bill's "kissing cousin" Catherine Cornelius, and Debra Schiff, the former flight attendant who insisted on her daily twenty minutes alone with the President. "It's the same in Arkansas," said the longtime FOB. "I used to ask Beth Coulson [an alleged lover of Bill's who was named to a state judgeship] if it was true, and she'd say with this grin, 'Bill always drops by the house when he's jogging—for "water." ' These women want their friends to know," she added, "and then they go right out and deny everything to the press. But they want to make sure *you* know."

The others aside, no one infuriated Monica more than Eleanor Mondale, the stunning blond daughter of former Vice-President Walter Mondale, who now worked as an entertainment reporter for CBS. During a visit to Los Angeles in the summer of 1996, Mondale stayed with Bill in his hotel room until 3:30 A.M., and then tried to dodge paparazzi when she went running with him the next day. When Monica confronted him with this, he snapped, "Do you think I would be stupid enough to go running with someone I was foolin' with?"

"Do you want me to answer that?" Monica replied.

On December 6, 1997, Monica arrived at the White House loaded down with gifts, including a Santa "Monica" Starbucks coffee mug, a sterling silver antique cigar holder, a tie, and a book about Theodore Roosevelt. Told that the President was meeting with his lawyers, Monica was kept waiting for forty minutes at the

Northwest Gate—until one of the uniformed Secret Service guards mentioned that Bill was actually in the Oval Office with the twice-divorced (one marriage lasted three months, the other sixteen) Eleanor Mondale.

"Livid," as one of the guards described her, Monica stormed off. When she later accused the President of cheating on *her* with Mondale, he angrily replied, "I am not having an affair with her. That is ridiculous. In fact, I set her up with her current boyfriend."

A month later, Monica would again have cause to be jealous. While vacationing in the Virgin Islands in January 1998, Bill and Hillary were photographed through the bushes sharing a tender moment on the beach, embracing affectionately and then dancing in their bathing suits.

The White House protested when the pictures were published, but many in the press were convinced the Clintons had actually staged the affectionate scene to counter the persistent rumor that their marriage was nothing more than a cold-blooded arrangement. Yet given the decidedly unflattering photos of presidential avoirdupois spread across the front pages of newspapers around the country, it was difficult to believe the exposure was intentional. "Ask any fifty-year-old woman," Hillary remarked convincingly, "how much she wants to have her picture taken in a bathing suit."

Monica rightly believed that this rarely seen glimpse of playful intimacy between Bill and Hillary was genuine, and it crushed her. Later, while watching the President deny that he had ever had sex with "that woman," Monica was devastated. "I felt like a piece of trash. I felt dirty, I felt used . . . " she said. "When I look back I was so young, so foolish, so trusting. How could he have messed with me so cruelly?" More than once, she thought of suicide.

Bill and Hillary were half a world away in Senegal, winding up a twelve-day tour of Africa, when Bob Bennett called with the news on April 1, 1998. Without warning, U.S. District Court Judge Susan Webber Wright had dismissed Paula Jones's case against the President on the grounds that, if he had sexually harassed her as she claimed, she could not prove that she had suffered any actual harm as a result.

"Is this an April Fool's joke?" Bill asked, incredulous.

"No, sir, Mr. President."

"You're not shittin' me?"

Repeatedly assured by this lawyer that it was no April Fool's joke, Bill relayed the news to Hillary, who began cheering. Back in Washington, the President's aides were already in a state of "delirium," as one put it. But Bill, still facing plenty of trouble from Kenneth Starr back home, thought it best not to be seen gloating publicly. He and Hillary canceled plans to dine that night at a restaurant, choosing instead to celebrate in their hotel suite. Even after she went to bed, the President stayed up with his aides, puffing on a cigar, playing a guitar, and beating a bongo drum that had been given to him by his African hosts.

Paula Jones, meantime, was driving down a California freeway when she got the news on her cell phone. She hung up the phone, pulled over to the side of the road, and cried.

For Bill and Hillary, there would be little cause for rejoicing in the coming months as Congress and the nation moved inexorably toward impeachment. In the aftermath of Bill's August 13, 1998, confession, after their Martha's Vineyard vacation ended and Chelsea went back to Stanford, Hillary was in a state of deep despair. On their trip to Moscow in September, she claimed she was "getting along fine." But it was plainly evident that there was real tension between them. Bill and Hillary did not make eye contact, avoided touching each other, and never spoke to each other. A top White House aide admitted at the time that the scandal had turned their marriage into "a tumble of emotions."

By October she seemed to have regained some of her old fighting spirit. Realizing full well that the 1998 congressional elections were going to be a referendum on her husband, Hillary devised a bold new campaign strategy. While Bill hunkered down in the White House, emerging for the periodic private fund-raiser, the First Lady, who had never been more popular, would go out and fight for the Democrats. Too proud to ever allow herself to be pitied as the wronged wife, she put on a resolutely upbeat face as she barnstormed the country. Along the way, she had somehow managed to find the time to pose for the cover of *Vogue*.

When the dust had settled, the Republicans had nearly lost the House, given up several governorships, and barely held their ground in the Senate. The GOP debacle would force Clinton archnemesis Newt Gingrich's resignation as House Speaker.

Bill and Hillary were a seamless partnership before the cameras, holding hands and smiling at a formal White House dinner two days after the elections. But there continued to be friction behind the scenes. On election night, Bill holed up with his aides in the office of his chief of staff, Erskine Bowles, surfing the Net for exit polls. Hillary, meanwhile, invited several girlfriends over to the White House theater to screen Oprah Winfrey's new film based on Toni Morrison's novel *Beloved*. On the night of one of their greatest election triumphs, the President and the First Lady behaved as if they had nothing to say to each other.

In the ensuing months, Hillary consulted constitutional scholars and met regularly with the President's lawyers. But she seldom spoke to her husband directly. As time passed and the First Lady made no public statements in support of the President, his supporters began to worry. So did the President. When his senior staff approached hers asking gingerly when such a statement might be forthcoming, they were coolly rebuffed. When and if such a statement were to be made, the President's men were told, it would be on the First Lady's terms—if at all.

Suddenly there was talk that Hillary had made the decision to protect her political future by distancing herself from Bill at a time when he needed her most. She was angry and hurt, of course. "She won't go public anytime soon with a full defense," said a family friend, "until she is convinced that her husband understands that what he's done was wrong and unacceptable. It's very personal." Said another: "She really didn't mind seeing him squirm a little."

Only hours before the Starr report was made public, Bill made a tearful repentance at a White House prayer breakfast. Referring to handwritten notes, he admitted that he had "not been contrite enough," and admitted that he "must wear the hair shirt for I have sinned." He also asked forgiveness from his family, friends, staff, cabinet, the American people—and "Monica Lewinsky and her family." He went on to tell the clergymen he would instruct his lawyers to "mount a vigorous defense" against the charges of perjury and obstruction of justice leveled against him.

Bill's misty-eyed mea culpa appeared to move Hillary, who told her staff that she was proud he was prepared to "do the right thing." But when they appeared together at the Democratic Business Council, they seemed ill at ease in each other's company; after she introduced the President, he hugged her awkwardly and she gave him a halfhearted pat on the back.

That Christmas season, as they fought to stave off the inevitable House vote to impeach, the atmosphere on the second floor of the White House remained decidedly chilly. Even their closest friends from Arkansas days shifted nervously in their seats when they dined upstairs with the Clintons. "They used to have these wonderful, spirited debates all the time," said one. "That was one of the things that made them so exciting." And now? According to their guests, "they are both sullen, anxious. She's giving him the silent treatment, and he keeps clenching his jaw . . ." Of the atmosphere in the family quarters, another friend simply sighed, "It's very different."

Impeachment notwithstanding, Hillary and Bill stood shoulder to shoulder in the Map Room—the room where he lied in his federal grand jury testimony—and worked a holiday season receiving line. They appeared happy and relaxed as they chatted with visitors and posed for snapshots, but once it was over they went their separate ways without exchanging a word. Later, when they toured Israel together, the Clintons were not holding hands as they used to, and at one point television cameras caught a telling moment when Bill reached for his wife and she seemed to instinctively recoil from his touch.

As an impeachment vote drew nearer in late December, however, Hillary went to Capitol Hill to rally the troops. In an emotional closed-door meeting with House Democrats, she declared that she was there as "a wife who loves and supports her husband" and that her husband was being "hounded out of office" by enemies "opposed to the Clinton agenda." The impeachment effort, she went on, "is not just about my husband. It is about the Constitution."

"She was determined and defiant," said New York Congressman

Jerrold Nadler. "Her message was that they've been pursuing him since the day he came into office." She received half a dozen standing ovations, and when she was finished, House Democrats stood in line to give her a hug. They walked away thinking, as one congressman put it, "If Hillary can forgive him and move on, then so can I."

Once again, Hillary was proving to be the real political warrior in the family—focusing her wrath not on the husband who betrayed her but on the political foes who sought to capitalize on that betrayal. As a friend of the Clintons told *U.S. News & World Report*, Hillary convinced herself the scandal was "nothing but a jihad to get him—and to get her. The 'enemies' thing is a very, very powerful and unifying force."

"She is married to a fellow who believes that politics is all about turning enemies into friends," wrote columnist Gloria Borger. "Her attitude, friends say, is that enemies are enemies for life and should be consigned to the outer darkness, then vaporized."

Even as their world appeared to be coming apart at the seams, it looked as if Bill had made strides in winning Hillary's forgiveness. "Of course I don't even know how to talk about what I believe Hillary has meant to the success of our endeavors," he said wistfully to a gathering of supporters. Then he reeled off a list of her accomplishments, her travels, "and just a thousand other things. And she has done it under circumstances I think are probably more difficult than anyone who has ever done it before . . ."

Hillary wiped a tear from her eye as he looked over at her. "I love her for it," Bill said, "but our country should love her for it as well."

To those in the audience, it appeared at that moment that he may have taken a major stride on the road to winning her back. It was, mused one of Hillary's oldest friends, "only a matter of time . . . She's over the moon in love with that guy."

It was not enough to forestall the inevitable. On December 19, 1998, a Saturday, the House of Representatives prepared to vote on the impeachment of William Jefferson Clinton. Bill, meantime, went on with business as usual, inviting a few close friends to the Oval Office to watch him tape his weekly radio address.

Before he began, however, the President was called out of the Oval Office. Congressman Robert Livingston, who had been chosen to succeed the controversial Newt Gingrich as House Speaker, had just announced to the nation that he was resigning from Congress because of his own past extramarital affairs. Livingston urged the President to "heal the wounds that you have created" by doing the same. "I must set the example," Livingston declared, "that I hope President Clinton will follow." It was a stunning move that, on its face, put more pressure on Bill to explain why he should not resign.

Yet when he returned to his friends gathered in the Oval Office, the President was elated. "I know it's terrible for me to say this," Bill Clinton said, "but Livingston is resigning, and it's SO GREAT! IT'S JUST TERRIFIC!" Then he and his small group of friends went into another room to watch the House vote as he became only the second president in history along with Andrew Johnson in 1868 to be impeached.

"The rest of us felt numb, but the President was upbeat, cheerful," said one of those friends who was in the Oval Office when Clinton burst into the room with the "great" news that the new House Speaker had resigned because of his own sex scandal. "He just watched while his enemies did themselves in one after the other. There was no way he would ever resign for any reason—it's just not him. So from his standpoint, the day he was impeached was a *good day* for him. Bill was like a kid in a candy store."

The President and Hillary both monitored television coverage of the vote closely but, as now had become the norm, apart—he in his West Wing offices and she upstairs in the family quarters.

Hillary, even more incensed about what she saw as a Republican effort to destroy both her and her husband, then joined Bill for another display of unity—and defiance. After the historic House vote, the President, his First Lady, and some two hundred of their smiling, waving congressional supporters staged a pep rally of sorts at the White House—"a display of egregious arrogance," Democratic Senator Robert Byrd later fumed, "the likes of which I have never seen."

Coupled with charges that he had ordered air strikes against Saddam Hussein to distract public attention from the impeachment à la the film *Wag the Dog*, the backlash worried Clinton's supporters. "He just doesn't get it" became the rallying cry for those who saw the President as unrepentant. They were right. "He sees himself," a bewildered advisor said, "as a victim surrounded by tormentors." When asked the day after the House vote how it felt to be impeached, Bill replied with a shrug, "Not bad."

In truth, the congressmen who marched to the White House that dreary December day were showing their devotion to Hillary as much as to the President. "She's so terrific," said Democratic Congressman Dennis Kucinich of Ohio. "It's lucky for America we have a woman with the strength to lead the nation right now. And everybody understands she is one of the leaders of the nation right now, as much as the President."

Like her parents, Chelsea put on a brave public face to mask her private pain. In addition to everything else, the First Daughter had just broken up with her boyfriend of six months, Stanford swimmer Matthew Pierce. But Chelsea, who was home in the White House at the time of the impeachment vote, stayed resolutely upbeat. Bursting into a room where her mother was entertaining friends that evening, Chelsea said, "I've got to run. I'm so late for a party, my friends are going to *kill* me."

> *It is therefore ordered and adjudged that the said William Jefferson Clinton be, and he hereby is, acquitted of the charges in the said articles.*

With those words, U.S. Chief Justice William Rehnquist ended the nation's yearlong impeachment nightmare on February 12, 1999. After a five-week trial that included the videotaped testimony of Monica Lewinsky, Vernon Jordan, and Clinton advisor Sidney Blumenthal, the Senate voted 55–45 to acquit the President on perjury charges and tied 50–50 on obstruction of justice charges—both falling far short of the two-thirds needed to convict.

While their countrymen sat glued to their television sets, the Clintons, rightly confident there would be no defectors among the Senate's forty-five Democrats, went about their business. Chelsea was back attending her regular classes at Stanford, while Hillary played host to a few close friends in the family residence. Bill, meanwhile, worked out in the White House gym, showered, then put on a fresh white shirt and a blue-and-white patterned tie. He then put a few finishing touches on the 129-word statement he would make to the press.

Standing alone and solemn-faced, Bill did not want a repeat of the scene that had followed the House vote to impeach six weeks earlier. "Now that the Senate has fulfilled its constitutional responsibility, bringing this process to a conclusion," he said, "I want to say again to the American people how profoundly sorry I am for what I said and did to trigger these events and the great burden they have imposed on the Congress and the American people.

"I also am humbled and very grateful for the support and the prayers I have received from millions of Americans over this past year," he went on. "This can be and this must be a time of reconciliation and renewal for America."

Sam Donaldson of ABC rose to ask if, "in your heart, sir, you can forgive and forget?"

"I believe any person who asks for forgiveness," the President replied, "has to be prepared to give it."

In the months following her father's Senate acquittal, Chelsea's welfare would weigh heavily on her mother's mind. At Stanford, where she finished up her sophomore year, Chelsea would get up before her seven roommates and sit alone in the kitchen reading about her parents in *USA Today*. Not even her closest friends dared bring up the impeachment, and in the words of one, "She doesn't let on at all." Observed longtime Clinton family friend Dr. Nancy Snyderman: "Chelsea has her mother's strength. She's been bred for it."

Yet Roger Clinton told *Paris Match* that the scandal had "profoundly affected" Chelsea, and it was clear that Hillary worried about the long-term effects. "When she talks about what this has done to Chelsea," said one FOH, "that's the only time you hear her voice cracking. That's the thing that grieves her and hurts her the most . . . I'd be surprised if she ever really forgives him for that."

Meantime, Hillary saw her own ratings in the polls soar in 1999 as Democrats urged her to seek a New York Senate seat in the year 2000. After a quarter-century standing by Bill, she had quite simply become the most popular figure—female or male—in public life. "The most important legacy of the Clinton years," said Democratic activist Mary Louise Oates, "will be Hillary Rodham Clinton."

Of course, the Senate was only one of several possibilities that would be open to Hillary after leaving the White House. If Al Gore were to succeed her husband as President, she could be almost assured of an appointment as ambassador to the United Nations. She could pen her memoirs for $5 million, accept one of several offers to become CEO of a major corporation, or teach law at a leading university. Then there were other Senate races, if she was willing to wait—one seat in Arkansas was coming up in 2002, and another in her home state of Illinois in 2004.

But as she weighed her options, none seemed more appealing than the rough-and-tumble of a Senate race against New York City's popular Republican Mayor Rudy Giuliani—perhaps with an eye on making her own try for the White House in 2004 or 2008. There was an analogy that Hillary found particularly compelling: The other carpetbagger who won a New York Senate seat was Robert F. Kennedy, who then ran for president.

When the idea was first broached by veteran New York Congressman Charlie Rangel, Bill did not need persuading. "He was more excited than I've ever seen him about anything," Rangel said.

"It's a decision she'll have to make," Bill said when asked about her running for office. "She'd be great if she did. I think she would be terrific in the Senate." Until now, the Clintons had disagreed about where to live after they left office. The Clinton Presidential Library in Little Rock would always be their base, but he wanted to spend the rest of the time hobnobbing with their show business friends in Los Angeles while she talked of settling in Manhattan. If Hillary ran for the Senate and won, she would be spending most of her time in the town she had come to loathe: Washington.

There were other, potentially more ominous problems lurking in the wings if she chose to run. Once again, all the scandals from Whitewater to Filegate would almost certainly be resurrected during a Senate campaign. And then there was Bill. "We all remember what happened back in 1980 when he lost the governor's race and was out of office for two years," said a close family friend. "Bill basically went crazy sexually. With Hillary busy representing New York in the Senate, we're all terribly afraid it'll happen again." Concurred a longtime advisor: "If Hillary runs and wins, Bill's ego won't be able to take it, and he'll have even less control over his urges than he does now. He'll definitely go off the deep end."

Whatever road she would choose, Hillary was buoyed at the prospect of pursuing her own dreams—and grateful for her husband's support. Not that she didn't count on it. "He probably has to do everything she wants," a longtime Arkansas friend conceded. "He is pretty much owned by her now."

On the contrary, to many it seemed that, emotionally at least, Bill still had the upper hand. At a Long Island dinner hosted by actor Alec Baldwin and his wife, Kim Basinger, the Clintons were noticeably frosty toward each other until she got up to speak. She surprised the crowd—and clearly Bill—by rhapsodizing about his achievements and dreams for the future. When she introduced him, the President jumped to his feet and embraced her, said one startled guest, "like Rhett Butler taking Scarlett O'Hara." Watching this, New York State Democratic Party Chairwoman Judith Hope observed, "He just keeps seducing this woman, over and over again. This kind of chemistry can't be faked. She can't resist him."

Hillary aside, Bill was not at all contrite about the mess he found himself in. Far from it. Privately, he raged at his enemies. "This is much ado about nothing," he told one old colleague. "I beat the odds." Agreed one advisor: "I think there's real honest regret for behaving stupidly and being shabby to his family . . . But he doesn't believe he lied or obstructed justice."

Even as Juanita Broaddrick stepped forward to accuse him of rape—an accusation both Bill and Hillary dismissed as politically motivated—Bill continued his desk-pounding tirades against his right-wing tormentors. In an interview with CBS's Dan Rather, Clinton made the confounding claim that he was "proud" to have set an example for America's young people during the impeachment by "defending the Constitution."

★   ★   ★

Arkansas FOB to Washington FOB: "I'm afraid that as long as Bill refuses to admit that he has a problem and gets some help, it's just going to start all over again."

Washington FOB to Arkansas FOB: "It already has."

Friday, February 26. The ballroom of Beverly Hills's Century Plaza Hotel. It has been only two weeks since the Senate impeachment verdict, but the crowd attending the Democratic National Committee Women's Leadership Forum fund-raiser is, the *Los Angeles Times* will later report, "rowdy." Donors wearing tiny saxophone pins in honor of tonight's main speaker gyrate to the high-voltage swing band Big Bad Voodoo Daddy. Clutching her evening bag, a striking, willowy young blonde gets up to leave and makes her way between the tables toward the exit. Once outside, she takes a few steps in the direction of the ladies' room when someone taps her on the shoulder. She turns and sees a tall man wearing a dark suit, an earpiece, and a solemn expression.

"Excuse me, miss," the stranger whispers, flashing his Secret Service identification. "The President would like to know if you could join him upstairs for a drink . . ."

The following month, an anguished military officer complains to her immediate superior that the President "groped" her following yet another glittering black-tie function in Washington. Her commanding officer tells her pointedly: "It didn't happen."

"They'll never split up," insisted a confidant of nearly thirty years, echoing the sentiments of most Clinton friends. "I mean *never.*"

Still, the crucial questions remain: Do Bill and Hillary love each other, or has it always been a calculated arrangement based on power? Yes—and yes. Just as Jack Kennedy admired Jackie for her grace, beauty, and courage even as he pursued other women, Bill is in awe of Hillary's intelligence, grit, and unwavering loyalty. To her, he represents not only an avenue to power—and by extension

[317]

a means of accomplishing great things—but above all else a figure of historical importance. Together, they became the most powerful married couple in history.

When this mutual respect was fractured by Bill's self-destructive behavior, their daughter was the glue that held the Clinton marriage together. In the end, Chelsea emerged as a hero in her own right. Betrayed and publicly humiliated by the father she adored, she nonetheless hid her private pain behind a brave smile and—like her mother—soldiered on. Even the President's most bitter political foes marveled at the dignity displayed by Hillary and Chelsea in this time of crisis. There was, as Arthur Schlesinger Jr. once said of Jackie Kennedy, a "gallantry" about them.

In the end, both women have needed such qualities to endure a private and public saga that has all the makings of a Greek tragedy. Hillary's fatal flaw is Bill, and Bill's fatal flaw is—and likely always will be—himself.

Acknowledgments

"You don't pick out who you fall in love with," my friend Katharine Hepburn told me. Indeed, my books about Hepburn and Spencer Tracy, Jack and Jackie Kennedy, and—saddest of all—Princess Diana, were devoted largely to exploring the mysterious forces that draw people to each other and the equally mysterious forces that hold them together, often against seemingly insurmountable odds.

Like *Jack and Jackie, Bill and Hillary* is the biography of a sometimes inspiring, often harrowing, always spellbinding relationship—a marriage of hearts and minds that has somehow survived scandal, betrayal, and heartbreak.

I am delighted to be working for a fifth time with my supremely talented friends at William Morrow. Once again, I am especially grateful to my editor Betty Kelly, who brought the same passionate commitment, insight, and editorial skill to *Bill and Hillary* that she did to *The Day Diana Died*. The folks at Morrow may be tired of my thanking them, but I'm going to anyway because each of them more than deserves it—particularly Bill Wright, Michael Murphy, Sharyn Rosenblum, Marly Rusoff, Alice Lee, Brad Folz, Debra Weaver, Lisa Queen, Fritz Metsch, Richard Aquan, Kathy Antrim, Kim Lewis, and Camille McDuffie of Goldberg-McDuffie Communications.

After sixteen years and seventeen books, Ellen Levine does not have to be told how much I depend on her counsel, support, and friendship—she is, as I have said before, simply the finest literary agent around. I am also indebted, as always, to her two gifted associates, Diana Finch and Louise Quayle.

My daughters, Kate and Kelly, delight and astound their parents on a more or less continual basis. Jeanette and Edward Andersen, my parents, are no less astounding to me—two members of the "Greatest Generation" who are, if anything, more curious than ever about the events shaping the world around them. Incredibly, it has been thirty-two years since my wife, Valerie, and I first met on the campus of the University of California at Berkeley. Those mysterious forces that hold people together have, if anything, grown stronger with time.

Additional thanks to David Leopoulos, Carolyn Yeldell Staley, Mary Ann Campbell, Dick Morris, Ann Henry, Juanita Broaddrick, Dolly Kyle Browning, Woody Bassett, Carl Whillock, Richard Atkinson, Morris Henry, Kathleen Willey, Guy Campbell, Eileen McGann, Harry Criner, Larry Klayman, Vada Sheid, Rosemary McClure, L. D. Brown, Larry Gleghorn, Debbie Goodsite, Wendy Rothman, Norman Curry, Jeanette Peterson, Ray Whelan Jr., Larry Nelson, Bernice Kizer, Joe Dillard, Barry Schenck, Michelle Lapautre, Betsy Loth, Rudy Moore, Claudia Mooser, Joe Newman, Margaret Whillock, Ernie Wright, Morris Henry, Lou Ann Vogel, Brownie Ledbetter, Brigit Dermott, Janet Lizop, Tom Freeman, Gary Gunderson, Bill Bushong, Lawrence R. Mulligan, Jeanette Walls, Larry Schwartz, Ray Whelan Sr., Hazel Southam, Tobias Markowitz, Wes Holmes, Tom Fitton, Jean Chapin, Esther Devine, Martie Smolka, Everett Raymond Kinstler, Ed Coulter, Thomas Mars, Michael Shulman, Joy Wansley, Yvette Reyes, Susan Rogers, Mary Sheid, Betty Monkman, the Gunn Memorial Library, the White House Historical Association, the John F. Kennedy Library, the New York Public Library, the Lyndon Baines Johnson Library, the Litchfield Library, the New Milford Library, the Southbury Public Library, the Boston Public Library, the Woodbury Library, the University of Arkansas, Oxford University, Yale University, Wellesley College, Georgetown University, the *Arkansas Democrat Gazette*, John Sykes, Archive Photos, Sygma, AP–Wide World, Globe Photos, Retna, Sipa, Corbis, Design to Printing, and Graphictype.

Sources and Chapter Notes

The following chapter notes are designed to give a general view of the sources drawn upon in preparing *Bill and Hillary,* but they are by no means intended to be all-inclusive. The author has respected the wishes of many interviewed sources—including government officials still serving in Washington as well as longtime Clinton family friends from Arkansas, Illinois, and Washington, D.C.—to remain anonymous and accordingly has not listed them either here or elsewhere in the text. The archives and oral history collections of, among other institutions, the John F. Kennedy Library, Wellesley College, Georgetown University, Yale University, Oxford University, Columbia University, the University of Arkansas, and the Lyndon Baines Johnson Library yielded a wealth of information. Court documents and sworn depositions generated by numerous civil and criminal investigations—ranging from the testimony of the Arkansas State Troopers in the Paula Jones case to the mountain of testimony and evidence contained in the Starr Report—proved valuable. Obviously, there have also been thousands of news report and articles concerning the President and the First Lady published since he was first elected to state office nearly a quarter century ago. These reports appeared in such publications as *The New York Times, The Washington Post, The Wall Street Journal, The Boston Globe, The Arkansas Democrat, The Arkansas Gazette,* the *Chicago Tribune,* the *Los Angeles Times, Vanity Fair, The New Yorker, Time, Life, Newsweek, The New York Observer, U.S. News & World Report, USA Today, The*

(London) *Times, Paris Match,* and *Le Monde,* and carried on the Associated Press, Knight-Ridder, Gannett, and Reuters wires.

Chapters 1 and 2

Interview subjects included David Leopoulos, Carolyn Yeldell Staley, Dolly Kyle Browning, Mary Ann Campbell, Harry Criner, Dick Morris, John Dunbar, Joe Newman, Bill Bushong, Cliff Jackson, Gared Mankowitz, Lou Ann Vogel, Larry Klayman, Ed Coulter, Betty Monkman, Brownie Ledbetter. Published sources included "Clinton Admits Lewinsky Liaison to Jury," *The New York Times,* August 18, 1998; "The Starr Report: The Independent Counsel's Complete Report to Congress on the Investigation of President Clinton," September 9, 1998; *U.S. News & World Report,* August 31, 1998; Gail Sheehy, "Hillary's Choice," *Vanity Fair,* February 1999; "How Low Can It Go?" *Newsweek,* September 28, 1998; David Maraniss, *First in His Class* (New York: Simon & Schuster, 1995); "Why She Turned, What He Can Do," *Time,* August 10, 1998; "Under Oath," *Newsweek,* August 24, 1998; Virginia Kelley, *Leading with My Heart* (New York: Simon & Schuster, 1994); Kenneth T. Walsh, "Portrait of a Marriage," *U.S. News & World Report,* August 31, 1998; "The Politics of Yuck," *Time,* September 14, 1998; George Stephanopoulos, *All Too Human* (New York: Little, Brown & Company, 1999); "Special Report: Clinton's Crisis," *Time,* February 2, 1998; Evan Thomas and Michael Isikoff, "How Strong Is Starr's Case?" *Newsweek,* September 21, 1998.

Chapters 3 to 5

For these chapters, the author drew on conversations with Juanita Broaddrick, Woody Bassett, Ann Henry, David Leopoulos, Carl Whillock, L. D. Brown, Larry Gleghorn, Vada Sheid, Richard Atkinson, Guy Campbell, Brownie Ledbetter, Harry Criner, Thomas Mars, Cliff Jackson, Mary Sheid, Ernie Wright, Larry Nelson, Bernice Kizer, Joe Dillard. Among the published sources consulted: David Freeman, "The First Friends," *Newsday,* January 6, 1993; Martha Sherrill, "The Education of Hillary Clinton," *The Washington Post,*

January 11, 1993; Meredith Oakley, *On the Make: The Rise of Bill Clinton* (Washington, D.C.: Regnery Publishing, 1994); Connie Bruck, "Hillary the Pol," *The New Yorker*, May 30, 1994; David Brock, *The Seduction of Hillary Rodham* (New York: The Free Press, 1996); Michael Kelly, "Saint Hillary," *The New York Times*, May 23, 1993; Judith Warner, *Hillary Clinton: The Inside Story* (New York: Penguin Books, 1993); Jim Moore, *Clinton: Young Man in a Hurry* (Fort Worth: The Summit Group, 1992); Michael Medved, "When Bill Met Hillary," *Sunday Times* (London), August 21, 1994; Charles Babcock and Sharon LaFraniere, "The Clintons' Finances: A Reflection of Their State's Power Structure," *The Washington Post*, July 21, 1992; Charles F. Allen and Jonathan Portis, *The Comeback Kid: The Life and Career of Bill Clinton* (New York: Birch Lane Press, 1992); Dolly Kyle Browning, *Purposes of the Heart* (Dallas: DOCC, 1997); Gail Sheehy, "What Hillary Wants," *Vanity Fair*, May 1992; Hillary Rodham Clinton, *It Takes a Village, and Other Lessons Children Teach Us* (New York: Simon & Schuster, 1996); Donnie Radcliffe, *Hillary Rodham Clinton: A First Lady for Our Time* (New York: Warner Books, 1993); L. J. Davis, "The Name of the Rose: An Arkansas Thriller," *The New Republic*, April 4, 1994; Francine Du Plessix Gray, "A Reporter at Large: The Moratorium and the New Mobe," *The New Yorker*, January 3, 1970; Ambrose Evans-Prichard, "Sally Perdue and Bill Clinton," *Sunday Telegraph* (London), January 23 and July 17, 1994; Ernest Dumas, *The Clintons of Arkansas: An Introduction by Those Who Knew Them Best* (Fayetteville: University of Arkansas Press, 1993); Micah Morrison, "Who Is Dan Lasater?" *The Wall Street Journal*, August 7, 1995; Lloyd Grove, "Hillary Clinton, Trying to Have It All," *The Washington Post*, March 10, 1992; Art Harris, "Gennifer Flowers," *Penthouse*, December 1992; Dorothy Rabinowitz, "Juanita Broaddrick Meets the Press," *The Wall Street Journal*, February 19, 1999; "The Children of Watergate," *Newsweek*, October 19, 1998.

Chapters 6 to 8

Information for these chapters was based in part on conversations with Mary Ann Campbell, Kathleen Willey, David Leopoulos,

Juanita Broaddrick, Eileen McGann, Guy Campbell, Wendy Rothman, L. D. Brown, Leslie Singer, Carolyn Staley, Dolly Kyle Browning, Everett Raymond Kintsler, Larry Nelson, Priscilla McMillan, Joe Dillard, Larry Klayman, Ernie Wright, Paula Dranov, John Sykes. Published sources included David Brock, "Troopergate: Living with the Clintons," *The American Spectator,* January 1994; David Maraniss, "The Woman Who Shaped the President Dies in Her Sleep," *The Washington Post,* January 7, 1994; Roger Morris, *The Clintons and Their America* (New York: Henry Holt, 1996); Ann Devroy and Susan Schmidt, "The Mystery in Foster's Office: Following Suicide, What Drove Associates' Actions?," *The Washington Post,* December 20, 1995; David Maraniss and Susan Schmidt, "Hillary Clinton and the Whitewater Controversy: A Close-Up; Her Public Record Suggests Conflicts with Self-Portrait of Naivete," *The Washington Post,* June 2, 1996; "Turning Fifty: Hillary Confronts a Birthday and a Newly Empty Nest," *Time,* October 20, 1997; Andrew Morton, *Monica's Story* (New York: St. Martin's Press, 1999); Jane Gross, "Clinton's Lost Half-Brother: To Neighbors, He's Just Leon," *The New York Times,* June 22, 1993; Alessandra Stanley, "A Softer Image for Hillary Clinton," *The New York Times,* July 13, 1992; Bob Woodward, *The Agenda* (New York: Pocket Books, 1995); "Hillary's Role: How Much Clout?," *Newsweek,* February 15, 1993; Maureen Dowd, "On Washington: A Cautionary Fable," *The New York Times,* February 13, 1994; Helen Kennedy, "Truth About Bill and Me: Ex-Miss America Says Encounter Was Consensual," the New York *Daily News,* March 31, 1998; Howard Kurtz, *Spin Cycle* (New York: Simon & Schuster, 1998); Dick Morris, *Behind the Oval Office* (New York: Random House, 1997); Martin Walker, *The President We Deserve* (New York: Crown, 1996); Michael Isikoff, *Uncovering Clinton* (New York: Crown, 1999); Susan Schindehette, "The Ties That Bind," *People,* February 15, 1999; "Monica and Bill: The Sordid Tale That Imperils the President," *Time,* February 2, 1998; "The Loser: Newt Hits the Showers," *Newsweek,* November 16, 1998; Gary Wills, "Inside Hillary's Head," *The Washington Post,* January 21, 1996; William C. Rempel and David Willman, "Starr Looks for a Pattern in Job Offers by Clinton Camp," *Los Angeles Times,* February 9 1998; Ann Douglas, "The Extraordinary Hillary Clinton," *Vogue,* December 1998; "The Fight of Their Lives," *Newsweek,* December 21, 1998; "Starr Probes Clinton's Personal Life—Whitewater Prosecutors Question Troops About Women, "*The Washington Post,* June 25, 1997; "We, the Jury," *Time,* September 21, 1998; Evan Thomas and Debra Rosenberg, "Hillary's Day in the Sun," *Newsweek,* March 1, 1999.

Bibliography

Aldrich, Gary. *Unlimited Access*. Washington, D.C.: Regnery Publishing, 1998.

Allen, Charles F., and Jonathan Portis. *The Comeback Kid: The Life and Career of Bill Clinton*. New York: Birch Lane Press, 1992.

Andersen, Christopher. *Jack and Jackie: Portrait of an American Marriage*. New York: William Morrow and Company, Inc., 1996.

————. *Jackie After Jack: Portrait of the Lady*. New York: William Morrow and Company, Inc., 1998.

Brock, David. *The Seduction of Hillary Rodham*. New York: The Free Press, 1996.

Browning, Dolly Kyle. *Purposes of the Heart*. Dallas: Direct Outstanding Creations, 1997.

Carville, James, and Mary Matalin. *All's Fair*. New York: Simon & Schuster, 1995.

Clinton, Hillary Rodham. *It Takes a Village, and Other Lessons Children Teach Us*. New York: Simon & Schuster, 1996.

————*Dear Socks, Dear Buddy*. New York: Simon & Schuster, 1998.

Drew, Elizabeth. *On the Edge: The Clinton Presidency*. New York: Simon & Schuster, 1994.

Dumas, Ernest. *The Clintons of Arkansas*. Little Rock: University of Arkansas Press, 1993.

Exner, Judith Campbell, as told to Ovid Demaris. *My Story*. New York: Grove Press, 1977.

Fulbright, J. William. *The Arrogance of Power*. New York: Random House, 1967.

Gallen, David. *Bill Clinton as They Know Him*. New York: Gallen Publishing, 1994.

Gitlin, Todd. *The Sixties: Years of Hope, Days of Rage*. New York: Bantam, 1987.

Isikoff, Michael. *Uncovering Clinton: A Reporter's Story*. New York: Crown, 1999.

Johnson, Rachel. *The Oxford Myth*. London: Weidenfeld & Nicholson, 1988.

Kelley, Virginia. *Leading with My Heart*. New York: Simon & Schuster, 1994.

Levin, Robert E. *Clinton: The Inside Story*. New York: S.P.I. Books, 1992.

Maraniss, David. *First in His Class*. New York: Simon & Schuster, 1995.

Moore, Jim. *Clinton: Young Man in a Hurry*. Fort Worth: The Summit Group, 1992.

Morris, Dick. *Behind the Oval Office*. New York: Random House, 1997.

Morris, Roger. *Partners in Power: The Clintons and Their America*. New York: Henry Holt, 1996.

Morton, Andrew. *Monica's Story*. New York: St. Martin's Press, 1999.

Nelson, Rex. *The Hillary Factor*. New York: Gallen Publishing, 1993.

Oakley, Meredith L. *On the Make: The Rise of Bill Clinton*. Washington, D.C.: Regnery Publishing, 1994.

Osborne, Claire G. *The Unique Voice of Hillary Rodham Clinton*. New York: Avon Books, 1997.

Radcliffe, Donnie. *Hillary Rodham Clinton: A First Lady for Our Time*. New York: Warner Books, 1993.

Reeves, Richard. *President Kennedy: Profile of Power*. New York: Simon & Schuster, 1993.

Starr, John Robert. *Yellow Dogs and Dark Horses*. Little Rock: August House, 1987.

Stephanopoulos, George. *All Too Human*. New York: Little, Brown & Company, 1999.

Stewart, James B. *Blood Sport: The President and His Adversaries*. New York: Simon & Schuster, 1996.

Walker, Martin. *The President We Deserve*. New York: Crown, 1996.

Warner, Judith. *Hillary Clinton: The Inside Story*. New York: Penguin Publishing, 1993.

Woodward, Bob. *The Agenda: Inside the Clinton White House*. New York: Pocket Books, 1994.

Index

suicide of, 4, 274–282, 286, 287, 291, 306
Frankin, Aretha, 257
Fray, Mary Lee, 140, 142, 144, 145–146, 147
Fray, Paul, 140, 141, 143, 144, 145–146, 148
Freeh, Louis, 278
Friedman, Richard, 34
Frost, David, 237
Fulbright, J. William, 61–62, 69–70, 71, 76, 77, 106, 112, 130, 132, 133, 141, 143, 156

Gaddy, William, 238
Garcia, Franklin, 122
Gash, Adele, 44, 271
Gash, Faye, 44
Geigreich, William, 152
Georgetown University, 65, 66–67
Gergen, David, 30, 282
Giancana, Sam, 155
Gieve, Katherine, 83
Gingrich, Newt, 291, 309, 312
Ginsburg, Ruth Bader, 278
Giuliani, Rudy, 315
Gladstone, William, 78
Gleckel, Jeffrey, 101–102
Gleghorn, Larry, 204, 205, 206
Glespeny, Michael, 131
Goldwater, Barry, 97
Goodwin, Tommy, 208
Gore, Al, 18, 248, 257, 258, 315
Gore, Tipper, 248, 257
Gracen, Elizabeth Ward, 193, 194, 219, 233
Greenberg, Stanley, 230, 246
Greer, Frank, 230
Greer, Germaine, 111–112
Grigsby, Ann Blythe, 81
Grunwald, Mandy, 1
Guernica (Picasso), 95–96

Hackler, Hugh, 127–128
Haldeman, Bob, 126
Hall, Arsenio, 249
Hammerschmidt, John, 126–127, 134, 140, 145, 146

Hamzy, "Sweet, Sweet Connie," 196–198, 232
Hargraves, Ruth, 152
Harrison Daily Times, 127
Hart, Gary, 217, 218, 220
Hatch, Orin, 29
Hawkins, Willard "Lefty," 106
Henley, Don, 196
Henry, Ann, 146–147, 150
Henry, Helen, 67
Henry, Morris, 150
Herbst, William P., 266
Hernreich, Nancy, 266, 290
Hershey, Lewis B., 80
Hinton, Karen, 198
Hobbes, Thomas, 78
Hodson, Philip, 79
Holmes, Eugene, 106–107, 108–110, 141, 245
Holt, Frank, 69
Holt, Mary, 69
Hope, Judith, 316
Hot Springs, Ark., 52
Hot Springs Sentinel Record, 63
Houston, Jean, 36
Hubbell, Webb, 262
Huber, Carolyn, 224, 239
Humphrey, Hubert, 74
Hussein, Saddam, 5, 273, 312–313
Hutchinson, Asa, 209
Hyland, Denise, 67–68, 69, 75, 76

Iraq, 273, 312–313
Ireland, Patricia, 296
Irons, Edith, 65
It Takes a Village (H. R. Clinton), 292

Jackson, Cliff, 78–79, 80, 106, 112
Jackson, Jesse, 13, 23–26
Jackson, Michael, 257
Jagger, Mick, 80
Jamieson, Jet, 64
Jefferson, Thomas, 256
Jernigan, George, 151
Johnson, Andrew, 312
Johnson, Lyndon B., 37, 61, 70, 74, 98, 99, 112
Jones, Clinton, 141